Sport in the Global Society

General Editor: J.A. Mangan

SPORT IN LATIN AMERICAN SOCIETY

SPORT IN THE GLOBAL SOCIETY
General Editor: J.A. Mangan

The interest in sports studies around the world is growing and will continue to do so. This unique series combines aspects of the expanding study of *sport in the global society*, providing comprehensiveness and comparison under one editorial umbrella. It is particularly timely, with studies in the cultural, economic, ethnographic, geographical, political, social, anthropological, sociological and aesthetic elements of sport proliferating in institutions of higher education.

Eric Hobsbawm once called sport one of the most significant practices of the late nineteenth century. Its significance was even more marked in the late twentieth century and will continue to grow in importance into the new millennium as the world develops into a 'global village' sharing the English language, technology and sport.

Other Titles in the Series

SPORT IN LATIN AMERICAN SOCIETY

Past and Present

Editors

J.A. MANGAN
University of Strathclyde

and

LAMARTINE P. DaCOSTA
Gama Filho University, Rio de Janeiro

FRANK CASS
LONDON • PORTLAND, OR

First published in 2002 in Great Britain by
FRANK CASS PUBLISHERS
Crown House, 47 Chase Side, Southgate,
London, N14 5BP

and in the United States of America by
FRANK CASS PUBLISHERS
c/o ISBS, 5824 N.E. Hassalo Street
Portland, Oregon 97213-3644

Website: www.frankcass.com

British Library Cataloguing in Publication Data

Sport in Latin American society : past and present
1. Sports – Social aspects – Latin America 2. Sports – Latin
America – History
I. Mangan, J. A. (James Anthony), 1939– II. DaCosta,
Lamartine P.
306.4′83′098
     ISBN 0-7146-5126-5 (cloth)
     ISBN 0-7146-8152-0 (paper)
     ISSN 1368-9789

Library of Congress Cataloging-in-Publication Data

Sport in Latin American society : past and present/editors, J.A.
Mangan and Lamartine P. DaCosta.
 p. cm.
Includes bibliographical references (p.) and index.
ISBN 0-7146-5126-5 (cloth) – ISBN 0-7146-8152-0 (paper)
1. Sports–Latin America–History. 2. Sports–Social aspects–Latin
America. I. Mangan, J. A. II. Costa, Lamartine Pereira da.
 GV586 .S66 2001
 306.4′83′098–dc21
       2001004347

This group of studies first appeared as a special issue of
The International Journal of the History of Sport (ISSN 0952-3367),
Vol.18, No.3, September 2001, published by Frank Cass

Printed in Great Britain by Antony Rowe Ltd., Chippenham, Wilts

Contents

List of Illustrations

Series Editor's Foreword

J. A. MANGAN

This is a novel and timely inquiry into history, space and 'genealogy'.[1] It deals with time and asymmetrical changes, locations and the contrasting evolutions of locations, and non-linear historical narratives that nevertheless link past, present and future. The words of Michel Foucault haunt this volume:

> We should not be deceived into thinking that ... heritage is an acquisition, a possession that grows and solidifies; rather it is an unstable assemblage of faults, fissures and heterogeneous layers that threaten the fragile inheritor from within and underneath.[2]

'Unstable heterogeneity'[3] is the key to unlocking the evolution of modern sport *and* modern society in Latin America. There is a pleasing irony in the fact that Latin American cultural genealogy is sometimes 'history in the form of a concerted carnival'.[4] In recapturing the pleasures, bravura and excesses – in short the occasional buffoonery of sport in Latin American history – some of the contributors depict, consciously or unconsciously, figures whose seeming unreality at times 'surpasses that of God, who started the whole charade'.[5] Consider the fans and football of Argentina! The whole story of this 'carnival' is far from complete in this slim volume. There will be more to come.

Latin American sport deserves a wider audience in the English language as well as thoughtful reflection on its significance for the nations, communities and individuals of the complex cultures of this vast continent. There the influence of modern sport grows decade by decade – politically, economically, culturally and emotionally.

There has been a recent miasma of prejudice, misunderstanding and myopia on the part of some academics with, on occasion, surprisingly limited attitudes towards the cultural history of sport.[6] *Sport in Latin American Society* is by way of an education for them. These essays reveal something of the richness, complexity and subtlety of the role of modern sport in its recent and present existence.

The intention of the contributors to *Sport in Latin American Society* is not to write a history of modern sport where the emphasis is inadequately on arguments and evidence that are seen as only contingently and almost irrelevantly located in the past. The informing inspiration has been to write a history of sport which attempts 'to recover the ... the past in its complexity and, in a sense which is neither self-contradictory nor trivial [and] *as far as possible in its own terms*' (emphasis added).[7] Stephan Collini and fellow colleagues have this aim for intellectual history – another formerly insufficiently appreciated historical subject. They have also issued an invaluable caveat, which is of equal relevance here, to the effect that with intellectual history now becoming an established and generally accepted sub-academic discipline, it would be unfortunate if this resulted in 'a new disciplinary trade union' characterized by parochialism, exclusiveness and demarcation disputes. They remark that their *History, Religion and Culture* is surely a symbol of cultural health whereas its contributors span various academic affiliations with the result that the sub-discipline is characterized by a 'healthy pluralism of approaches'.[8]

The history of modern sport too should be eclectic in both its analysts and audience. Furthermore, since the history of modern sport is substantially about intellectual history, there is considerable scope for a strong disciplinary association between 'the history of ideas' and the 'history of sport' in Latin America – and elsewhere.[9]

J. A. MANGAN

International Research Centre for Sport, Socialisation, Society
University of Strathclyde
September 2001

NOTES

1. David Matless, *Landscape and Englishness* (London: Reaktion Books, 1998), Introduction, p.9.
2. Ibid., p.20.
3. Ibid., p.21.
4. Ibid.
5. Ibid.
6. Not by any stretch of the imagination could anyone find the distinguished historian David Cannadine guilty of such shortcomings. His work is rightly inspirational. However, he surprisingly fails to appreciate the significant role of modern sport in imperial history in *Ornamentalism: How the British Saw Their Empire* (London: Allen Lane/The Penguin Press, 2001). As I wrote in *The Games Ethic and Imperialism: Aspects of the Diffusion of an Ideal* (Penguin/Viking 1986 and Frank Cass, 2000), Victorian and Edwardian English games were concerned 'with ethnocentricity, hegemony and patronage, with ideals and idealism, with educational values and aspirations, with cultural assimilation and adaptation, and most fascinating of all, with the dissemination throughout the Empire of a hugely influential moralistic ideology' (Introduction [p.7]). These games were replete with influential imperial rituals, symbols and myths. They were paradoxically pragmatic 'ornaments' of empire.
7. Stefan Collini, Richard Whatmore and Brian Young (eds.), *History, Religion and Culture: British Intellectual Life 1750–1950* (Cambridge: Cambridge University Press, 2000), p.3. The editors were commenting on the ill-informed reaction in some academic quarters to 'Intellectual History'.
8. Ibid., p.4.
9. See J. A. Mangan, 'The History of Modern European Sport as a History of Modern European Ideas' in *Sport, Europe, Modernisers: Middle-Class Revolutionaries* (London and Portland, OR: Frank Cass, forthcoming 2002).

Emulation, Adaptation and Serendipity

J.A. MANGAN

Modern sport, especially soccer, has taken large swathes of Latin America by storm. *Sport and Latin American Society* celebrates the 'infancy', 'adolescence' and 'maturity' of modern sport on the sub-continent. The volume is not comprehensive. It cannot be. For one thing, space does not permit it. For another research, as yet, does not allow it. Therefore, the volume is consciously eclectic, knowingly tentative and clearly exploratory. However, one fact remains starkly clear; this volume deals with a significant phenomenon.

Modern sport is important to the lives of countless millions in Latin America just as it is elsewhere in our contemporary world. It offers an ecstasy as potent as any religion, an escapism as real as any cinema, an enjoyment as intense as any carnival. It is the tool of governments, the toy of oligarchs and the passion of peoples.

At the centre of the following narrative of innovation and consolidation, is Europe. For one good reason:

> What occurred in the course of Europe's expansion had a profound impact on the modern history of all continents. Since the fifteenth century west Europeans have sent forth their inhabitants, their several versions of the Christian faith, their attitudes toward nature, their languages, intellectual and political controversies, consumer goods, diseases, death-dealing and life-enhancing technologies, commercial institutions, government bureaucracies, and values. Entire regions were directly incorporated, in a kind of global enclosure movement, into overseas empires.[1]

The sound point has been made that in some respects 'it makes sense to consider Western Europe a single entity when analysing the cumulative impact on other peoples of what is appropriately termed European imperialism',[2] but that at the same time, in other respects, it is important 'to disaggregate Western Europe into its numerous states'.[3] The reason is obvious: Western European imperialism involved various national imperialisms. This is as true of European cultural imperialism – and of sport within it – as it is true of European political and economic imperialism.

As a generalization, it may be true that Europeans in their imperial strategies, tactics and actions persistently attempted to undermine 'the modes of production, social institutions, cultural patterns, and value systems of indigenous peoples'.[4] What is striking, fascinating and different in the case of Latin America is that the English, the main progenitors of much of modern global sport, a phenomenon not to be underestimated in its political, economic, cultural and emotional impact on the modern world, on their arrival in the nineteenth century certainly made no persistent effort either to undermine the then indigenous play patterns or their values among the then indigenous peoples. The reason is clear; there was no moral imperative born of the reality of imperial political control or subscription to imperial protestant evangelical ethics. In Latin America, the English, and to a far lesser extent in numbers and influence, the Scots, in their pleasure, leisure and morality linked to play, were concerned mostly with themselves. This is abundantly clear in the case of Argentina and in the light of present and developing knowledge, seems to have been the case elsewhere.

Once again there is undoubtedly some, or even considerable, truth in the assertion that the challenge facing European imperialists was 'to persuade or coerce indigenous leaders, if not the populace as a whole, to adopt what Europeans believed to be their clearly superior religion, moral code, language, literature, artistic tradition, legal system and technology'.[5] In the case of the transportation of modern sport notably from England, but also from other parts of Britain, to Latin America, there was no such challenge. The challenge was willingly taken up by many Latin Americans without any European coercion and not a great deal of persuasion. In the second half of the nineteenth century, adaptation to new fashions was 'essentially a one-way process'.[6] The Latin American communities placed the burden of making any necessary adjustments willingly on their own shoulders. European culture, including English games, was seen as superior, desirable, commendable and to be assimilated. Of course, desirability and admiration varied in intensity from place to place but the generalization that the challenge was indigenous not 'imperial' rings true.

In any consideration of nineteenth-century European global dominance, as David B. Abernethy states, a number of crucial questions are worth asking. What does the history of European empires reveal about the nature of power? What does it reveal about transfers of power from one group to another? What does it reveal about relationships across the divides of race, ethnicity and culture? Furthermore, what does it reveal about the persistence (or equally lack of persistence) of continuity in the face of social change? Finally, what does it reveal about the role of change agents in situations of seeming stability? *Sport in Latin American Society*, directly and indirectly, if understandably incompletely, both asks and answers these questions. If the answers are provocative, incomplete, even unsatisfactory (at present), speculative and contestable, it is argued here that they are well worth attempting. No doubt in time, with more interrogative balls rolling ever more faster and accurately, more speculative and contestable pins will be knocked over. Academic interrogation gets better and better with practice.

There is an interesting point to be raised with regard to sport in Latin America. What is modern and what is not? As has been pointed out, new states, both in Latin America and elsewhere, 'emerged not from some vague traditional status, after all, but from lengthy extensive interaction with some of the world's most economically and technologically advanced countries'.[7] This is certainly the case in many instances but modernity is relatively straightforward in the case of sport and Latin America. It refers mainly to the major modern activities engaged in the modern way from the beginning of the second half of the nineteenth century onwards.

Globalization also raises its head in relation to Latin American modern sport. Globalized sport is not simply a twentieth-century phenomenon of globalization. It is an earlier manifestation. Consider the sports of England in the late nineteenth century, especially soccer. Nineteenth-century imperialism, sport and globalization are inseparably linked. Without the former the latter would not exist. As Abernethy pithily states (quoting Raymond Betts): 'The landscape of the post-colonial world resembles a beach after the tide has receded; it is still strewn with what the European had earlier floated in.'[8]

Of course, some beaches have more than one tide ebbing and flowing and no consideration of the introduction of major modern sport to Latin America would be complete without consideration of the United States and its influence in this regard. The North American tide came both at the same time and after the European tide and it flooded different areas more extensively. This North American tide receives due consideration in *Sport in Latin American Society*.

The flotsam and jetsam from both tides, as is the way with such things, were taken 'off the beach' to the 'hinterland' and shaped and used in the manner and practice of the local beachcombers before being taken further and further inland by visitors to the 'seaside' or travellers from the 'seaside' to the hinterland. In this way modern sport, an initially alien cultural flotsam and jetsam, became the furniture of local communities across the continent. Then, to return to my earlier metaphor, modern sport entered its 'adulthood'. South America re-taught Europe, and to a lesser extent, North America to play. A process of reverse cultural osmosis was, and still is, at work – but only up to a point. European and North American populations make wider use of their own modern sport, have generally better facilities and a more equitable distribution of resources. Here is the challenge in its maturity to Latin America in the twenty-first century.

In *The World and The West: The European Challenge and the Overseas Response in the Age of Empire*, Phillip Curtin remarks that the *past* itself has been a preoccupation for many historians within Western culture with the result that the more basic question of how societies change through time has been hardly approached.[9] This question is certainly tackled in *Sport in Latin American Society*. In fact, it is a central concern.

Curtin also remarks that 'the rise of the West did not merely introduce a new principal player in patterns of global interchange; it introduced a whole new era in world history. Empires had risen and fallen in the past but no society had even approached the European degree of control over the whole world.'[10]

This volume deals with the background of the Late Age of European Empire but also with its influence and consequences. European technology, economies and imperialism *per se* are not its concern. *Sport in Latin American Society* is concerned with culture and cultural change and with a further concern – sport as it meshes with 'a people's whole way of life'.[11]

Sport in Latin American Society will discuss a European Recreational Revolution that precipitated a Global Recreational Revolution as a consequence of European control – both direct and indirect. This discussion will consider North American modern sport as essentially a derivative European sport, creatively and imaginatively adapted to North American cultural needs, inclinations and imperatives. It will also carefully consider the Latin American emancipatory and self-assertive response to both. In short, it will be as complex as the situation requires.

Like Curtin's book, *Sport in Latin American Society* is in part a set of case studies. Its approach is based on 'the conviction that theory and broad generalizations often conceal so many exceptions that they are in danger of becoming only vague reflections of reality'.[12] Theory and generalization, of course, have their part to play in assisting understanding. This volume does not reject these practices but supplements them because case studies 'can only be a partial reflection of the broader processes of history ... and make it possible to stay closer to empirical data on which all good history must be based.'[13] Furthermore, they permit close exploration of different situations and circumstances clustered around a common theme and offer the possibility of posing a variety of questions in response to a variety of conditions. Thus it could be 'that the sum of partial truths, arrived at by asking a variety of different questions about the past, may lead to a better understanding of how human societies – [and cultures and their sports] change through time'.[14]

Sport in Latin American Society, as should now be clear, is a study in complex cultural history or it is nothing. While *Sport in Latin American Society* will deal with the 'infancy, adolescence and maturity' of sport there, it is fully appreciated that these divisions are not absolute. They overlap. They are related to activities, classes, races, sexes, countries and cultural, economic and political circumstances.

As has been rightly said elsewhere, the emergence of the West to 'a position of dominance is one of the most important developments in world history in recent centuries'.[15] It has become a guiding paradigm for most analyses of history, economics and politics. In consequence, for those beyond Europe 'the central fact of their lives has been the challenge of the West and the appropriate responses to it, politically, economically and culturally'.[16] Several consequences of this response in the specific setting of Latin America may be noted. By way of example, the hiatus between the intentions of the colonizer and the actions of the colonized but, more particularly, the fact that 'cultural borrowing from the West was rarely a matter of wholesale invasion. The borrowed cultural items were filtered into an existing cultural matrix.'[17] Of course, this was hardly the end of it. The globalization of world cultures was not a one-way street: 'western borrowing from the non-West is less obvious to Westerners because it, too, was fitted into a familiar Western cultural matrix.'[18] For example, the Latin American influence on the sport of the West through football has been profound.

Sport in Latin American Society offers a forum for a variety of perspectives on the evolution of modern sport in Latin America: European, North American and Latin American. No single perspective has exclusive access to a complex reality. The invitation to commentators with a range of analytical insights and utilization of their accumulated expertise offers the opportunity for subtlety of perspective. The European may stress future challenge; the Northern American might lay emphasis on past hegemony; the Latin American may be concerned with continuous emancipation: cumulatively they may provide a sophistication of analysis that ensures the complexity of the evolutionary process is at least approached.

No commentator, of course, should be too stridently certain about what are good and what are bad approaches. Most bring something by way of insight to the subject. Over-defensive rebuttal can be as much a myopic weakness as over propagation.

> To search for a truly 'scientific' history is to pursue a mirage. Insofar as it has succeeded in generating new methods and techniques, this quest has of course been enormously beneficial. But every time a new wave of historians comes along and declares its method – whether it is philiogy, as in the nineteenth century, or economics, sociology, anthropology, psychology, statistics, linguistics or literary theory, as in the twentieth – to be the one true 'scientific' way of studying the past, rendering all previous historical methods outmoded at a stroke and consigning all previous historical writing to the realm of myth, anyone who is on the receiving end of this kind of rhetoric is entitled to a healthy degree of scepticism. For such claims have never been able to establish themselves for very long.[19]

As Isaiah Berlin observed many years ago, there exists in history a far greater variety of methods, procedures and approaches than are asserted in textbooks on scientific methods. Consequently, ecumenical humility is as useful in modern historical departments as it is in theological colleges.

By way of example, in the specific setting of the Latin American nations, it is sensible to recall Richard Graham's calmly unsensational appraisal of the influence of the British in Brazil.

> By 1914 Brazil had begun to move toward a modern society. The British had done a lot to bring about this onset of modernization, although they had also given some support to those forces that opposed it. Acting neither with altruism nor with malice, but driven by the ambitions and desires instilled in them by their own modernizing society, the British played a large part in initiating change in tropical Brazil.[20]

It is to be hoped that in the enthusiasm for and impassioned pursuit of the currently fashionable theme of Latin American 'emancipation', the Latin American historian and, perhaps more to the point, the social scientist playing the part of historian, does not throw the historical baby out with 'the bath water', nor 'refill' the bath with entirely fresh water without appreciating that it has been 'filled' on an earlier occasion by thoughtful historians both European, American and Latin American – deeply interested in the reality of the European and North American influence on Latin America; an interest that has enriched the history of Latin America as well as the histories of Europe and North America.

NOTES

1. D.B. Abernethy, *The Dynamics of Global Dominance: Europeans Overseas, 1415–1980* (London: Yale University Press, 2000), p.6.
2. Ibid., p.9.
3. Ibid.
4. Ibid., p.10.
5. Ibid.,
6. Ibid., p.12.
7. Ibid., p.14.
8. Ibid., p.17.
9. P.D. Curtin, *The World and the West: The European Challenge and the Overseas Response in the Age of Empire* (Cambridge: Cambridge University Press, 2000), p.vii.
10. Ibid., p.viii.
11. Ibid., p.xi.
12. Ibid.
13. Ibid.

14. Ibid.
15. Ibid., p.275.
16. Ibid.
17. Ibid., p.276.
18. Ibid.
19. Richard J. Evans, *In Defence of History* (London: Granta Books, 1997), pp.73–4.
20. Richard Graham, *Britain and the Onset of Modernization in Brazil: 1850–1914* (Cambridge: Cambridge University Press, 1968), p.324.

1

The Early Evolution of Modern Sport in Latin America: A Mainly English Middle-Class Inspiration?

J.A. MANGAN

To begin in a sense at the end with three significant quotations:

The Consequences of the 'Expansion of Europe'

The rise and fall of the modern colonial empires have changed dramatically the human geography of the planet. The 'expansion of Europe' which began in the late fifteenth century ... led, sometimes intentionally sometimes not, to the destruction of entire peoples who had been born and reared in colonies and whose futures, and sense of identity, were markedly divergent from those of either the European invaders or the societies of the Aboriginal populations. In its final phase it also created new states, and new political forms, or renewed and transformed versions of older political types, one of which – democratic republicanism – was to become the dominant ideology of the modern industrialised world.[1]

And;

From European Hegemony to American Hegemony

In the nineteenth century [there] was the Industrial Revolution, of which Great Britain was the driving force. She effortlessly displaced Spain and Portugal in South America in order to sell her industrial products and to control the commercial networks. The new states ran into debt to acquire the marvels of British production and the British were satisfied with simply doing business. Thus a sort of new colonial pact got under way: it linked the interests of European industrialists to the local leading classes. But soon the former had gained control over the economy of the country. Great Britain was actually the ruling power in Peru and in Argentina; German capitalists secured the coffee trade in Guatemala; American companies took possession of the sugar-cane lands in Cuba.[2]

And;

Aspects and Effects of the Unification of the World

One of the leading features of colonization was to set in motion the process of the unification of the world.[3]

One further quotation of significance:

An Absence of Moral Hegemony

In 'Latin' America the British had not imparted a moral or ideological tone to their economic domination. Granted, they averred they were acting in the name of civilization in Africa or elsewhere, but not in 'Latin' America. Here they conducted business, as usual, and they were satisfied with concrete advantages ... on the contrary, the Americans wanted to export their original puritanism ... The 'Yankees' wanted to lead the South Americans to a 'healthy' management of their business ... what to the South Americans appeared like hypocritical cunning, designed to control their budget and their country, was actually something more than a mere tactic. It was a real strategy ... educational moralism was used to justify very evident material advantages, but its main goal was to perpetuate a relationship of domination.[4]

Now statements on colonialism of insight, clarity and shrewdness:

Colonialism was neither monolithic nor unchanging through history ... It is tempting but wrong to ascribe either intentionality or systematicity to a congerie of activities and a conjunction of outcomes that, though related and at times coordinated, were usually diffuse, disorganized, and even contradictory.[5]

And;

... in certain important ways, *culture* [emphasis added] was what colonialism was all about. Cultural forms in newly classified 'traditional' societies were reconstructed and transformed by and through colonial technologies of conquest and rule, which created new categories and oppositions between colonizers and colonized, European and Asian, modern and traditional, West and East, even male and female.[6]

And;

> ... many ... now believe that colonialism is what culture is all about. And if this is so, there are grounds to suggest that the interdisciplinary study of colonial histories and societies provides the basis for major theoretical advances in the elaboration of a new, critical 'historical anthropology'.[7]

This essay is a study in 'historical anthropology' linking man, history, culture, sport as culture and cultural imperialism, cultural hegemony and cultural emulation.[8] Of course cultural influence frequently, if not invariably, goes hand in hand with political or commercial dominance. As has been noted of Latin America:

> Cultural export through political dominance was achieved partially within Latin America's various colonial empires, but cultural export ... through commercial competition and dominance has become more the case over the last century, as new technologies, monopolistic structures, and power imbalances have given rise to 'general processes of cultural dominance and then of cultural dependence.'[9]

Three books on imperialism and colonialism pregnant with imaginative possibilities for the cultural analyst justifiably intrigued, startled and even mesmerized by the power of modern sport[10] to induce global rapture, to engage innumerable national societies, to intoxicate or enrage countless communities large and small, have provided the introductory insights set out earlier: *Lords of all the World: Ideologies of Empire in Spain, Britain and France c.1500–c.1800* by Anthony Pagden, *Colonization: A Global History* by Mark Ferro and *Colonialism and Culture* edited by Nicholas B. Dirks.

THE ROLE OF THE ENGLISH MIDDLE CLASS

A preliminary remark of some importance – Allen Guttmann, a profoundly thoughtful analyst of the significance of modern sport, has striven laudably to provide a mature analytical model that explains the phenomenon of modern 'Ludic diffusion'. He offers three concepts: cultural imperialism, cultural hegemony and cultural emulation.[11] All three play a part in what follows.[12] They must be used with prudence, they are not discreet and further, different weight might usefully be given to each term as circumstances demand. It is a sophisticated analytical trio.

At the onset, it is helpful to be reminded that Latin America:

> is physically and culturally most complex. Among some 30 countries, populations reach from Caribbean micro-states of 100,000 to Brazil's nearly 140 million. Economic activities encompass primitive subsistence agriculture, extensive commercialised farming and sophisticated mechanized industry. Similarly, standards of living range from Venezuela's oil-financed $4000 annual per capita gross national product to Haiti's impoverished £320. Argentina, Cuba and Costa Rica boast of literacy rates of 90 per cent or higher, while a dozen countries or more struggle to stay above 50–60 per cent. The majority of Latin Americans speak Spanish but Brazil's legions communicate in Portuguese and significant minorities speak French, Dutch, English and various Amerinidian languages such as Quechua, Aymara, Guarani and distinct Mayan dialects. Political systems cover the spectrum from open democracies [Costa Rica, Venezuela, and more] through dictatorships [Paraguay] to the socialist states of Cuba and Nicaragua.[13]

Before taking up the paint brush to sketch in the beginnings of modern sport in Latin America, or more specifically Argentina, it might be helpful to make it quite clear that late nineteenth and twentieth century imperialism has been more associated with financial capital and cultural creations than conquest and conquistadors and that these modern forms of imperialism can be influential even in situations of political independence. This situation constitutes imperialism without colonization and, it has been suggested, has been developed 'in its purer form in Latin America'.[14]

I shall paint in one small historical part of this complex canvas – the early role of the English middle class[15] in the diffusion of modern sport in Latin America. It is a relatively neglected part, this role of the English middle class in the evolution of modern sport – in England and beyond England, in Empire and beyond Empire in, for example, Latin America.

Regarding Latin America, there is at least one paradox; namely 'the efforts of Latin Americans to employ basically European cultural forms [including sports] to implement a fundamentally European construct – the construction of a nation state … all for the purpose of differentiating themselves from Europeans, North Americans and perhaps each other.'[16] I shall point up a further paradox – namely, that while the Anglo-Saxon *Homo Ludens Imperiosus* considered games as part of the imperial civilising process,[17] in Latin America such a powerful belief is far less evident. Indeed, in one location where the English public school was most admiringly recreated, Argentina, which has been called 'The Forgotten Colony', apparently it was mostly non-existent.

For the English, modern games in Argentina were a means of fashioning a cultural umbilical cord to their mother country. For the English these games were initiated mostly by themselves and for themselves, energetically pursued and had no wider major purpose. They had, however, an important serendipitous cultural outcome. This too will receive brief attention. It may have been the desire of some intellectuals, educators and politicians such as the Argentines Domingo F. Sarmiento and Juan Baptista Alberdi (who 'considered English "the language of liberty, industry and order" and wanted it taught in all Argentine schools'[18]) to advance civilized behaviour in Latin America by means of the espousal of European political, social, cultural and educational practices, including for some, the sports mainly of the English middle classes but that was certainly not the intention of the English, or other Britons, in Argentina to the extent that it was in Empire.

In the brief space at my disposal, I will concentrate on the English middle class and its indirect influence on, and purpose in, Latin America with close and specific reference to Argentina. This chapter will demonstrate briefly how this influence was perhaps surprisingly out of step with its influence and purpose within the British Empire.

ADAPTION, ADJUSTMENT, RECONSTRUCTION AND REINTERPRETATION

Paul Henderson has summed up as neatly as anyone the pre-1914 relationship between Great Britain and Latin America:

> For much of the nineteenth century and the early part of the twentieth, Britain was, economically, the dominant foreign power in Latin America. Though British influence was evident in the eighteenth century and the independence period, it reached its peak in the years 1870–1914. In the major countries of the region

that influence appeared unassailable. Yet World War I ushered in a period of decline and by 1945 Latin America, now facing the hegemony of the United States, possessed little real significance for the British government and business interests.[19]

He goes on to remark that the issue of British informal imperialism and Latin American consequent dependency[20] looms large in any consideration of this relationship. In short, 'most of Latin America, in its relations with the metropolitan countries of the North Atlantic, found itself in an increasing state of economic and cultural dependence with these two dimensions being functionally intertwined'.[21] Some write predominantly of economics; I speak essentially of culture in order to recognize the fact that 'there is no shortage of analyses by which both British and Argentine scholars, many of a collaborative nature, exploring the economic aspects of the relationship, but the cultural dimension with its wider social implications has gone largely uncharted … but even commercial relations have cultural implications.'[22]

Within this setting and with regard to sport as a cultural phenomenon of no mean significance, it has been correctly stated that 'for Latin America, as with the rest of the world, the center of modern sport innovation was principally England and secondarily France and the United States'.[23] To recognize this is not to suggest slavish imitation, inflexible obeisance and fawning reproduction. The need for careful and thorough consideration of indigenous adaptation, adjustment, reconstruction and reinterpretation has been made in various quarters and is fully acknowledged.[24] Furthermore, there is always the danger of Edward Said's 'possessive exclusivism' and while there should rightly be an exploration of a global trajectory of modernization, there should be no failure to continue to study 'the fragmentary, the local and the subjugated'.[25] Nevertheless, recognition of England's role in modern 'Ludic diffusion' in Latin America will permit the recording of the reality of the early moments of an eventual and extraordinary indigenous cultural manifestation – modern sport itself in Latin America – and at the same time it will allow a study of cultural diffusion, assimilation and adjustment, as well as continuity and change, and purposes and functions in response to specific external and internal needs, inclinations and desires.[26] One important aspect of this continually adjusting and adapting state of affairs in the specific setting of Latin America has been described as follows:

even sports introduced by dominant and/or imperialist forces, including corporate-sponsored mass institutions, can be manipulated by elements within the recipient society to forge, if not a truly residual or emergent subculture, at least an enclave which permits the fulfilment of needs or the expression of values at variance with some of the hegemonic structure ... But ... it is usually the hegemonic culture that defines the limits and terms within which these variants can ... develop.[27]

The reason has been explained as follows: 'Among the factors determining the [diffusion] process, the most important is the relative, economic and the cultural power of the nations involved'.[28] In short, a nation that exercises political or economic power often, although not always, intentionally and unintentionally, also exercises cultural power.[29]

Now to concentrate on the early spread of modern sport and English middle-class culture as its inspiration. To set the scene, first three sweeping comments which, for all that, throw a penetrating beam of light on the contribution of the English middle class as the pre-eminent early international innovator – for the most part, the Scots, Welsh and Irish followed in its wake, certainly at home and often abroad[30] – and its lasting relationship to the global evolution of much of modern sport:

> By 1900, [in England] games, ... had become more highly organized and team-oriented than at any time in the past. The main authors of this development were the urban middle class who were guided and inspired by public-school practices, so that sport was seen to have crucially important social and moral attributes.[31]

And;

> China is to hold its first university boat race, three decades after the fledgling sport of college rowing was wiped out by the Cultural Revolution. A leading Chinese sports official yesterday outlined his dream of promoting scientific 'urban' rowing, invented by the public schoolboys and undergraduates of Victorian Britain,* over the rural Chinese tradition of dragon boat racing. [He] hailed Western-style rowing as 'the fruit of industrial civilisation', as opposed to dragon boat racing, which he described as 'agricultural.'[32]
> [*The main centres were in England – namely Henley, Oxford, Cambridge, Durham and London.]

And;

> 'We must thank the English people because they invented all modern sports'.[33]

Such statements, whether or not appreciatively exaggerated, spotlight a widely accepted fact that, as Allen Guttmann put it in an admittedly hyperbolic statement, 'From the British Isles, modern sports went forth to conquer the world.'[34] Guttmann has also stated that 'from the eighteenth century until the middle of the twentieth, Great Britain's role in the development of modern sports was more important than any other nation'.[35] Of course, he would be even closer to the truth if he had replaced 'Great Britain' with 'England'. What is missing from these unquestionably accurate observations is that not wholly but inconsiderable measure, this development was a late nineteenth century metropole middle-class phenomenon in which the English schools of the privileged had a large, if not exclusive, part to play.[36] It is worth repeating that middle-class motives were complex and diverse, accidental and deliberate. As this consideration of Latin America reveals, the consequences were both intended and unintended. Furthermore, motives and outcomes were both predictable and unpredictable as well as various, hence the value of a triadic analysis involving the concepts of cultural imperialism, cultural hegemony and cultural emulation in addition to a consideration of the role of politics and economics and the power of the 'powerless' (who are never wholly powerless) to reinvent and reconstruct original imported phenomena in their own image.

THE EARLY SPREAD OF MODERN SPORT

Ian Bradley has remarked that

> The persistent fascination with the class system in England, and the persistence of the system itself, have produced a large number of books on the working classes but comparatively few on the middle classes. Somehow bank managers and school teachers do not have the same romantic appeal to historians and sociologists as miners and railwaymen.[37]

However, among cultural historians interested in an accurate record of evolution of modern sport as a major manifestation in modern world cultures, perhaps the time of the middle class has finally come! These are 'tell-tale' signs. In a series of observations, Mike Huggins makes the case for a timely re-evaluation of the role of the English middle class in the evolution of modern sport:

> From the second half of the nineteenth century onwards English middle-class sport increasingly functioned as a powerful cultural bond, moral metaphor, and political symbol. It had a major impact on recreational culture, career access and the formation of class cultures and relationships. Yet, as J.A. Mangan has pointedly remarked, discussion of the huge contribution of the middle classes 'to national and world sport as a political, cultural and social entity' and, more broadly ' to British, imperial and global culture' is, with a few notable exceptions, either consciously neglected, or inappropriately unfashionable. Currently their contribution is inexcusably undervalued and under-appreciated. Its manifestations constantly receive ritual reference yet frequently are not carefully considered or enterprisingly explored. *All of us should know better* [emphasis added].[38]

Huggins has a serious and sensible request:

> It is high time that sports historians began to put the Victorian middle classes under the same detailed scrutiny to which working-class participation in sport has been subjected. Cultural historians, particularly the influential and prolific J.A. Mangan, have performed this task in the context of middle-class education, investigating the origins of manliness, the games ethic in the public schools, its diffusion into other areas of education in Britain and abroad, and the links with imperialism and militarism. Education, of course, lay at the heart of British culture and the athleticism of the Victorian and Edwardian public school has fully merited the close scrutiny it has received. But the task of exploring middle-class sporting culture still needs to be addressed more completely in the field of post-education.[39]

Others have also had their say on the subject:

> Jeffrey Richards, the distinguished cultural historian, has remarked that in recent years that, 'while the working classes have received close attention, the middle classes, their values and life styles have been comparatively neglected.' It has been further suggested by J.A. Mangan that the middle classes and the middle-

class mythical heroes of the playing field are firmly out of fashion,
and that it is salutary, therefore, that they have, at least, one
recorder 'to ensure historical balance, to rescue from conscious
neglect a section of society which contributed hugely to national
and world sport as a political, cultural and social entity.' Indeed, a
recorder may be even more salutary in order to avoid future
justifiable accusations of contemporary 'inverted snobbery'! It is
for this reason that: 'In a period in which it is modish to embrace
anti-elitism and eschew elitism, it is important in the interests of
historical completeness that the middle–class athletic hero is not
written out of cultural history.'[40]

What of the English middle class in Latin America? Georges
Clemenceau, the distinguished French politician, travelled throughout
South America in the first decade of the twentieth century and, rather
curiously given his intense chauvinism, recorded his impressions in an
English language publication, *South America Today*, published in 1911 by
T. Fisher Unwin. Unabashed by this exegetical oddity, Clemenceau
wrote off 'the Northern races' as incidental to South American Latinism.
He wrote with Gallic self-flattery and ready self-belief:

> In the Argentine …, the Northern races prove merely a useful
> element of methodical intelligence and tenacity, which is in time
> engulfed by the great Latin wave. There are important German
> colonies in Brazil, and even in the Argentine. Both English and
> North Americans have prosperous manufactories there. Yet in a race
> that has preserved integrally its Latinity, all this is of but secondary
> interest, and the tendency remains to travel steadily in the track of
> people of Latin stock, among whom it may without presumption be
> said that the French exert the most powerful influence.[41]

To some degree, the fact that he required an English publisher arguably
gives the lie to his bold assertion. Equally, when Clemenceau wrote of
sport, for example, it was Argentine game shooting on the pampas, that
excited him. Everything else, including soccer, failed to attract his
attention. In view of the limitations of his analysis of the relative
significance of European cultural diffusionists, perhaps this is just as well![42]
  Happily, as has been noted, rather more precisely and presciently:

> Even before the mid-1800s, British technology, capital, personnel
> and culture were penetrating the urban areas on both sides of the Rio

de la Plata estuary, a process which would intensify and geographically spread as the British played an ever greater role in the
region's import-export economy, in its banking and transportation
sectors, and in its emerging educational system, and in its evolving
recreational and leisure activities. Above all through the founding of
schools and of athletic and social clubs, the British introduced those
sports which back home had become rationalised and popularised as
part of the larger pattern of industrialization: cricket, rugby, soccer
[association football], polo, horse racing [clock-wise on grass],
fencing, rowing, cycling, gymnastics and track and field.[43]

In his valuable if, in certain respects, somewhat irritatingly limited
article in *Studies in Latin American Popular Culture* in 1994, Richard
McGehee, writing of the early evolution of sport in Guatemala and
Mexico, included a throw-away sentence claiming that:

> The earliest ... activity took place in social and sports clubs whose
> members were young men of the higher social classes, and in some
> cases, entirely [composed of] foreigners.[44]

The reasons are obvious: they had leisure, they had money for facilities
and equipment, they had opportunities to travel and to observe,
participate and imitate. One of the eventual results was that that the
Buenos Aires *Herald* (one of two English-language city newspapers) in
May 1900, celebrated the fact that 'English sports and pastimes have
taken root in Argentine soil, and become the favourite outdoor
amusements of Argentines of *all* [emphasis added] ranks and ages.'[45]
However, it is equally clear from the attendance at association football
matches, not to mention polo and rugby events, that, at least at this time,
these events attracted the *crème de la crème* of society. The President of
the Republic, together with an escort of Lancers, attended one match
between Alumni (the English High School team) and a visiting English
professional club in 1904, while a similar match the following year
attracted many of the best known families and ladies were well
represented.[46] The 'higher social classes' led the way.

There is every reason to believe that McGehee's comment on the
infancy of modern sport in two of its nations is relevant to much, if not
indeed the whole, of Latin America. Joseph L. Arbena has written of the
introduction of European, initially at least substantially English, modern
sports, that:

By 1900 Buenos Aires ... and corresponding environs were the sites of frequent sporting competitions among national populations, resident foreign communities and visiting European athletes at the same time that at least the upper echelons of these South American areas were adopting broader European economic processes: the first geographically outward, the second socially downward. In *most* cases these sports entered Latin American countries through a capital or major port city and via middle to upper class foreigners or locals who had travelled in Europe or the United States.[47]

This is a perceptive comment and it would be both fascinating and valuable to locate and discuss these foreigners and locals more fully than has been done. For example, it might be illuminating to trace the possible influence of Argentines who attended the Catholic English public schools of Ampleforth, Downside and Stonyhurst[48] in the second half of the nineteenth century, at that time these schools were coming under the influence of the then rampant English public school athleticism (games cult).[49]

There is a pressing need in Latin American cultural studies of sport, it is suggested, since 'history is the child of narrative',[50] for 'the construction of a narrative that has a *beginning* [emphasis added] middle and end, and which is structured around a sequence of events that take place over time'.[51] There is no reason, it is further suggested, that this involves rejection of dialogue with other disciplines, regulation of traditional biographical approaches, dismissal of consideration of the mentalities of past societies. These can, and should, be woven into the narrative. Total history may be a challenging, even an impossible task but the thoughtful effort at woven approaches could enrich the understanding of the Latin American past with regard to the introduction, as well as the assimilation and consolidation of modern sport.

The absence of an adequate discussion of 'infancy' by McGehee, despite the clear value of his research and reflection, is certainly a source of exasperation. Future cultural historians of Latin American and its sport could, and should, learn from this omission. In attempting to repair this omission, Latin American historians should not ignore the historic role of the middle classes, nor marginalize them, nor minimize their role in the growth of one of the most powerful, influential and significant components of contemporary Latin American and international culture – modern sport.[52] Myopic tendencies referred to earlier, adopted in academia in the 'birthplace of modern sport', should be resisted in the interest of academic completeness, integrity, balance and accuracy.[53] Middle-class Latin American innovators, and others from beyond Latin America, should be tracked down, their sources of inspiration and action beyond their own shores should be documented and their actions on Latin American shores should be traced and described. Rediscovery is both a historical element and agent of identity. The historian of sport, as much as other historians, is a cartographer of culture. Equally, cultural history is as much about the diffusion, assimilation, adaptation of, and resistance to, sport in 'infancy' as it is about intermediate 'adolescent' consolidation[54] or later, independent 'maturity'. To say this in no way implies a desire to wilfully neglect other classes or indeed any dimension of the evolution of modern sport. It merely makes clear the need for balance in the interests of a completeness of analysis and understanding.

AN INFORMAL BRITISH EMPIRE

There was, it seems, a British Informal Empire in Argentina between 1806 and 1914,[55] but it differed markedly from the formal Dominions of Australia, Canada, New Zealand and South Africa. Anglo-Argentine relations 'were primarily economic market relationships from which political power was absent'.[56] The Argentine economic connection with Great Britain between 1880 and 1914 was for the latter of greater importance than its connection with Egypt or China and, perhaps, even greater than with India as a source of foodstuffs and raw materials, a market and a place for the investment of capital.[57] Regarding Great Britain, it has been further noted that 'until the Great Depression of the 1930s, Argentina can be classed with Australia, Canada and the United States (and also with New Zealand and South Africa) as a frontier of enterprise, a source of raw materials and foodstuffs, a market for capital and consumer goods, and an area of investment opportunities which yielded profits from enterprises and rents from property holding'.[58] However, in one vital respect Argentina differed from Australia, Canada and the United States: Argentina never received British immigrants on a scale capable of seriously modifying the Latin character of the community, nor of its political culture.[59] This is a point of some importance.

It must be made quite clear that as early as 1806, Britain had attempted both direct and indirect, military control. It failed: 'a very small and most incompetently-led British expedition at the beginning of the nineteenth century only just missed turning the country into a British colony.'[60] In the end, Britain settled for economic and financial control, advantageous to investors, entrepreneurs and consumers. Thus in 'a very real sense Argentina was the first community, substantially dependent economically on Great Britain, to achieve Dominion status'[61] – informally, of course. This state of affairs, it is argued, lasted from 1806 until 1914. After 1806 the next date of significance in Argentine-British relations was 1862 when, following the final unification of Argentina by General Mitre, the Congress 'laid the legislative basis for the influence of foreign merchandise and capital.'[62] The details are not important here.[63] What is important is the fact that confidence in London investors was won and 'within 10 years at least £23,000,000 had been raised in the London market for investment in Argentina'.[64] By 1890, British investment stood at £174,000,000 and the Argentine economy was 'in the position to substantially influence the entire structure and course of the affairs of Great Britain'.[65] And as illustrated earlier, eventually it did.

With investment came middle-class entrepreneurs, merchants and technicians and their culture. Early evidence suggests that they were predominantly English although they did include a number of Scots, Irish and Welsh.[66] Apropos of this fact, it has been suggested in Latin America, perfectly reasonably, that the early English connection with association football's growth was strong but it has also been suggested that any associated cultural influence on Latin America by way of the spread of most of modern sport is more difficult to measure.[67] This is a curious statement in that, if anything, with regard to the early spread of much of modern sport, not merely soccer, the influence of the English (and to a lesser extent the other British) was clear, specific and lasting in the sense that many modern sports came via them or those they had influenced. Times changed, circumstances changed and sport changed but the initial influence of the English, and others from Britain, is clearly obvious and in terms of the historical record, lasting, in its way. In the early moments of the spread of modern sport throughout Latin America it was mostly their sports that were played. However much these sports have changed, for better or worse, they were a mainly English legacy. This much is clear, as is the fact that the consequences for countless millions in Latin America have been quite remarkable.

It would be surprising if there had been no associated cultural relationship parallel to the economic and financial Anglo-Argentine relationship in the second half of the nineteenth century. The economic and financial relationship was not an impersonal one involving simply paperwork, shares and capital. It involved human beings. In the case of the construction of the Argentine railway system, for example, 'Great Britain supplied most of the capital, technicians and equipment, and the fuel was British coal'.[68] These middle-class technicians, along with others, bankers, businessmen, educationalists and the like brought their culture with them and surrounded themselves with it. However, many did not stay. It should always be remembered that the British were among the smallest of the immigrant communities. 'In 1914, out of a population of nearly eight million, Britains numbered fewer than 28,000 in a registered foreign-born population of 2.3 million. Many of these were from the lower middle and working class, which included a large proportion of Irish immigrants.' However, even more important in political terms is the fact that 'The British were visitors ... only a minority assimilated.'[69]

As Sir David Kelly recorded 'Young English immigrants came in without impediment ... and if they wished, retired to England, either with their whole capital, or with the (as it seemed then) certainty of having their incomes or pensions remitted to them as though they had merely moved from Birmingham to London'.[70] It was the middle and upper middle classes who were frequently 'transient'. Once wealth was acquired, it was taken home. When the wealth and its holders departed 'it was a community of managers, not of proprietors that remained'[71] along with a few missionaries and a few teachers; no soldiers or administrators were among them. Thus the British played little part in politics. Their eyes were on home and since their opinion of Argentine politics was low, they kept their distance.[72] Profit not politics was their concern.

Where they had influence, in view of urban capitalist trends and associated technological and cultural developments in the birthplace of the industrial revolution, logically, therefore, was in commerce, transportation, education and sport. The massive British investment, mentioned earlier, had to be supervised, monitored and protected, with the result that 'with the British railways, British shipping, British meat-packing companies, British-owned farms, British wheat brokers, British importers, British exporters, British banks, British public services, British insurance, British schools, the British community in Argentina

was the most numerous outside the physical boundaries of the Empire'.[73]
There is some truth in the assertion that Argentina was an unclaimed
colony. This community was never too concerned with cerebral
pursuits.[74] In this it had much in common with the community of
compatriot middle-class public school products remaining at home. It is,
therefore, perhaps no surprise that it 'introduced most sports to the
Argentines'[75] but had little lasting intellectual influence.

AN UNCLAIMED COLONY

In May 1841 British and North American businessmen in Buenos Aires
formed the Society of Foreign Residents. The British comprised the
strongest national group.

> The Society was the forerunner of [the] Strangers' Club, the oldest
> social club in South America, renowned for many years for having
> the town's most influential merchants among its members. With
> the Society, the life and business, social calendar and sporting
> fixtures of Buenos Aires were all decided by members who used
> their marriages, churches, Masonic lodges, clubs and European
> trading houses to compete for an ever increasing share of
> Argentina. Out of the Society grew a business organisation: a
> fraternity of stockbrokers formed early in the 1850s. So proud of
> their power were they that they called the group 'El Camoati',
> which is a South American wasp with a fierce sting. The sporting
> world was an extension of the Society and members started the
> Foreign Amateurs Race Sporting Society – which had its earliest
> meetings in 1849 – that became the predecessor of Argentina's elite
> Jockey Club.[76]

Andrew Graham-Yooll puts the situation crisply:

> The British took their sports wherever they went, primarily for
> their own enjoyment, although they did teach the natives the
> secrets of their forms of amusement. Some sports were assimilated
> whilst others remained specifically British. Cricket remains a
> British community activity, although with enough interest in
> Argentina to make two divisions. Soccer is a national sport in
> Argentina. Rugby has five divisions in Buenos Aires, in addition to
> a schools division and several provincial leagues. British sports

became an important part of national life and the only aspect of the British community that put Britons in close social and cultural contact with Argentines. Nevertheless even in teaching all the sports to Argentines, the Briton kept to himself.[77]

Some sports came early, others came late. 'The first to be taken to Argentina, by a wide margin of several decades, was cricket. Officers who were captured in the invasion of 1806 played the game, it appears, for the first time in Argentina in the neighbourhood of San Antonio de Areco.'[78] In 1831 the first cricket club was established by English residents. It survived until 1839. In the early 1850s there was a permanent pitch at Palermo de San Benito on the north side of the city by the river. It was the home of the club that succeeded the first, called the Anglo-Potemo Club and, in its way, 'a sacred place: the area was to become the cradle of Argentine sport'.[79] In the late 1850s a third club was founded. It survives to this day as the Buenos Aires Cricket and Rugby Club on the fashionable Alvear Avenue. Other early clubs were the Flores Cricket Club and the Buenos Aires Zingari Cricket, Athletic, Sport Club, both established in the late 1870s. In time, clubs were set up in the provinces. These clubs were inward-looking; they were for the pleasure of the ex-patriot members. They were initially mostly exclusive to these members. Only a few North Americans, Europeans and prominent Argentines were welcome as players and members although the wider population was welcome to watch!

In 1874 the English language newspaper *The Standard* contained the first description of polo at the estancia of one David Anderson Shennan. Polo, it appears, prospered in all farming districts 'where English-speakers were influential'.[80] In 1854 a polo match between teams from Bahia Blanca and Buenos Aires took place at the Buenos Aires Polo Club. The other and smaller Argentine English-language newspaper, *The Herald*, recorded the event.

Soccer was played in the city somewhat earlier. *The Standard* announced the creation of the Buenos Aires Football Club in May 1867. Pablo Alabarces has described the event attractively:

> Football was born in Argentina on 20th June 1867 … the newspaper, the Standard, published in English by members of a community on the up (quantitatively as well as qualitatively …) had announced a football game for May 25th, 'Birthday of the Fatherland'. The rain forced suspension until the next holiday,

June 20th, 'Day of the Flag' ... the Brothers Thomas and James
Hogg ... wanted to play football, but players were lacking. Finally,
the first game was played with eight a side on the cricket field of
Palermo Cricket Club. The sixteen protagonists were, of course,
British.[81]

In this way Argentine soccer began. It grew steadily due to the influence
of ex-patriot schools, their social and sports clubs and their company
clubs.[82] Within a few years there were numerous clubs and a league was
established in 1891.[83] As mentioned above, the innovators of 1867
included Thomas and James Hogg, prominent young members of the
middle class.[84] Their father, the Yorkshireman Thomas Hogg, was a key
figure in the introduction of modern sport to Argentina. Overall, his
contribution was far more significant than the Scot Alexander Watson
Hutton, discussed below. Hogg may quite reasonably be called the
'father of modern Argentine sport'. He founded a cricket club in Buenos
Aires in 1819 (and a British Library, College and commercial centre)
while his son, also named Thomas, founded a swimming club, and with
his brother James created the Buenos Aires Athletic Club (its first
meeting was on 30 May 1867) took part in the first rugby match played
in Buenos Aires in May 1874. Furthermore, it appears that he initiated
the first golf club in Latin America.[85]

The Argentine Football League was formed in 1893. Its first
president was an Edinburgh University educated Scot, Alexander
Watson Hutton. He is known as the 'Father of Argentine Soccer' and
was headmaster of the prestigious Buenos Aires English High School
which for a number of years fielded a highly successful team known as
the 'Alumni'.

Buenos Aires English High School was opened in 1884. Hutton came
to Argentina initially as headmaster of St. Andrew's Scots School, the
oldest English-language school in Buenos Aires (founded in 1838).
Hutton brought current Anglo–Saxon practices with him: 'Not the least
of these was the introduction of sports into the curriculum. This was to
be one of the most important aspects of Hutton's own High School,
which had a gymnasium and a tennis court. The school formed the
Alumni soccer club which dominated the association football
championships for several years. It is still referred to as a model in
Argentine soccer history.'[86] Other 'English' schools elsewhere in
Argentina also formed soccer clubs.[87] Incidentally, St. Andrew's Scots

College has retained its tradition of English games. The present headmaster, A.G.T. Fisher, has written recently: 'Here at St. Andrew's we follow a very traditional English style of sporting activities linked to games, most importantly including rugby, hockey, athletics, cross-country running, swimming, soccer and the recent reintroduction of cricket.'[88]

In June 1873, rugby was first played in Argentina. Later a committee with the British Consul in the chair and including Thomas Hogg formally adopted the rules of Rugby Union. Initially the game was more popular than soccer but the Argentine government banned it in 1875 due to the excessive casualties. Rugby was reintroduced in 1886. One typical team founded in 1902 was the San Isidor Athletic Club – made up initially of English railway employees of the Buenos Aires – Rosario line – which in the second half of the twentieth century has gained a reputation for excellence.

Rowing made an early appearance in the 1860s and there was certainly an English Boat Club in 1870 although the official birthday of rowing in Argentina is accepted as the date of the first regatta on the River Lujan in February 1871. The next major regatta attracted the President of Argentina, an admirer of Anglo-Saxon sports, and the ubiquitous British Consul, Ronald Bridgett, as well as the British Minister, Lionel Sackville-West. Sackville-West, a keen rowing enthusiast, was the first president of the Buenos Aires Rowing Club, while Bridgett was the club's captain.

Tennis, it seems, first appeared in 1881. The Buenos Aires Lawn Tennis Club, the most famous of the Argentine tennis clubs, was formed some ten years later and was ultimately responsible for the River Plate Championship which, in time, would become one of the major tennis events in South America.

Golf had its first course at the famous Hurlingham Club in 1892. Athletics was introduced by Dr Andrew Dick of the British Hospital and boxing was part of the activities of the Anglo-Saxon inspired athletics clubs. Hockey at club level entered the capital city in 1911 by means of the Buenos Aires Hockey Club. It had been introduced to Argentina by an English man, Herbert Brookhouse, in 1905, who was responsible for the organization of a league championship in 1908. Women's hockey began at St. Catherine's School in 1907.

There is no need to continue to offer a possibly tedious list of people, dates, venues and occasions associated with the coming of modern sport to Argentina in the second half of the nineteenth century. The purpose has been to simply provide unequivocal evidence of the mostly English middle class nature of the innovations and innovators and to lay emphasis again on the self-absorbed non-missionary purpose of the founders, organizers and participants. The record surely has now been established. The reasons for it were rehearsed earlier; they do not require repetition. What has been revealed above is a rich and innovative cultural lode. The veins of an essentially English, in its origins and its introduction, middle-class cultural influence that has lasted to the present are threaded throughout the Argentine. Latin America has added its own cultural veins, to produce a rich mine of the fused non-indigenous and indigenous.

To provide a splash of colour to an academic text; few things could bring home more vividly the extent of the existence of self-absorbed English middle-class sport in Argentina than this record of a competition between two 'all-rounders' of the Hurlingham Club recorded in W.H. Kroebel's *Argentina: Past and Present*:

GREAT SPORTING EVENT
ON
1st November 1892

BETWEEN TWO MEMBERS OF THE
HURLINGHAM CLUB
TO COMMENCE AT 9.30 A.M.

1. Bat Fives – best of 3 games.
2. Racquets – best of 3 games.
3. Lawn Tennis – best of 3 sets.
4. Foot Race – one round, cinder track.
5. Pony Race – one round, race-course.
6. Boxing – 5 rounds, 3 minutes; 1 minute time.
7. Fencing – best of 3 points.
8. Cricket – single wicket.
9. Quoits – best of 3 games of 15.
10. Golf – 9 holes.
11. Shooting – 7 pigeons.
12. Billiards – best of 3 games of 100.

'The competition', Kroebel records, 'was faithfully carried out, and each event closely contested.'[89]

ST. GEORGE'S COLLEGE

There remains one further task and that is to establish a further and unequivocal dimension to English middle-class innovation by means of a consideration of St. George's College, Quilmes. St. George's was modelled exactly on the English public school – indeed it was 'a complete replica of a typical English Public School'[90] – initially self-contained, self-confident and self-absorbed in its maintenance of its essentially English culture. It has been claimed that:

> British schools in Argentina (and in Latin America) are fundamental in transmitting British ideas and attitudes but still no adequate study of them exists, nor a comparative study assessing their importance vis-à-vis other foreign schools. Were French Lycées the most prestigious academically? Were British schools admired more for their character building qualities than for academic achievement? Once in the 'tram-lines' of a particular national mode of thought it is difficult to break away. This aspect of the sociology of knowledge merits closer attention than it has received. Universities in Britain have more influence today on Argentines whereas up to the 1930's public schools would have been more important.[91]

To what extent is this true? Again inquiries would be invaluable to determine the full nature and extent of any influence.

The minds of the young are relatively malleable. All societies and cultures devote much time and effort to create educational systems to ensure the perpetuation of desirable social and cultural values. Educational institutions endorsed by the state or an elite are, therefore, significant agents of indoctrination into pre-eminent and prevailing beliefs, values and actions. All this is surely incontrovertible.

If this is so, it is illuminating to examine an English school in Buenos Aires to see to what extent it was a self-supporting, self-proclaiming, self-assured instrument of Englishness and to what extent it was an incidental, even accidental, instrument of Argentine cultural change. Self-evidently, at this temporal remove, this is not exactly an easy task but despite the difficulties, it is worthwhile in the pursuit of an understanding of the complex nature of the cultural diffusion, assimilation and adaptation of modern sport in a variety of locations, as well as an understanding of attempts at the construction of a secure, self-reliant identity in an alien place.

St. George's College, Quilmes, Argentina was founded in 1898. Its origins lay in confident patriotism – the belief in a system of education which had 'a hallmark essentially its own'.[92] The school's historian wrote, in the opening page of its history that in 'our English Public Schools there is a secret which other nations envy and that is the training of character, to which is due our national success'.[93] It was this 'secret' that was responsible for the foundation of the school.

St. George's was established with the capital of English residents in Buenos Aires. England's patron saint was chosen as its patron. The school was widely known as 'Little England' and was open to all 'English-speaking boys in the Argentine and neighbouring republics'[94] to provide 'a first-class education on the same basis as that given at an English public school'.[95] The headmaster was obliged to be a priest of the Anglican church, a common requirement of English public schools at the time.[96]

St. George's struggled financially for a good ten years but held a healthy portfolio of assets: a chapel, continually extended games fields, a feeder preparatory school, a prize for the finest Christian gentleman, a house system, eventually an Officer Training Corps and a dining hall in which were to be found martial, patriotic paintings[97] – the 'Roll Call' recalling an episode at the Battle of Inkerman and 'The Fight for the Standard' recalling an action at the Battle of Waterloo, donated by John Miller, one of the founders, 'a fine type of robust manhood, a thorough patriot and a grand old English gentleman'.[98]

The 'Englishness' of St. George's was much admired by the English themselves. When the Rt Revd Edward Francis Evey of Harrow and Trinity College, Cambridge, newly Bishop of the Falkland Isles, made a visit to the school, he expressed pleasure at seeing 'such a fine English-looking set of boys'.[99] He became a strong supporter of the school and its Official Visitor. The visits of Her Majesty's Ministers and later His Majesty's Ambassadors to distribute prizes for sport and work were a regular feature of school life.[100] In 1903 the Minister, Sir William Haggard, distributed the school prizes and expressed his pleasure at coming to the College as 'it seemed to him quite a part of England with the green trees, English voices and faces'.[101] In 1909 the Minister, Sir Walter Townley, distributed the Sports prizes and remarked on the strong relationship of the Old Boys with the school, which demonstrated, in his view, 'that indefinable bond called *esprit de corps*, which was such a noticeable thing in English Public Schools'.[102]

Central to the institutional life of an English Public School is the chapel. It is therefore no surprise that the school historian devoted an entire chapter of his work to St. George's Chapel and began with a statement that 'The school chapel and all that it stands for and implies, has been, through all English history, down to our own time, an essential part of an English Public School.'[103] Within the Chapel, St. George's had an obligatory commemorative marble tablet celebrating the imperial self-sacrificial subaltern: 'The Reredos was erected by his parents and sisters to the Glory of God and in ever loving memory of Phillip Noel Stevenson, only son of Canon and Mrs. J.T. Stevenson, and Lieutenant in the Bombay 1/109th Infantry, Indian Army, who, while leading his company at Asa Khan, North-West Frontier, was killed in action on January 14, 1920: aged 19. "Greater Love hath no man than this, that a man lay down his life for his friends."'[104]

All the early masters 'were chosen from England'.[105] Regrettably some created unspecified problems and provided 'the greatest difficulty'[106] in the early life of the college; they are not named in the school history. Those mentioned in the history were, invariably and inevitably, praised for their enthusiasm for, and involvement in, sport. Indeed in the climate of the time it would have been hard for masters to be appointed without it.[107] There was also the obligatory games-master – the first, T. Knight-Adkin, was 'always very breezy, a keen sportsman and a good friend to the boys'.[108] A number of the staff came from, or returned to English public and preparatory schools and links with England and English elite education were in this way continually being renewed and strengthened. Several of the staff became headmasters of the 'English' schools in Argentina[109] and helped spread English public school games, manners and practices throughout Argentina. Clearly a study of these peripatetic diffusionists would be of some interest and importance in tracing the English middle-class influence on Argentine secondary education and on society, both in the capital and the interior.

In all probability, the boys themselves were equally significant as diffusionists. They came from six South American republics – Argentina, Brazil, Bolivia, Chile, Paraguay and Uruguay. Also of significance in this regard was the fact that initially, many of the pupils at St. George's 'proceeded to the Public Schools and Universities of England'. Some of these certainly returned to Argentina with their enthusiasm for sport reinforced.[110] Others too, such as the Argentine gilded youths, the Etonian sons of Don Miguel Alfredo Martines de

Hoz, played their part.[111] It was not simply passing sailors and visiting businessmen who spread 'the gospel of games' and English pastimes. Following English practice, St. George's had its preparatory school, formed in the image of the senior school in which, in consequence, game-playing masters were greatly in evidence.[112] Thus the cult of games, or athleticism at it was known at the time, invigorated by moral purpose, was assimilated at an early age by the pupils. Unsurprisingly the school history in its coverage of distinguished Old Boys makes frequent mention of their athletic ability, clearly inferring that character acquired on playing fields played its part in their later success in life.

One hundred and forty Old Boys of St. George's volunteered for service during the Great War; fourteen died in uniform. The school considered itself one with the Public Schools across the Atlantic in the need to do its patriotic duty. At the unveiling of the Roll of Honour in the Peace Memorial Gymnasium after the war, the Minister, Ronald Macleay, stated in his address that the names on the memorial tablet constituted 'a record of duty nobly done and a tribute to the traditions of loyalty and patriotism and to the high ideals of manliness and courage inculcated in this English School'[113] as well as an 'overmastering affection for the land of their origin'.[114] He requested that when the 'young Georgians' glanced up at the Tablet they would say to themselves 'I will play games hard and practice in this gym' in order to be ready for enterprises requiring the strength and health.[115]

Armistice Day was celebrated with an English public school ceremonial: 'A whole day cricket match against the Old Georgian Club'.[116] Through such rituals the school demonstrated that it was wholly convinced that it stood virtuously apart. It considered these manifestations of masculinity English rather than Latin American and with confident ethnocentricity, it was convinced that its masculinity in its subscription to 'fair play', was quintessentially English. In this way continuity of values was confirmed. This conviction suggests that a comparison of Latin American and English masculinities and the role of sport in their definition and determination, has much to recommend it.[117]

On the anniversary of the Armistice, it became the practice 'to read in Chapel the Roll of those who made the supreme sacrifice, and to place above the memorial tablet a crown of flowers, and to drape it with the St. George's flag'[118] linking school with England in perpetuity. Other symbolic gestures were made such as on the Coronation of Edward VII

on 9 August 1902 which was celebrated with a service at St. John's
Anglican Church sports in the city at the Hippic Club, a bonfire and a
display of fireworks. The Coronation of George V on 22 June 1911 was
similarly celebrated with equal enthusiasm. The school history records
complacently state that the Argentine, like all South American
Republics, is proverbial for numerous fiestas, but the College has been
content to observe only May 25 its Day of Independence in 1810.[119] St.
George's was an English Protestant school in a Latin American Catholic
country and its cultural accommodation would only go so far. The
Englishness of St. George's remained unadulterated until at least the
retirement of the founding headmaster Rev. Canon J.T. Stevenson
(author of the school history) in February 1935. He was praised by Mr
H. Taylor, Honorary Treasurer of the College Company in the
following words: 'You in only six years of loving labour, have built a
great edifice of which every Englishman in this country may well be
proud.'[120] In his farewell speech Stevenson produced sincere and decent
platitudes wholly typical of the English public school headmaster: 'your
greatest capital in life is your character ... never ask a favour of yourself
in sport, but if another ask it of you, given it him with courtesy and
chivalry. It is always a joy to me when I hear that Old Georgians play
the game in business and sport ... I am jealous that this excellent
tradition should be ever and fully maintained.'[121] Within three months
of his retirement Stevenson was awarded the CBE for his services
to education.

Among other things, the Chapel sermon in the English public school
system was an opportunity for reminders of the special nature of the
public school and public schoolboy by convinced eulogists of 'Anglo-
Saxonism'. It was no different at St. George's. Those published in the
school history make reference to 'the best traditions of our old English
Public Schools', 'the happy features of English Public Schools life', 'the
[English] Public School tradition ... of clean honour and unselfish
service', the fact that St. George's College ranked equality with 'the
great English Public Schools which ... still play a great part in the next
English life' and the business of the school in a foreign country was
described as 'to turn out boys of the English Public school type' with the
result that the boys were, in fact, 'wonderfully English'.

The confident insularity of St. George's College in the late
nineteenth and early twentieth centuries comes through clearly in
everything set out above. Convinced of its special superiority, it stood

removed from the Latin American community. One visitor to the school
wrote: 'You have a really magnificent school. Not only does the number
of boys testify to its position in the estimation of the British community
but I hear on all sides that its greatest achievement has been to create
among the boys the true English Public school spirit and to give them
ideals hard to acquire in a Latin-American country.'[122] This aloofness
was shared by their adult compatriots, who eschewed living 'in centrally
located ornate palaces, preferring the dullness – and coolness – of the
suburbs, Hurlingham and Temperley, relieved by the playing of the
games they introduced – polo, tennis, golf, soccer and rugby'.[123] In
Edward Said's term, these English possessed in their self-chosen
isolation, 'an essentialist representation' of the Latin American.
however, for the Argentine, this ethnocentric self-confidence was
arguably not without its power to impress and attract.[124]

St. George's existed in itself for itself. It had no imperial, moral,
cultural or political mission – either direct or indirect. Yet despite this,
and in a sense because of this, it proved one of the agents of cultural
transmission which brought the English Games Cult to, and spread it
throughout, Argentina and other countries of Latin America. Of course,
the full extent of this still remains for the historian to discover.
Unquestionably, the school's confidence in itself and its athletic
activities and their value engendered a degree of admiration and
certainly emulation among Argentines.[125] To a degree, St. George's
assured aloofness was its attraction. Together with English middle-class
merchants, bankers, technicians and others from Britain and those of the
Latin American middle classes who were educated in England, who
travelled in England, who lived for a time in England, as well as
elsewhere in Britain, the school was an early source and a fine illustration
of Shakespearian 'strange eventual history' of an extraordinary and
peaceful Latin American revolution – modern sport for recreation,
health and education. It has been wisely observed that 'It is essential …
to avoid facile assumptions about unidirectionality'.[126] It is also sensible
to appreciate that stimuli may not only be confusingly diverse but
sometimes unintentional.

THE ARRIVAL OF MODERN SPORT

In the twentieth century, Latin America, like too many other areas of the
world, has been a place of diplomatic turmoil, social inequality, political

paranoia, capitalist exploitation and class conflict.[127] However, it may be stated factually and without sentimentality, that it has also been a place where, despite all this and through all this, people have survived and even thrived, worked, loved and played. Modern sport has brought to their play, as well as a measure of disillusion and disappointment, marvellous opportunities for illusion and pleasure. In its absence no doubt traditional activities, indigenous or otherwise, would have provided distraction but fortunately there has been no void and they have not. That is the reality whatever the causes or consequences. Modern sport, with its warts and beauty spots, is the reality – and on the balance sheet, while there are things to criticize, there are also many things to applaud. The English middle class, with others, have played a not insignificant part in its arrival.

It has been written that while the Imperialists have left India, they have left behind mental, as well as physical traces of their occupation, 'mind tracks' as well as train tracks.[128] Should the same be said of the Anglo Saxon in Latin America? Should it be said similarly of Argentina? Soccer seduced the masses *and* the middle classes; other sports remained middle-class but all these initially novel sports were embraced by one level of society or another; a massive cultural transformation occurred. It was to be supplemented substantially by North American cultural influences but that is another story.[129]

In any consideration of cultural diffusion, to adapt and to correct one commentator, what matters is not only what happens to a cultural form when it arrives, but that it arrives.[130] It has been observed that the reception of foreign movements and tendencies has been an integral part of Argentine culture and instead of interrupting the purity of improbable autonomous developments, this receptivity has added a dynamic element to the development of artistic creation.[131] This statement is extremely apt in the case of sport. It is not a matter of sets of cultural alternatives with associations of superiority and inferiority. The reality is more subtle than that. It is a matter of advantaged cultural hybridity. Furthermore, it is not unreasonable to suggest the same is true of the other nations of Latin America or indeed the world. The point has been made, 'with epigrammatic forcefulness', that 'the history of all cultures is the history of cultural borrowing'.[132] In Argentina the absorption and adaptation of those modern sports established and developed mainly in England and the other nations of Britain in the late nineteenth century, is clearly an illustration of this receptivity: 'Culture is never just a matter of ownership, of borrowing and lending with absolute debtors and creditors, but rather of appropriations, common experiences, and inter-dependency of all kinds.'[133]

It scarcely needs to be stated that the sometimes substantial variation between Latin American nations and their different enthusiasms for various kinds of sport, perhaps with the exception of soccer, makes generalizations regarding the 'infancy', 'adolescence' and 'maturity' of their sport difficult to achieve. However, perhaps the safest generalization is that the route modern sport took was via the middle classes of (mainly) England and the other nations of Britain and Latin America. It is hoped that future Latin American analysts and their inquiries will determine how far this is true.

It has been argued with good sense that 'the next generation of analysts of Latin American sport must dig deeper into untouched archives and other sources'[134] in order to reveal new areas of inquiry, to explore ways in which sport can illuminate cultural migration and emigration, indigenous assimilation and adaptation and to investigate sport as an indicator and reflector of cultural change. There is good reason for this, namely to understand the origins of assuredly one of the most significant, far-reaching and influential of twentieth-century cultural innovations – the coming of modern sport.

A. Hennessy and J. King expressed the hope that their book would 'open up a neglected field of [cultural] study – even among professional Latin Americans – and make some contribution towards increasing mutual understanding'.[135] This chapter has the same ambitions. In the specific area of the Argentine, Richard Graham's sober appraisal of the influence of the British in Brazil seems most apposite: 'By 1914 Brazil had begun to move toward a modern society. The British had done a lot to bring about this onset of modernization, although they had also given some support to those forces that opposed it. Acting neither with altruism nor with malice but driven by the ambitions and desires instilled in them by their own modernizing society, the British played a large part in initiating change in Brazil.'[136] Perhaps it is worth recalling that even Edward Said appears to appreciate the balanced view of C.L.R. James, lover of cricket, 'whose early formation in British colonial schools brought forth a wonderful appreciation of English culture, as well as serious disagreements with it'.[137] An understanding of the roots of the present buried in the past, consolidates and confirms identity. In this regard there is still much for the Latin American historian interested in the history of sport embedded in culture to discover about its origins and those responsible. This is a far from unimportant task. For one thing is unequivocally clear that 'Modern sport [has] – for better and for worse – become the heritage of humankind.'[138]

AN APPROPRIATE CODA

To add a final daub of colour from my brush – regarding the rejection of a facile assumption of diffusional unidirectionality[139] – there is a world class Argentinean rugby player who plays in Europe at club level in France and at international level for Italy: Diego Dominguez. His genius has enhanced European sport; he is an outstanding illustration of the 'back and forth' diffusion of modern sport.[140]

NOTES

1. Anthony Pagden, *Lords of All The World: Ideologies of Empire in Spain, Britain and France c.1500–1800* (New Haven: Yale University Press, 1995), p.1.
2. Mark Ferro, *Colonization: A Global History* (London: Routledge, 1997), p.350.
3. Ibid., p.345.
4. Ibid., p.346.
5. Nicholas B. Dirks, *Colonialism and Culture* (Michigan: University of Michigan Press, 1992), p.3.
6. Ibid., p.7.
7. Ibid., p.11.
8. See Allen Guttmann, *Games and Empires: Modern Sports and Cultural Imperialism* (New York: University of Columbia Press, 1994), pp.6–10. With this book Guttmann has made a major contribution to cultural inquiries into modern sport and its global diffusion.
9. Joseph Arbena, 'Sport and Social Change in Latin America', unpublished paper, 14.
10. For a detailed definition of modern sport, see Guttmann, *Games and Empires*, pp.2–3.
11. Ibid., pp.178–9.
12. Ibid.
13. Arbena, 'Sport and Social Change in Latin America', 1.
14. Ferro, *Colonialization*, p.9.
15. The term 'English middle class' is used here as a generic term embracing the lower middle, middle and upper middle classes.
16. See Joseph Arbena, 'Nationalism and Sport in Latin America, 1850–1990: The Paradox of Promoting and Reforming "European" Sports', in J.A. Mangan (ed.), *Tribal Identities: Nationalism, Europe and Sport* (London and Portland, OR: Frank Cass, 1995), p.230, for an elaboration of this argument.
17. See J.A. Mangan (ed.), *The Cultural Bond: Sport, Empire, Society* (London and Portland, OR: Frank Cass, 1992), pp.1–2.
18. John King, 'The Influence of British Culture in Argentina' in Alistair Hennessy and John King (eds.), *The Land That England Lost* (London: British Academic Press, 1992), pp.159–60.
19. Paul Henderson makes this point in a review of Rory Miller, *Britain and Latin America in the Nineteenth and Twentieth Centuries* (London: Longman, 1993) in *Bulletin of Latin American Research Review*, 14, 2 (1995), 88.
20. The full extent of this dependency is under scrutiny and a source of academic contention, see

especially Miller, *Britain and Latin America in the Nineteenth and Twentieth Centuries*, pp.274–5 and 238–44.

21. Arbena, 'Nationalism and Sport in Latin America', p.15.
22. Hennessy and King (eds.), *The Land that England Lost*, p.2.
23. Ibid.
24. See, for example, the discussion in J.A. Mangan's Prologue to *The Cultural Bond*, pp.7–9.
25. Partha Chatter, *The Nation and its Fragments: Colonial and Postcolonial Histories* (Princeton: Princeton University Press, 1993), p.xi, quoted in Anna Green and Kathleen Troup, 'Postcolonial Perspectives', in *The Houses of History* (Manchester: Manchester University Press, 1998), p.281.
26. In his review essay 'Sport and Colonialism in Latin America and the Caribbean' (*Studies in Latin American Popular Culture*, 10 [1991], 257–71), Alan Klein lays considerable stress on the unquestionably important topic of colonial sport as cultural resistance. However, while he takes Brian Stoddart to task for an over-emphasis on cricket as cultural hegemony in his West Indian studies, he himself displays a clear tendency to lean too far in the other direction in his preoccupation with sport as cultural resistance. The reality, of course, is that sport can be a sophisticated manifestation of cultural involvement. It can be as much a force for cultural integration as a face for cultural polarization. For discussions of these two faces of cultural involvement, see, for example, J.A. Mangan 'Braveheart Betrayed? Cultural Cloning for Colonial Careers', *Immigrants and Minorities*, 173, 1 (March 1998), 189–208, which deals with the Scottish middle class's eager adoption of the English public school games ethic as a castemark, ensuring imperial careers, and J.A. Mangan and Nam Gil Ha, 'Confucianism, Imperialism and Nationalism: Ideology, Modern Sport and Korean Society 1876–1945' in J.A. Mangan (ed.), *Europe, Sport, World: Shaping Global Societies* (London and Portland, OR: Frank Cass, 2000), which provides evidence on the part of Koreans of the extensive use of sport in the early twentieth century in an effort to resist Japanese attempts to destroy a separate Korean cultural identity. The coin has two façades.
27. Arbena, 'Nationalism and Sport in Latin America', 23.
28. Guttmann, *Games and Empires*, p.177.
29. Ibid.
30. For a good example, see Mangan, 'Braveheart Betrayed? Cultural Cloning for Colonial Careers'.
31. Harry Hendrick, *Images of Youth* (Oxford: Oxford University Press, 1990), p.137.
32. *Daily Telegraph*, 20 July 1999, 5.
33. Juan Antonio Samaranch, quoted by Mihir Bose in 'Inside Sport', *Daily Telegraph*, 11 Dec. 1999, S6.
34. Guttmann, *Games and Empires*, p.2.
35. Ibid., p.2.
36. See J.A. Mangan, *Athleticism in the Victorian and Edwardian Public School: The Emergence and Consolidation of an Educational Ideology* (Cambridge: Cambridge University Press, 1981; Falmer: Falmer Press, 1986; London and Portland, OR: Frank Cass, 2000).
37. Ian Bradley, *The English Middle Classes Are Alive and Kicking* (London: Collins, 1982), p.11.
38. Mike Huggins, 'Second Class Citizens? English Middle-Class Culture and Sport 1850–1910: A Reconsideration', *International Journal of the History of Sport*, 17, 2 (March 2000), 1.
39. Ibid., 2.
40. J.A. Mangan, 'Regression and Progression', Introduction to the 2000 edition of *Athleticism in the Victorian and Edwardian Public School* (London and Portland, OR: Frank Cass, 2000), p.33.
41. Georges Clemenceau, *South America Today* (London: T. Fisher Unwin, 1911), pp.81–2.
42. Ibid., pp.180–84. This is not to overlook the impact and popularity of French culture (see King, 'The Influence of British Culture', 162–3) but to make it clear that the English influence was underestimated by Clemenceau!
43. Arbena, 'Nationalism and Sport in Latin America', 17.
44. Richard McGehee, 'Sports and Recreational Activities in Guatemala and Mexico, Late 1800s to 1926', *Studies in Latin American Popular Culture*, 13 (1994), 22.
45. See T. Mason, *Passion of the People: Football of the People* (London: Verso, 1995), pp.16–17.
46. Ibid.

47. Arbena, 'Nationalism and Sport in Latin America', 16.

48. See King, 'The Influence of British Culture', 162.

49. See Mangan, *Athleticism*, and especially the discussion of Stonyhurst, pp.59–67 and passim.

50. The term is that of Francois Furet, 'From Narrative History to Problem-orientated History' in *In the Workshop of History*, trans. Jonathan Mandelbaum (Chicago: University of Chicago Press, 1984), p.54.

51. Green and Troup, 'The Question of Narrative' in *The Houses of History*, p.204.

52. For an early discussion in the English language of their role in this regard see J.A. Mangan and Victor de Melo, 'A Web of the Wealthy: Modern Sport in the Nineteenth-Century Culture of Rio de Janeiro', *International Journal of the History of Sport*, 14, 1 (April 1997), 168–73.

53. See Huggins, *Second Class Citizens*, also J.A. Mangan, ' "Muscular, Militaristic and Manly": The British Middle-Class Hero as Moral Messenger', *International Journal of the History of Sport*, 13, 1 (1996), 44.

54. See Mason, *Passion of the People*, pp.24–5. Mason concentrates on 'adolescence' at the expense of 'infancy'. 'Infancy' is an important and relevant part of the story too.

55. H.S. Ferns, 'Britain's Informal Empire in Argentina, 1806–1914', *Past and Present*, 1, 4 (1953), 60.

56. H.S. Ferns, 'Argentina: Part of an Informal Empire?' in Hennessy and King (eds.), *The Land that England Lost*, p.50.

57. Ferns, 'Britain's Informal Empire', 60.

58. Ferns, 'Argentina; Part of an Informal Empire?', 49.

59. Ibid.

60. Sir David Kelly, *The Ruling Few* (London: Hollis and Carter, 1952), p.110.

61. Ferns, 'Britain's Informal Empire', 63.

62. Ibid., 70.

63. Ibid.

64. Ibid.

65. Ibid., 71.

66. Some significant modern sports, for example, rugby, cricket and athletics, owe much, if not everything, to the games cult and games systems of the late Victorian and Edwardian English public schools – wholly middle-class institutions. Irish, Scottish and Welsh schools followed in their footsteps with time. Irish, Scottish and Welsh schools certainly adopted the games system later than many English public schools and they were, of course, far fewer since the English middle class was very much larger than those of Ireland, Scotland and Wales. It is wholly reasonable to suggest that the English middle class as a group moved overseas in larger numbers, had greater capital, more establishment roles and more influence, both culturally, politically and economically, than those of Ireland, Scotland and Wales. At a time when the nations of Britain are increasingly asserting their separateness, there could well be a case for separating the role and influence of the English middle-class 'imperialism' – formal and informal – from the Irish, Scots and Welsh. This article is a step in that direction in academic anticipation of things to come. Hennessy and King, incidentally, made a related point as early as 1992: 'At a time when the United Kingdom may be becoming more disunited, analysis needs to focus on those strains and tensions which have always existed between the English, Irish, Scots and Welsh'. They added that 'In studies of the British diaspora insufficient attention has perhaps been paid to the different experiences and responses of Britain's major ethnic groups'. This is my point exactly with regard to the English! In passing, it should also be remembered that many of the Irish, Scots and Welsh middle class, especially the upper middle class, attended English public schools and universities and their members were often greatly influenced by their experiences. Nor should it be forgotten that universities, as well as schools, in these countries took up some of the general 'recreational' practices of the English public schools and Oxford and Cambridge and established their own modern games, clubs, facilities, playing fields and teams of one kind or another. Regarding early evidence of English middle-class involvement in Argentina, while research is certainly incomplete, Hennessy has written that 'The 1825 Treaty permitted the building of an Anglican church which came to be attended by respectable merchants, the majority of whom were English' (p.19) and again 'Many English came as merchants and stayed as landowners'(p.21).

67. Mason, *Passion of the People*, p.25.
68. George Pendle, *Argentina* (London: Royal Institute of International Affairs, 1961), p.57.
69. Andrew Graham-Yooll, *The Forgotten Colony* (London: Hutchinson, 1981), p.16.
70. Kelly, *The Ruling Few*, p.111.
71. Graham-Yooll, *The Forgotten Colony*, p.17.
72. Ibid.
73. Ibid., p.18.
74. Ibid.
75. Ibid., p.19.
76. Ibid., p.115.
77. Ibid., p.188.
78. Ibid., p.189.
79. Ibid.
80. Ibid., p.193.
81. Pablo Alabarces, 'Argentine National Identity and Football: 'the Creole English' – Adventures of a Scot on the River Plate', Conference paper delivered at the British Society of Sports History, Brighton: 2–3 June 1999.
82. Ibid., 4.
83. See Alabarces, 'Argentine National Identity and Football', passim.
84. Members of a family of Yorkshire textile merchants.
85. See Guttmann, *Games and Empires*, pp.57–8. Incidentally, Graham-Yooll puts the date of the first rugby match in Argentina a year earlier.
86. Graham-Yooll, *The Forgotten Colony*, p.130.
87. Ibid., pp.194–5.
88. Letter to J.A. Mangan dated 26 April 2000. This information, as well as helpful additional material, including an attractive and useful published school history, was greatly appreciated. Information on St. Alban's College, founded by the Rev. G.H. Knight-Clarke, as Quilmes Grammar School in 1907 was also generously supplied by the present headmaster, John R. Vibert. A printed note from Mr Vibert on Knight-Clarke records that 'Possessed of a very strong character indeed, it was he who laid down the ethical, moral, academic and sporting bases that made St. Albans such a positive influence in Argentine Education through the years'.
89. W.H. Kroebel, *Argentina: Past and Present* (London: Paul, Trench and Trubner, 1910), p.163.
90. Kelly, *The Ruling Few*, p.110.
91. Hennessy and King (eds.), *The Land that England Lost*, p.44.
92. J.T. Stevenson, *The History of St. George's College, Quilmes, Argentina 1898–1935* (London: Church Missionary Society, 1936), p.1.
93. Ibid., p.2.
94. Ibid., p.7.
95. Ibid.
96. It is generally accepted that Frank Fletcher was the first lay headmaster of an English public school. He was appointed headmaster of Marlborough in 1903, see Mangan, *Athleticism*, Epilogue.
97. The English public schools, as public schools elsewhere in Britain, imbued their pupils with strong martial, patriotic and imperial values which helped promote the late Victorian militaristic attitude of many of the middle class. Despite the curious protestations to the contrary of at least one English sports historian, this reality is now surely beyond dispute and succinctly summarized by, for example, Robert H. MacDonald in *The Language of Empire: Myths and Metaphors of Popular Imperialism, 1880–1918* (Manchester: Manchester University Press, 1994), p.2: 'By the 1890s, it is clear, British society was saturated with nationalistic and militaristic ideas. The Queen and the army moved to the centre of the imperial stage, a cult of heroes and a heroic national history was celebrated in popular literature and had infiltrated school text books, the music halls exploited patriotic sentiments in song and tableaux.' Those who appear to dispute this, at least in part, simply have not read widely and deeply enough in the relevant literature. For a comment on this state of affairs, see especially Mangan, 'Regression and Progression', Introduction to the 2000 edition of *Athleticism*, and also J.A. Mangan, 'The Nordic World and Other Worlds' in H. Meinander and J.A. Mangan (eds.), *The Nordic World: Sport in Society* (London and Portland, OR: Frank Cass, 1998), pp.184–90. For evidence of public school martial indoctrination, for which

there are now a number of sources, see especially J.A. Mangan, 'Play Up and Play the Game: the Rhetoric of Cohesion, Identity, Patriotism and Morality' in *Athleticism*, pp.179–203; J.A. Mangan, 'Concepts of Duty and Propsects of Adventure: Images of Empire for Public Schoolboys', in *The Games Ethic and Imperialism*, pp.44–70; J.A. Mangan, 'Moralists, Metaphysicians and Mythologists: The 'Signifiers' of a Victorian and Edwardian Sub-culture' in Susan J-Bandy (ed.), *Coroebus Triumphs: The Alliance of Sport and the Arts* (San Diego: University of San Diego Press, 1988), pp.141–62; J.A. Mangan, 'Noble Specimens of Manhood: Schoolboy Literature and the Creation of a Colonial Chivalric Code' in Jeffrey Richards (ed.), *Imperialism and Juvenile Literature* (Manchester: Manchester University Press, 1989), pp.173–94; J.A. Mangan, 'The Grit of our Forefathers: Invented Traditions, Propaganda and Imperialism' in John M. MacKenzie (ed.), *Imperialism and Popular Culture* (Manchester: Manchester University Press, 1986), pp.113–39; J.A. Mangan '"Duty unto Death": English Masculinity and Militarism in the Age of the New Imperialism', in J.A. Mangan (ed.) *Tribal Identities: Nationalism, Sport, Europe* (London and Portland, OR: Frank Cass, 1996), pp.10–38, J.A. Mangan, 'Muscular, Militaristic and Manly: The British Middle Class Hero as Moral Messenger' in Richard Holt, J.A. Mangan and Pierre Lanfranchi (eds.), *European Heroes: Myth, Identity, Sport* (London and Portland, OR: Frank Cass, 1996), pp.28–47, J.A. Mangan 'Gamesfield and Battlefield: A Romantic Alliance in Verse and the Creation of Militaristic Masculinity' in J. Nauright and J. Chandler (eds.), *Making Men* (London and Portland, OR: Frank Cass, 1998), pp.141–57. For the wider cultural and educational context in which these articles and chapters are set, see Mangan, *Athleticism*; Mangan, *The Games Ethic*; and also J.A. Mangan (ed.), *Benefits Bestowed?: Education and British Imperialism* (Manchester: Manchester University Press, 1988); J.A. Mangan (ed.), *Making Imperial Mentalities: Socialisation and British Imperialism* (Manchester: Manchester University Press, 1990); and J.A. Mangan (ed.), *The Imperial Curriculum: Racial Images and Education in the British Colonial Experience* (London: Routledge, 1993).

  98. Stevenson, *A History of St. George's College*, p.35.
  99. Ibid.
100. Britain had a legation with a Minister in Buenos Aires until 1927 when it was raised to an Embassy.
101. Stevenson, *A History of St. George's College*, p.165.
102. Ibid.
103. Ibid., p.41.
104. Ibid., p.48.
105. Ibid., p.67. In fact some came from other parts of Britain. See, for example, pp.69 and 70.
106. Ibid.
107. See Mangan, *Athleticism*, Ch.5.
108. Stevenson, p.7. Knight-Adkin abandoned scholastic life for commerce and eventually owned an estancia.
109. For example, J.E. Green, A.S. Cuff, G. Thomas and J. Cavendish, all of whom, except Cavendish, were applauded in the school history for their keenness for games.
110. One example is F. Dickinson (1899) who left to attend Shrewsbury School (as did his brother A. Dickinson) and returned to own citrus plantations in Misiones. He was a successful athlete in both schools (see Stevenson, p.83).
111. Kelly, *The Ruling Few*, p.122.
112. There was one difference: Miss Gwendoline Stevenson, educated at The Ladies' College, Cheltenham, taught the smaller boys (see Stevenson, p.78).
113. Stevenson, *A History of St. George's College*, p.97.
114. Ibid.
115. Ibid.
116. Ibid., p.99.
117. For regional interpretations – British and Argentine respectively – of the role of sport in defining and determining masculinity see J.A. Mangan, 'Social Darwinism and Upper-class Education in the late Victorian and Edwardian England' in J.A. Mangan and James Walvin, *Manliness and Morality: Middle-Class Masculinity in Britain and America, 1800–1940* (Manchester: Manchester University Press, 1987), pp.135–59; and J.A. Mangan, 'Duty unto Death: English Masculinity and Militarism in J.A. Mangan (ed.), *Tribal Identities: Nationalism, Europe, Sport*, pp.10–38; and E.P. Archetti, 'Playing Styles and Masculine

Virtues in Argentine Football'; M. Melhuis and K.A. Stolen (eds.), *Machos, Mistresses, Madonnas: Contesting the Power of Latin American Imagery* (London: Verso, 1996), passim; and E.P. Archetti, 'The Moralities of Argentinian Football' in S. Howell (ed.), *The Ethnography of Moralities* (London: Routledge, 1997a), pp.98–123.

118. Stevenson, *A History of St. George's College*, p.101.
119. Ibid., p.153.
120. Ibid., p.230.
121. Ibid., p.229.
122. Ibid., p.210.
123. Hennessy and King, *The Land that England Lost*, pp.4–5.
124. See Edward Said, *Orientalism: Western Conceptions of the Orient* (New York: Pantheon Books, 1978), p.1.
125. The school was officially inspected by Argentine schoolmasters. Some were greatly impressed and clearly wished the school be widely imitated.
126. Guttmann, *Sports and Empires*, p.117.
127. No one has made this point more forcefully than E. Bradford Burns, in *Latin America: A Concise Interpretative History* (Englewood Cliffs, NJ: Prentice-Hall, 1986). He writes of the recent past, for example, 'The majority of Latin Americans are undernourished, under-employed, undereducated, and underpaid'. See also Stanley J. Stein and Barbara Stein, *The Colonial Heritage of Latin America* (New York: Oxford University Press, 1970), and Eric R. Wolf and Edward C. Hanse, *The Human Condition in Latin America* (London: Oxford University Press, 1972).
128. Green and Troup, 'Postcolonial Perspectives', *The Houses of History*, p.279.
129. Joseph Maguire in *Global Sport: Identities, Societies, Civilizations* (London: Polity Press, 1999), states quite correctly that 'England is viewed as the 'cradle' of modern sport' (p.56) and goes on to remark that 'People in different societies have proved to be remarkably receptive to and emulating of 'English' customs and pastimes!' (p.56). However, he also makes the pertinent remark that: 'Sports such as association football, golf and tennis are examples of these processes at work. There are, however, two qualifications to be made to this argument. The sports mentioned also highlight the "European" influence on the development of 'English' sports, that is the development of golf, for example, was strongly influenced by events in the Netherlands and Scotland. The role of the French in the development of tennis also cannot be underestimated. Indeed, some of the technical terms associated with tennis are derived from French. In addition, if consideration is also given to sports such as basketball and volleyball, which spread across the globe at a later stage in the sportization process, account has to be taken of the Americanization of sporting terms' (pp.57–8). His comment, however, does raise the questions of how 'modern' is 'modern' and when does 'modernity' begin.
130. See Allen Guttmann, *Games and Empires*, p.187.
131. King, 'The Influence of British Culture in Argentina', 170.
132. Quoted in Guttmann, *Games and Empires*, p.184.
133. Edward W. Said, *Culture and Imperialism* (London: Chatto and Windus, 1993), p.262.
134. Robert M. Levine, 'Sport as Dramaturgy – for Society: A Concluding Chapter' in Joseph L. Arbena (ed.), *Sport and Society in Latin America: Diffusion, Dependency and the Rise of Mass Culture* (New York: Greenwood Press, 1988), p.145.
135. Hennessy and King, *The Land that England Lost*, p.6.
136. Richard Graham, *Britain and the Onset of Modernization in Brazil: 1850–1914* (Cambridge: Cambridge University Press, 1968), p.324.
137. Said, *Culture and Imperialism*, p.295.
138. The expression is Allen Guttmann's – see *Games and Empires*, p.187. I have amended sports (an American expression) to sport in this quotation.
139. Again the expression is Allen Guttmann's – see *Games and Empires*, p.174.
140. Once again the expression is Allen Guttmann's – see Guttmann, *Games and Empires*, p.173. Guttmann is unquestionably one of the most stimulating, as well as pellucid, of commentators on modern sport in contemporary cultures and his *Games and Empires* is an essential source for all those who wish to explore the fascinating and significant topic of the global diffusion of modern sport. He has the odd critic (see, for example, the Epilogue of this volume) but also many admirers.

2

The Later Evolution of Modern Sport in Latin America: The North American Influence

JOSEPH L. ARBENA

That the diffusion of sports has been a feature of the last several centuries seems undeniable.[1] In the post-1492 era of European expansion and colonialism, the Portuguese, Spanish, English, French and others carried various games, sports and forms of recreation to areas previously untouched by European society. In Latin America through the eighteenth century, this meant mainly Iberian card games, animal combats, numerous equestrian activities – including bullfighting – and early versions of Basque ball games.[2] To use Allen Guttmann's terminology, all these activities fit into the pre-modern category. In short, they were more games and diversions than true sports, lacking consistency and structure across time and space.[3]

By the mid-1800s, the sports entering the Latin American realm, whether from North America or from Europe and the United Kingdom, increasingly displayed characteristics associated with the evolving modern societies from which they came: greater structure and discipline, more standardized rules across larger geographical areas, emerging bureaucratic administration, rationalized training methods and decision making, evaluation based more on skill and performance than race, class, or gender, and signs of massification and commercialization.[4]

Some Latin American thinkers became convinced that the imported sports, whatever the source, could serve to teach the behaviour necessary to accelerate modernization in their still laggard societies, though they generally much preferred amateur over professional types, and could serve to demonstrate that their countries and select groups within them were achieving new levels of sophistication and status.[5] The Mexican philosopher-politician-educator, José Vasconcelos, linked play, games, physical education and sport to the improvement of health and morality and thus to the betterment of Mexican youth and society, through the discipline of 'team-work' and the rejection of body-destroying sensual habits, such as unhealthy eating, alcoholism and insufficient physical activity.[6] The Argentine lawyer, politician and sports administrator, César Viale, likewise argued that muscularity and athleticism were the way to improve a nation's health, virility and power. His fellow countryman Próspero Alemandri also asserted that sport would strengthen those virtues that ensure the best in life.[7] In Brazil, it has been suggested that the acceptance of *futebol* and, even earlier, horse racing and rowing, was part of a larger process of conscious importation of foreign customs and habits aimed at the imposition of social control and the inculcation of discipline and qualities necessary to function in a hierarchical and eventually industrial society.[8] However, as Victor Andrade de Melo and Julio Frydenberg suggest, different socioeconomic groups soon learned to inject different meanings into their sports and to find in them the roads to different ends.[9] And, arguably on some occasions at least, physical education as opposed to sport might better serve those purposes.[10]

Of course, the perceived link between sport and moral behaviour was not new to the nineteenth century. There were the earlier Spanish efforts to suppress the Mesoamerican ball games tradition and the Puritan struggles to protect the Sabbath from alleged corruption, but these newer campaigns were more comprehensive and constructive. Their purpose was to improve attitudes and behaviour through sport, physical education and recreation rather than to limit undesirable actions by controlling or even eliminating offending sports.[11] The North American influence on sports and physical culture in Latin America can be understood only in this wider context of an already ongoing process of dissemination, assimilation and adaptation that had its origins to a large extent in Britain and its Empire.[12]

THE NORTH AMERICAN INFLUENCE

Surely the North American sport that has had the greatest impact on Latin America over the longest period of time is baseball,[13] which evolved out of a variety of English stick and ball games. The outline of the modern game was first drawn in New York City in the mid-1840s. It spread rapidly, alongside the explosion of the US economy, the growth of cities, the rise of a middle class, the introduction of revolutionary technology, faster and more extensive transportation and communication networks, the desire for more recreational and leisure activities, more discretionary time and money and the construction of a unique national identity.[14]

As it evolved with the expanding American population and economy, baseball was carried to Latin America by a motley collection of US workers including sailors, engineers, miners, merchants, educators and missionaries, by Latin American students and other visitors to North America and by United States entrepreneurs such as Albert G. Spalding. The first group took the game mainly as a recreation, the second as a recreation but also as a means to spread American values and institutions and the third in the hope of profiting from anticipated new markets among spectators and buyers of equipment. Of course, the motives of each group often overlapped.[15]

Cuba, to a degree, illustrates all three groups in action. By the mid-1800s, numerous Americans were regularly visiting Cuban ports and plantations where baseball increasingly filled their free time. Simultaneously, large numbers of Cubans went to the United States to study or to escape from the ever more despised Spanish colonial administration. After 1850, these two facts, combined with favourable Cuban impressions of American progress, led the more nationalistic Cubans to embrace baseball as a symbol and expression of their rejection of things Spanish and of their admiration for the political, technological and economic advances of the United States. Eventually, Americans found in Cuba a deep enough baseball culture to scout talent, take frequent barnstorming tours, establish spring training camps and accept a Havana club into a high-level minor league.[16]

In the end, Cuba itself became the carrier of baseball to nearby foreign lands – various Caribbean islands and such mainland areas as the Mexican Yucatán and the Venezuelan coast – where its association with the dynamic island may have been as important as its American roots. Before 1959 Cuba was the only significant source of Latin players in the major leagues, although a few Dominicans, Puerto Ricans, Venezuelans and Mexicans did play in the minors and the Negro leagues prior to the re-integration of the National Game in the 1940s.[17]

There is no denying that the United States, like other sports exporters, has long seen political and patriotic messages in sporting competitions. However, the Cubans needed no model to instruct them that baseball, like all sports, can be used for political ends. The inspiration for the post-1959 Castro regime to make sport a symbol of its Revolution came as much from Cuba as America.[18]

Despite baseball's unquestionable importance in Cuba, other sports – boxing, basketball, track and field, volleyball – attract significant attention.[19] This is not the case in the Dominican Republic, 'the last place in the free world where baseball is the unchallenged national pastime'[20] and, since 1959, probably the Latin country that has had the greatest impact on North American major league baseball.[21] Beyond the Dominican, baseball has gained national prominence in Puerto Rico, Nicaragua and Panama, shares the spotlight with soccer in Mexico and Venezuela and fills an important niche in Colombia, Costa Rica and the Dutch Antilles.[22] On a smaller scale it has been played for numerous decades in Argentina and Brazil and recently the United States Embassy in La Paz supported the construction of what may be the world's highest ballpark at some three miles above sea level in the Bolivian Andes.[23]

In 1997, 201 Latinos spent time in the major leagues: 89 Dominicans, 42 Puerto Ricans, 39 Venezuelans, five Cubans and a scattering of others from several other circum-Caribbean countries. The 2000 season began with Latinos filling over 20 per cent of major league rosters.

While the success of Latino *beisbolistas* in North America may elevate national pride and even dollar earnings back home, it has also been argued that this uneven relationship – similar to the movement of *futbolistas* to Europe and of Caribbean cricketers to Mother England – is nothing more than a modern version of neocolonial extraction of a valuable natural resource. The exporting country is left materially and culturally poorer, as the major share of the profits remain in the hands of the metropolitan owners, spectators and media giants.[24] Still, certainly in the Cuban case and even, to some degree, in the Dominican case the suggestion is that, despite the appearance of a contradiction, surpassing the masters at their own game can allow a people to express their own unique character and define their own national identity,[25] with the result that baseball (like other sports) has become a vehicle for expressing and working out aspects of the post-1959 tensions between Cuba and the United States.[26] To an extent then, the adoption and adaptation of baseball in Latin America is more an expression of multi-dimensional transcultural fusion than of imposed cultural imperialism.[27]

It is as well to remember that the American boxing establishment has also been accused of exploiting Latin athletic talent, profiting from the riches generated by successful fighters before dumping them when they pass their prime.[28] If boxing originally reached Latin America more directly from Britain and Europe than the United States, selected US boxers such as Jack Dempsey and Muhammad Ali were admired in the south. Despite the earlier accusations, Latin American fighters such as Julio César Chávez have continued to seek their fortunes in North American rings.[29] But even if they are not leveling accusations of severe economic exploitation, Latin American players and fans alike have often maintained that North Americans do not fully understand or appreciate Latin American athletes and discriminate against them on racial and cultural grounds.[30]

THE AMERICAN VERSION OF FOOTBALL

American football is almost as distinctly American as baseball. However, although the American version of football was being played in neighbouring Mexico at least as early as the 1920s and perhaps before,[31] the game has touched very few areas south of the Río Grande. It has been played in Panama, especially in the old Canal Zone at high schools attended by youth from the north, but only in Mexico do local men, and recently a few women, play it regularly in schools and clubs.[32] Mexico hosts National Football League pre-season exhibition games, participates in university-level international competitions[33] and sends players of notable skill to NFL rosters.[34] Recent Mexican interest in the NFL Super Bowl surely reflects that century-long connection to the game, though in Mexico, as in those countries where American football is rarely performed – I have participated in Super Bowl Monday parties in New Zealand – a colourful global event may also be just an excuse to party in the same way as Anglos in the United States have learned to celebrate the Mexican national holiday, Cinco de Mayo. Nevertheless, a 1995 Super Bowl party in Buenos Aires reportedly inspired some 80 fans to form the Asociación Argentina de Football Americano and to start an eight-team competition of the much less physical 'flag ball' variation of the sport a year later.[35] The failure of American football to gain wide acceptance in Latin America, even where rugby football has found a niche, may derive from such circumstances as climate and cost – the equipment is both hot and expensive, from nationalism (it's just *too* American!) and from the possibility that it is truly a post-modernist game and thus not suitable to the masses in a region not so far beyond Ford and the industrial age.

A CHALLENGE TO BASEBALL'S SUPREMACY

In recent years the one sport that has challenged baseball as the most widely diffused American sport in Latin America is basketball, invented in 1891 by James Naismith at Springfield College, MA, in order to fill the gap between autumn's American football and spring's baseball. Roundball, or the cage game, as it may still be known to an older generation, did indeed provide at first a seasonal variation in both urban and rural areas. However, it eventually proved appealing all year round in the cities where, in part because of spatial considerations, it displaced baseball as the dominant sport.[36] The game's spread across the hemisphere may be attributed to various factors: the simplicity of the game, the balance between individuality and teamwork, the role of the YMCA and innumerable American educational institutions, international television broadcasting and the dominance in the recent US game of non-white players with whom many Latin American youth can more easily identify.[37]

Not only have Latin American countries developed their own basketball programmes at various levels but players from the south are now playing on North American college and professional teams – not in the same numbers as baseball players but in sufficient numbers to have an impact.[38] Their success in the land of basketball's birth, and still of its greatest talent, has generated considerable national pride back home. This pride is demonstrated by the recent example of the Mexican Eduardo Nájera, who in the 1999–2000 season, helped the University of Oklahoma achieve national ranking and was later drafted high by the Dallas Mavericks of the National Basketball Association.[39] Nájera joins a growing number of emigrants from south of the United States border, such as Felipe López (Dominican Republic), Tim Duncan (St. Croix, United States Virgin Islands) and Patrick Ewing (Jamaica) who have achieved star status in their homeland for performing in sports other than soccer, baseball, boxing or cricket.[40] Nájera is helping to reverse a pattern of several decades that has seen US players, unable to sign professional contracts at home or to catch on in stronger European leagues, take lower paying positions with clubs in the Southern Cone countries of Argentina, Chile and Uruguay.

OTHER NORTH AMERICAN TRANSFERS

Two other sports of United States origin whose presence in Latin America is obvious but whose history has not been seriously pursued are volleyball and professional wrestling (*lucha libre*). Like basketball, volleyball was invented in Massachusetts in the 1890s by someone with ties to the YMCA. However, volleyball did not spread nationally or internationally as rapidly as basketball. For many decades it remained more a scholastic and recreational game than a sport. It gained recognition from both the National Collegiate Athletic Association and the Olympic movement only after the mid-twentieth century. Within Latin America, volleyball has proven acceptable as both a masculine and feminine sport and at least in Brazil, Cuba and Peru has earned teams international recognition. In the last decade, beach volleyball, a California inspired variation, has generated both a form of professionalism and Olympic status. Brazilian men and women have not only led their Latin neighbours but have often been the equal of their North American competition. On the beaches near Sydney in September 2000, the Brazilian men's team won a silver medal and the women a silver and a bronze. Incidentally, the Brazilian women also captured bronze on the indoor courts.[41]

Professional wrestling, considered by many more theatre than sport though involving a degree of physical training and aptitude, is especially prominent in Mexico, but is found in almost all of Latin America, most notably in urban areas.[42]

In general terms, in the past, these and other sports and related behaviour and values were often tied to the erratic spread of United States-based physical education, a result of Latino students studying in the north or, more significantly in the first half of the twentieth century, a consequence of the efforts across the hemisphere of the YMCA. Men such as Federico W. Dickens, a product of Springfield College and labelled 'the founder of Argentine sport' by Enrique Carlos Romero Brest, accelerated the diffusion of American sport culture, a diffusion that blended conveniently with the attitudes of Vasconcelos and others mentioned earlier.[43] In turn, the early Latin American converts to these imported values, such as the elder Brest, helped diffuse these views to other Latin American countries.[44]

Both on and off the field/court one interesting indicator of the intrusion of all these imported sports into the local culture has been seen and heard in the host languages. Over the long term, this process of linguistic adoption, modification and fusion has taken at least four forms: the direct incorporation of English terms; the Hispanicization (or Brazilianization) or phonetic transcription of English words; the invention of more or less equivalent terms by analytic translation; and the use of figurative, synthetic, or phonetic translation, sometimes creating false cognates.[45] This impact on language has been most extensive among peoples who have embraced soccer but the influence of baseball in certain areas has been noticeable as well.[46] Other sports, notably golf and boxing, have likewise modified vocabularies and linguistic images. In virtually all cases, whatever the sport or its origin, the new force has been tied to English. This might be considered enrichment, although in some cases it has provoked heated criticism and campaigns to defend more traditional forms of Spanish and Portuguese.

Other signs of North American intrusion through sports into the Latin American milieu include frequent sightings of t-shirts, sweatshirts and caps carrying the logos of professional and university teams and/or the names and numbers of well-known players. In addition, many Latin American radio and TV stations broadcast North American sporting events, while local news stands carry a variety of imported sports magazines or local language publications that focus on North American sports. While some highlight the performance in the United States of Latin American athletes, many report results independent of nationality. With minor exceptions, the reverse is not yet true.

THE FEMALE DIMENSION

The relatively recent expansion of women's sports in Latin America, especially of the non-elite types, is a consequence of various domestic and international forces of which the North American examples are clearly a part.[47] Over the last quarter century, the Federal legislation known as Title IX, passed in 1972, has raised the level of female participation in scholastic sports and contributed to the growth of women's professional leagues. With or without similar legislation, both for political and social reasons, a similar surge in women's sports has been observable in Europe and parts of Asia. One additional consequence has been the rise in television coverage of women's sports, from the Olympics and the women's soccer World Cup through the professionals to the schools, some of which have reached Latin American audiences. The consequence, combined with local demands for greater gender equity, has been at least some expansion of women's sports in the southern hemisphere.

However, the results in Latin America have been uneven. Certainly Cuba is most conspicuous, although even there women generally do not receive as much support as men.[48] Several countries have fielded competitive basketball and volleyball teams and have sent outstanding individual athletes to both amateur and professional international events. Others have shown some promise in soccer. Still, the fact that the Mexican women's national soccer team, for example, had to recruit Mexican-American women from the United States in order to have even a hope of being competitive during the run-up to the 1999 World Cup suggests that Mexico, like many of its neighbours, was learning from outside but still lagging behind many Latin and non-Latin countries.[49] This is despite the fact that Mexican females have experimented in boxing and shown some promise in weightlifting, including an Olympic gold medal in the 58 kg division at Sydney 2000.[50]

RECIPROCITY OF SPORTING INFLUENCE

As suggested above, the movement of sporting influences has not all been in one direction. Most notably there has been a northbound flow of a multitude of talented professional and amateur athletes. Several historical examples suggest that this intra-hemispheric process is complex. By the mid-nineteenth century, charreada (or charrería), a derivative of sixteenth-century Spanish equestrian activities, had become a unique form of horsemanship tied to the working practices of Mexico's rural north but that was also gradually evolving as a recreational form. Today charreada is a major source of national pride and cultural identity both inside Mexico and within Mexican-American enclaves in the United States. It almost certainly is a major source of North American rodeo, though it places much greater emphasis on style rather than speed or endurance.[51]

Shortly after the Second World War, when baseball in the United States was enjoying a rise in popularity and attendance, the Mexican entrepreneur Jorge Pasquel led a vigorous campaign to turn the Mexican League into a major league, or at least a high level minor league. He offered high salaries and benefits to white and black Americans, as well as Latinos from around the Caribbean, to join teams in his league, of which the most important was his own Veracruz club. Over a dozen players defected from Major League Baseball although all eventually returned to the United States, several playing again in the majors after a period of punishment. Pasquel's action combined with increased efforts to organize the players and challenge the restrictive reserve clause, forced the North American owners to make a number of concessions to the players, concerning treatment during spring training and, most importantly, the pension system.[52]

Overlapping this struggle was the impact on race relations in the United States of decades of interaction among whites, blacks and Hispanics of various shades on Caribbean baseball diamonds. Beginning in the 1920s and increasing through the next two decades, North American ball players, both black and white, often spent the winter months honing their skills and padding their wallets in the baseball hotbeds of Cuba, Puerto Rico, the Dominican Republic and Venezuela, as well as Mexico. Though barred by law and by custom from playing, travelling or socializing together in the United States, these men repeatedly ignored US law and custom while in foreign lands where they learned first hand that the myths of Negro inferiority were groundless. Unquestionably, such experiences facilitated the acceptance by some whites of black players into organized baseball after the Second World War and the signing of Jackie Robinson.[53]

Not surprisingly, the North American sports of baseball, football and basketball are not the only ones in which Latin Americans have been conspicuous on the northern scene. The recent growth of scholastic and club soccer and the at least partial success of Major League Soccer since the 1994 World Cup can be attributed in part to the role of Latino players and to the enthusiasm of Latin fans. This growth provides a reflection of the growing Latino immigration into the United States. If Eduardo Galeano is proved wrong in his prediction that in the United States 'soccer is the sport of the future and it always will be', this will be in large part due to the expanding Latin American presence.[54]

Of course, even before baseball and soccer attracted Latin American athletes to the United States, a few highly capable individuals had built much of their careers in the North. For example, Mexican Pancho González and Ecuadorian Pancho Segura were among the pioneers on the early professional tennis tour promoted mainly by Jack Kramer. Equally, whether they were exploited or properly rewarded, various boxers, many from Cuba, put their bodies on the line in American rings.

CONCLUSIONS

On the basis of these limited observations, a few general conclusions might be offered about why some sports originating in the United States were acceptable in some places but other sports were not acceptable in other places and the consequences of such imbalance. As noted above, proximity to the United States itself and a larger pattern of interaction with United States society seem to have been influential factors in the first transfers. In addition, the frequency of travelers in both directions raised the likelihood of sports diffusion. More recently, global media has increased contacts and offered at least a greater chance for borrowing. However powerful the Yankee society and economy, some of this transfer came with the encouragement and approval of Latin Americans themselves. In addition, sports diffusion from the United States to Latin America has carried with it more than just the playing of different games; it has involved the transfer of certain attitudes and values. It can be asserted that as the movement of talent/labour from south to north has increased the Latin American presence in North America if in unbalanced proportions, any influence has been mutual in human, cultural and economic terms. This has had its impact on playing style and human relations. These movements in recent decades are clearly part of the larger process of globalization (perhaps hybridization) of sport, society and the economy, a process applauded by some and condemned by others.[55]

Except in specific cases, it is often difficult to determine if in Latin American sports culture, as opposed to the sports themselves, was imported from Europe or North America – and if so, from which. Were these aspects of the evolving sports culture consciously imitated by Latin America innovators or did they result naturally from the modernization of the sports structure within the larger national and international context? For example, what provoked the creation of such journalistic institutions as Argentina's *El Gráfico* or Brazil's *Placar*? Obviously, much remains to be investigated. In the future, as some of these influences move in reverse, there must be due sensitivity to their impact on the original source areas.

In closing, a personal comment on the process of sports diffusion. I have written elsewhere, and Guttmann has concluded likewise, that whilst observable extrinsic features of sports are always important, we must not ignore those intrinsic qualities that make certain sports so appealing to certain populations: required skill levels and intelligence, body co-ordination, internal rhythm and harmony, movement of the ball and other implements, colourfulness of the performance package and such like.[56] There are some things in life that we do simply because we enjoy them, 'things we love [because] they make us feel alive, arouse our deepest sentiments, and make us laugh and cry'.[57]

In short, we must avoid getting too rigidly enmeshed in the pursuit of theory. There is a risk of taking ourselves too seriously and of losing touch with the truly human in us all. Mario Vargas Llosa concludes that the problem in trying to intellectualize sport is that 'reality overtakes theory'. While theories are rational and logical, 'in society and individual behaviour, unreason, the unconscious and pure spontaneity will always play a part'.[58] Ariel Dorfman advises that 'if you reduce everything to politics and ideology, you end up totalizing, squeezing the mystery out of life and explaining away too easily what at times has no explanation'.[59] Jorge Valdano and Eduardo Galeano likewise both warn that soccer – and I extend this to all sports – may be ruined by the pseudo-scientists who fail to understand its emotional reality and threaten to destroy it with excessive seriousness, ultimately producing boredom.[60]

I end with the insightful words of one of the leading novelists of our generation, Paulo Coelho, who counsels us that 'One is loved because one is loved. No reason is needed for loving.'[61] That is certainly true of people and may, at least in part, be true also of sport.

NOTES

1. Earlier versions of this chapter were presented at the VII Congresso Brasileiro de História da Educação Física, Esporte, Lazar e Dança, Gramado, RS, Brazil, 29 May–1 June 2000 and the III° Encuentro Deporte y Ciencias Sociales, Buenos Aires, Argentina, 13–15 Oct. 2000.
2. Joseph L. Arbena, 'Sports' in Barbara A. Tenenbaum (ed.), *Encyclopedia of Latin American History and Culture*, Vol.5 (New York: Charles Scribner's Sons, 1996), pp.171–5; Francisco López Izquierdo, *Los toros del nuevo mundo (1492–1992)* (Madrid: Espasa-Calpe, 1992); Ricardo M. Llanes, *Canchas de pelotas y reñideros de antaño* (Buenos Aires: Municipalidad de la Ciudad de Buenos Aires, 1981).
3. Allen Guttmann, *From Ritual to Record: The Nature of Modern Sports* (New York: Columbia University Press, 1978).
4. Joseph L. Arbena, 'Sport in Latin America and the Caribbean', in Simon Collier *et al.* (eds.), *The Cambridge Encyclopedia of Latin America and the Caribbean* (New York: Cambridge University Press, 1992), pp.463–6.

5. William H. Beezley, *Judas at the Jockey Club and Other Episodes of Porfirian Mexico* (Lincoln: University of Nebraska Press, 1987).
6. For a summary of Vasconcelos' ideas and those of other Mexicans, see Joseph L. Arbena, 'Sport, Development, and Mexican Nationalism, 1920–1970', *Journal of Sport History*, 18, 3 (1991), 350–64. For a general overview of Mexican physical education and its role in shaping the social structure, see Luis López Cabrera *et al.*, 'Ensayo histórico de la educación física en México' in Horst Ueberhorst (ed.), *Geschichte der Leibesübungen*, Vol.6: *Perspektiven des Weltsports* (Berlin: Bartels & Wernitz, 1989), pp.1095–112.
7. César Viale, *El deporte argentino (contribución a su desarrollo y prosperidad)* (Buenos Aires: Librería de García Santos, 1922) and *La educación física obligatoria impulsaría la grandeza nacional* (Buenos Aires: Talleres Gráficos de la Penitenciaria Nacional, 1924); Próspero G. Alemandri, *Moral y deporte* (Buenos Aires: Librería del Colegio, 1937).
8. Matthew G. Shirts, 'Futebol no Brasil ou Football in Brazil?' in José Carlos Sebe Bom Meihy and José Sebastião Witter (eds.), *Futebol e cultura. Coletanea de estudos* (São Paulo: IMESP/DAESP, 1982), pp.87–99; Lincoln Allison, 'Association Football and the Urban Ethos', in John D. Wirth and Robert L. Jones (eds.), *Manchester and São Paulo: Problem of Rapid Urban Growth* (Stanford, CA: Stanford University Press, 1978), pp.203–28.
9. Victor Andrade de Melo, 'Posibles representaciones sobre el turf en la sociedad carioca del siglo XIX', *Lecturas: Educación Física y Deportes*, 3, 9 (1998); Julio Frydenberg, 'Prácticas y valores en el proceso de popularización del fútbol, Buenos Aires 1900–1910', *Entrepasados: Revista de Historia*, 6, 12 (1997), 7–27.
10. Angela Aisenstein, 'El deporte en el discurso pedagógico: Una mirada desde la historia del curriculum. Argentina 1880–1961'. Paper presented at the VII Congresso Brasileiro de História da Educação Física, Esporte, Lazar e Dança, Gramado, RS, Brazil, 29 May–1 June 2000.
11. Amy Bushnell, ' "That Demonic Game": The Campaign to Stop Pelota Playing in Spanish Florida, 1675–1684', *The Americas*, 35, 1 (July 1978), 1–19; Elliott J. Gorn and Warren Goldstein, *A Brief History of American Sports* (New York: Hill and Wang, 1993).
12. See the chapter by J.A. Mangan in this volume, pp.9–42. It discusses this aspect of the wider context of the process of the dissemination, assimilation and adaptation of modern sport with specific reference to Latin America. J.A. Mangan, *The Games Ethic and Imperialism: Aspect of the Diffusion of an Ideal* (London and Portland, OR: Frank Cass, 1999) and Allen Guttmann, *Games and Empires: Modern Sports and Cultural Imperialism* (New York: Columbia University Press, 1994). J.A. Mangan (ed.), *The Cultural Bond: Sport, Empire, Society* (London and Portland, OR: Frank Cass, 1992) is also interesting because it continues the theme of sport's emotional hold on human beings.
13. To avoid an excess of words and possibly awkward constructions, in the context of this chapter I am applying the term 'American' to things associated with the United States.
14. Benjamin G. Rader, *Baseball: A History of America's Game* (Urbana: University of Illinois Press, 1992); John P. Rossi, *The National Game: Baseball and American Culture* (Chicago: Ivan R. Dee, 2000); Jules Tygiel, *Past Time: Baseball As History* (New York: Oxford University Press, 2000).
15. Peter Levine, *A.G. Spalding and the Rise of Baseball: The Promise of American Sport* (New York: Oxford University Press, 1985); William Schell, 'Lions, Bulls, and Baseball: Colonel R.C. Pate and Modern Sports Promotion in Mexico', *Journal of Sport History*, 20, 3 (Winter 1993), 259–75.
16. The most detailed and comprehensive survey of Cuban baseball history is found in Roberto González Echevarría, *The Pride of Havana: A History of Cuban Baseball* (New York: Oxford University Press, 1999). Greater focus on just the origins of baseball, its connection to emerging Cuban national identity and eventual struggle for independence from Spain is provided by the same author in 'Literature, Dance, and Baseball in the Last Cuban Fin de Siècle', *South Atlantic Quarterly*, 95, 2 (Spring 1996), 365–84; and by Louis A. Pérez, Jr., 'Between Baseball and Bullfighting: The Quest for Nationality in Cuba, 1868–1898', *Journal of American History*, 81, 2 (Sept. 1994), 493–517. Pérez expands his impressions of the place of baseball in Cuban society in *On Becoming Cuban: Identity, Nationality, and Culture* (Chapel Hill: University of North Carolina Press, 1999). Two recent and equally stimulating pictures

are provided in Mark Rucker and Peter C. Bjarkman, *Smoke: The Romance and Lore of Cuban Baseball* (Kingston, NY: Total Sports Illustrated, 1999) and Milton H. Jamail, *Full Count: Inside Cuban Baseball* (Carbondale: Southern Illinois University Press, 2000).

17. Samuel O. Regalado, *Viva Baseball! Latin Major Leaguers and Their Special Hunger* (Urbana: University of Illinois Press, 1998).
18. Paula J. Pettavino, 'Novel Revolutionary Forms: The Use of Unconventional Diplomacy in Cuba', in Georges Fauriol and Eva Loser (eds.), *Cuba: The International Dimension* (New Brunswick, NJ: Transaction, 1990), pp.373–403.
19. Paula J. Pettavino and Geralyn Pye, *Sport in Cuba: A Diamond in the Rough* (Pittsburgh: University of Pittsburgh Press, 1994).
20. Tom Verducci, 'The Power of Pedro', *Sports Illustrated*, 92, 13 (27 March 2000), 54.
21. Alan M. Klein, *Sugarball: The American Game, the Dominican Dream* (New Haven, CT: Yale University Press, 1991); Rob Ruck, *The Tropic of Baseball: Baseball in the Dominican Republic* (Westport, CT: Meckler, 1991).
22. Peter C. Bjarkman, *Baseball with a Latin Beat: A History of the Latin American Game* (Jefferson, NC: McFarland & Company, 1994).
23. Héctor Pastrian, *Béisbol; reseña histórica internacional y argentina* (Buenos Aires: Federación Argentina de Béisbol, 1977); *International Baseball Rundown*, 9, 7 (Oct./Nov. 2000).
24. See Alan M. Klein, 'Baseball as Underdevelopment: The Political Economy of Sport in the Dominican Republic', *Sociology of Sport Journal*, 6, 2 (June 1989), 95–112.
25. See González Echevarría, *Pride of Havana*, on Cuba; and Klein, *Sugarball*, on the Dominican Republic.
26. S.L. Price, *Pitching Around Fidel: A Journey into the Heart of Cuban Sports* (New York: The Ecco Press, 2000).
27. Silvia Spitta, *Between Two Waters: Narratives of Transculturation in Latin America* (Houston: Rice University Press, 1995).
28. Urbano Fernández, 'La leyenda viviente de Chocolate', *Cuba Internacional*, 13, 139 (June 1981), 48–51.
29. On Dempsey's popularity in Mexico, see Richard V. McGehee, 'The Dandy and the Mauler in Mexico: Johnson, Dempsey, *et al.*, and the Mexico City Press, 1919–1927', *Journal of Sport History*, 23, 1 (Spring 1996), 20–33.
30. David G. LaFrance, 'A Mexican Popular Image of the United States Through the Baseball Hero, Fernando Valenzuela', *Studies in Latin American Popular Culture*, 4 (1985), 14–23; Murray Chass, 'Roberto Clemente', in Danny Peary (ed.), *Cult Baseball Players: The Greats, the Flakes, the Weird, and the Wonderful* (New York: Simon & Schuster, 1990), pp.294–300.
31. Luis Amador de Gama (ed.), *Historia gráfica del fútbol americano en México, I: 1936–1945* (México, DF: Olmeca Impresiones Finas, 1982).
32. An expression of that continuing Mexican interest is the magazine *Yarda 50: La Revista del Futbol Americano de México* which began publication in 1999. Issue 3 (p.10) carries an article by Marely Marín on 'Futbol Americano Femenil'.
33. Francisco Ponce, 'Qué horror, caray', *Proceso*, 1184 (11 July 1999), 76.
34. Mario Longorio, *Athletes Remembered: Mexicano/Latino Professional Football Players, 1929–1970* (Tempe, AZ: Bilingual Press, 1997).
35. *Buenos Aires Herald*, 3 Aug. 1997, 21.
36. James Naismith, *Basketball: Its Origin and Development* (Lincoln: University of Nebraska Press, 1996 [1941]).
37. Jay R. and Joan D. Mandle, *Caribbean Hoops: The Development of West Indian Basketball*, Vol.8 in Caribbean Studies (Langhorne, PA: Gordon and Breach, 1994).
38. John Bale, *The Brawn Drain: Foreign Student-Athletes in American Universities* (Urbana, IL: University of Illinois Press, 1991). On the larger pattern of athletic talent migration, see John Bale and Joseph Maguire (eds.), *The Global Sports Arena: Athletic Talent Migration in an Interdependent World* (London and Portland, OR: Frank Cass, 1994), specific chapters on the Latin American involvement in this process are authored by Alan Klein and Joseph Arbena.
39. Grant Wahl, 'One Tough Hombre', *Sports Illustrated*, 92, 3 (24 Jan. 2000), 60–63; John Gustafson, 'Mas macho', *ESPN: The Magazine*, 3, 3 (7 Feb. 2000), 94–97; Marc Stein, 'A Tex-Mex Treat', *ESPN: The Magazine*, 3, 24 (27 Nov. 2000), 128.

40. For examples, see Richard Brunelli, 'This Dunkin' Dominican Stands Tall', *Caribbean Travel & Life*, 15, 2 (2000), 86–7; Steve Wulf, 'Special Delivery', *Sports Illustrated*, 82, 2 (16 Jan. 1995), 48–56.

41. Michael Bamberger, 'Sand Blast', *Sports Illustrated*, 87, 12 (22 Sept. 1997), 50–51. In Argentina, the beach variety has also made some progress; see Julio Chiappetta, 'Arena, sol y juego', *Noticias de la Semana* (10 Jan. 1993), 144–5. Olympic results are summarized in *Sports Illustrated*, 93, 16 (18 Oct. 2000); volleyball thus represented one-third of Brazil's dozen total medals. A comment on the earlier success of the Peruvian women's volleyball team is found in Abelardo Sánchez León, 'The History of Peruvian Women's Volleyball', *Studies in Latin American Popular Culture*, 13 (1994), 143–52.

42. Sources, though not all scholarly, on professional wrestling in Mexico include *Blue Demon: Memorias de una máscara* (México, DF: Clío, 1999); Rafael Olivera Figueroa, *Memorias de la lucha libre* (México, DF: Costa-Amic Editores, 1999); Heather Levi, 'Sport and Melodrama: The Case of Mexican Professional Wrestling', *Social Text*, 15, 1 (Spring 1997), 57–68.

43. Jorge Saraví Riviere, *Aportes para una historia de la educación física, 1900 a 1945* (Buenos Aires: IEF No.1, 1998), p.69. On the YMCA's role in Mexican sport, see Maurice A. Clay, 'Sport and Physical Education in Mexico' in William Johnson (ed.), *Sport and Physical Education Around the World* (Champaign, IL: Stipes, 1980), pp.405–23. The importance of travel in both directions in the diffusion of modern sports throughout Latin America is stressed in Richard V. McGehee, 'The Impact of Imported Sports on the Popular Culture of Nineteenth- and Early Twentieth-Century Mexico and Central America' in Ingrid E. Fey and Karen Racine (eds.), *Strange Pilgrimages: Exile, Travel, and National Identity in Latin America, 1800–1990s* (Wilmington, DE: Scholarly Resources, 2000), pp.85–111.

44. See Georgina Silva Baquero, *Tratado de educación física* (Quito: Editorial Casa de la Cultura Ecuatoriana, 1962).

45. Joseph L. Arbena, 'Sports Language, Cultural Imperialism, and the Anti-Imperialist Critique in Latin America', *Studies in Latin American Popular Culture*, 14 (1995), 129–41; see also Arbena, 'Sport and Sport Themes in Latin American Literature: A Sampler', *Arete: The Journal of Sport Literature*, 5, 1 (Fall 1987), 143–59.

46. For an implicit commentary on the 'brutalization' of Colombian Spanish as a result of the spread of baseball jargon, see Roberto Montes Mathieu, 'El cuarto bate', in *El Cuarto Bate* (Bogotá: Plaza & Janes, 1985), 29–38.

47. Some observations on the historic factors hampering the development of women's sports in Latin America are offered by Joseph L. Arbena in 'In Search of the Latin American Female Athlete: A Bibliographical Odyssey'. Paper presented at the annual meeting of the North American Society for Sport History, Auburn, AL, 24–27 May 1996. For summaries of the careers of a few women who overcame the odds and succeeded in the sports field, see Liliana Morelli, *Mujeres deportistas* (Buenos Aires: Editorial Planeta, 1990).

48. See Pettavino and Pye, *Sport in Cuba*.

49. John Philip Wyllie, 'Both Sides Now', *Soccer Digest*, 22, 1 (April/May 1999), 56–60.

50. Francisco Ponce, 'Sólo para ellas', *Proceso*, 1179 (6 June 1999), 69; Fabiola Zamorán, 'Soraya Jiménez, primera pesista mexicana en Juegos Olímpicos', *Proceso*, 1212 (23 Jan. 2000), 76–7; José Luis Tapia, 'Se gana Soraya el oro y el respeto', *Reforma* (16 May 2000), 1D.

51. Kathleen M. Sands, *Charrería Mexicana: An Equestrian Folk Tradition* (Tucson: University of Arizona Press, 1993) and idem., '*Charreada*: Performance and Interpretation of an Equestrian Folk Tradition in Mexico and the United States', *Studies in Latin American Popular Culture*, 13 (1994), 77–100; Mary Lou LeCompte, 'The Hispanic Influence on the History of Rodeo, 1823–1922', *Journal of Sport History*, 12, 1 (Spring 1965), 21–38.

52. Teódulo Manuel Agundis, *El verdadero Jorge Pasqual. Ensayo biográfico sobre un carácter* (México, DF: Gráfica Atenea, 1956); Alan M. Klein, 'Baseball Wars: The Mexican Baseball League and Nationalism in 1946', *Studies in Latin American Popular Culture*, 13 (1994), 33–56. Mark Winegardner, *The Veracruz Blues* (New York: Viking, 1996), provides an entertaining fictional account of several aspects of this story.

53. Donn Rogosin, *Invisible Men. Life in Baseball's Negro Leagues* (New York: Atheneum, 1985); Jules Tygiel, *Baseball's Great Experiment: Jackie Robinson and His Legacy* (New York: Oxford University Press, 1983).

54. Eduardo Galeano, *El fútbol a sol y sombra* (Montevideo: Ediciones del Chanchito, 1995).

55. A more positive view of the benefits of this mixing even for sports teams is found in G. Pascal Zachary, *The Global Me. New Cosmopolitans and the Competitive Edge: Picking Globalism's Winners and Losers* (New York: Public Affairs, 2000). Much more critical is Eduardo Galeano, *Upside Down: A Primer for the Looking-Glass World*, trans. Mark Fried (New York: Metropolitan Books, 2000 [1998]). See also Joseph Maguire, *Global Sports: Identities, Societies, Civilizations* (Cambridge: Polity Press, 1999).

56. Guttmann, *Games and Empires: Modern Sports and Cultural Imperialism*; Joseph L. Arbena, 'History of Latin American Sports: The End Before the Beginning?', *Sporting Traditions*, 16, 1 (Nov. 1999), 23–31; Joseph L. Arbena, 'Meaning and Joy in Latin American Sports', *International Review for the Sociology of Sport*, 35, 1 (March 2000), 83–91.

57. Juan Sasturain, 'Desde el túnel' in *El día del arquero* (Buenos Aires: Ediciones de la Flor, 1986), p.5.

58. Mario Vargas Llosa, *Making Waves*, ed. & trans. John King (New York: Farrar, Straus and Giroux, 1996), p.167.

59. Ariel Dorfman, *Heading South, Looking North: A Bilingual Journey* (New York: Farrar, Straus and Giroux, 1998), p.259.

60. Jorge Valdano, *Los cuadernos de Valdano* (Madrid: Aguilar, 1997), pp.23–4; Galeano, *El fútbol a sol y sombra*.

61. Paulo Coelho, *The Alchemist: A Story About Following Your Dream*, trans. Alan R. Clarke (New York: Harper Flamingo, 1998 [1988, 1993]), p.123.

3

Tribulations and Achievements: The Early History of Olympism in Argentina

CESAR R. TORRES

Arguably, from the industrial revolution until after the Second World War, Great Britain played the dominant role in the development and diffusion of modern sport.[1] Introduced by colonial authorities, military men, merchants and educators, modern sport rapidly spread across the world. Argentina, whose nineteenth-century economy was heavily influenced by British entrepreneurs, was no exception to this rule. Cricket was first introduced during the failed 1806 and 1807 British invasions of Buenos Aires. In the next decade British expatriates, mostly English, systematized the practice of their sports in Argentina.[2] Although it took some years for the newly independent nation to accept these novel practices, clubs started to flourish. By the end of the nineteenth century modern sport had become an integral part of Argentine culture. As early as the mid-1880s, Thomas Turner, an English traveller, observed that English expatriates 'have established a few healthy institutions in Buenos Aires – cricket, football, rowing, polo'.[3] By the end of the nineteenth century, of course, modern sport had seduced enthusiasts on all continents.

Baron Pierre de Coubertin, a student of the classical world, was certainly seduced by English sports and their ideology. Meshing together his devotion to classical antiquity, his admiration of *fin de siècle* English sport, his desire to inculcate national vigour into French youth and his intention to promote international peace and reconciliation, in 1894, Coubertin founded the International Olympic Committee (IOC) and in 1896, organized the first modern international Olympic Games in Athens. Although he drew inspiration from English models such as Rugby School, Coubertin started the IOC without their help. The subsequent survival of the Olympic Games required not only the consolidation of modern sport but also international participation and the globalization of Coubertin's project.[4]

During the 35 years after 1880, Argentina was politically and economically dominated by a landed elite that controlled the state apparatus. As such, it seemed to be in a privileged situation to spearhead the diffusion of Coubertin's Olympic internationalism throughout South America during the early years of the Baron's ceaseless and steadfast strivings. Three factors favoured the Argentines. First, Argentina was one of the world's great agricultural nations, enjoying a remarkable degree of economic growth in the half century after 1860. This economic development was accompanied by an increasing democratization of Argentine politics – a movement that gained momentum with the approval of the Saenz Peña Law of 1912 which granted universal male suffrage. Second, the Argentines had embraced modern sport. Lastly, and more importantly, the country was represented by an IOC member from the very beginning of the IOC. Coubertin had included Argentina's José B. Zubiaur in his original 1894 governing council in order to enlarge the demographic composition of the IOC. The Baron also hoped that Zubiaur would advocate the Olympic ideal in South America.[5]

Despite its advantageous early role and the chance it offered to incorporate Argentina into Coubertin's project, the country only enjoyed its first official participation in the Olympics of 1924 in Paris – the year after the Argentine Olympic Committee (AOA) was established. At first glance this fact may suggest that the Olympic movement expanded at a slow rate in Argentina in spite of its fortunate circumstances. However, even though the institutionalization of Olympism in Argentina was a relatively late development, there was an enthusiastic conversion to the idea of the Olympics after the establishment of the IOC. This conversion marks the first major step in the diffusion of Olympism in Argentina. Certainly Olympism took time to take root; the diffusion of the Olympic ideal began in the 1900s but institutionalization of the ideal took place extremely slowly. Cultural diffusion was driven both by the gradual adoption of new ideologies, attitudes and values, and by the gradual acceptance of new social practices, habits and structures.

This essay analyses the reception and spread of Olympism in Argentina. The establishment of Olympism reveals the struggle within factions of the powerful oligarchy to control sport in Argentina.

Although the core of the elite was a relatively stable group, those who believed that Olympic excursions would provide a great opportunity to situate Argentina in the Western-defined community of nations faced significant opposition. Modern sport in general, and the Olympics in particular, was subjected to multiple, sometimes bluntly opposed, interpretations. In addition, due to the grandiosity of their Olympic projects, promoters of Argentine Olympism largely depended on the state to realize their aspirations. For those in Argentina who viewed modern sport and the Olympics as important aspects of Western-style modernization the road was not only long but also tedious and very often frustrating to travel.

AN EARLY ENCOUNTER PRODUCES UNEXPECTED CONSEQUENCES

Argentina's and, arguably, Latin America's first connection with Baron Pierre de Coubertin occurred at a time when he had already been enormously impressed by English sport but had not yet conceived the idea of reviving the Olympic Games.[6] This particular stage in Coubertin's ideological development was to influence the encounter as well as prefigure the early diffusion of Olympism in Argentina.

In 1888, Coubertin established the Comité pour la Propagation des Exercises Physiques (Committee for the Propagation of Physical Exercises). This institution, which was intended to promote the benefits of physical exercise for a well-rounded education, managed to include an International Congress for the Propagation of Physical Exercise as part of the official programme of the 1889 Paris Universal Exposition. Argentina took the Universal Exposition seriously and sent a large delegation, including Alejo Peyret and José B. Zubiaur, to demonstrate that the country was travelling the route of progress. It was in the charmed setting of *fin de siècle* Paris and through these two prominent educators that Argentina first encountered Coubertin's early passions.[7]

Alejo Peyret was a Frenchman who emigrated to the Río de la Plata in 1852 after participating in France's failed Revolution of 1848. Following a three-year residence in Montevideo, Uruguay, he moved to Argentina where he died in 1902 he devoted almost 50 years of his life to the improvement of his adopted country. He gained a reputation as a journalist but more so as an educator. In his time as a teacher, he taught at Argentina's prestigious Colegio Nacional de Concepción del Uruguay

(National School of Concepción del Uruguay) and Colegio Nacional de Buenos Aires (National School of Buenos Aires). At the time of the Universal Exposition, Peyret had been recently appointed to the post of General Inspector of Tierras y Colonias de la República (Lands and Colonies of the Republic), an important position which he maintained until a few years before his death. It did not matter that Peyret was not a native Argentine; his extraordinary capabilities and continuous and faithful service to Argentina made him an unrivalled national representative to the Universal Exposition.[8] As the writer and educator Godofredo Daireaux wrote, '[Peyret] has served the Argentine Republic morally and materially like the best of its own sons'.[9]

Peyret probably instilled his passion for education and devotion to national organization and progress into the young José B. Zubiaur, an Argentine of strong persuasion, when Zubiaur was a student at the Colegio Nacional de Concepción del Uruguay, an institution to which Zubiaur, as headmaster, would later introduce sport. Zubiaur, born in humble circumstances in 1856, was a leading educator in Argentina at the time of the Universal Exposition. Indeed, Zubiaur was serving the National Ministerio de Justicia, Culto e Instrucción Pública (Ministry of Justice, Religious Affairs and Public Instruction) as Supervisor of Escuelas Nacionales y Colegios Normales (National and Normal Schools). However, above and beyond this position, he had an inexhaustible passion for the improvement of public education and the building of a strong Argentina – especially through physical education and sport.[10]

With a shared commitment to the enhancement of the school system and a love for Argentina, Peyret and Zubiaur embarked on the long trip to France. Among other duties, they were required to attend both the International Congress for the Propagation of Physical Exercise and the International Pedagogical Congress on Primary Instruction. Because Zubiaur's interests included all topics related to education, once he learned about the former Congress, in which Coubertin served as general secretary, it was virtually certain that Zubiaur would attend it. The Congress, designed to generate interest in physical exercise as a powerful tool for moral education, highly praised English sport and physical education and had a huge impact on Peyret and Zubiaur. Peyret wrote in his official report that the Argentines 'must not have any trepidation in adopting, propagating, generalizing, an institution [physical education] of such physical, moral and social scope'.[11] Much along the same lines,

Zubiaur offered a clue to both his own views on sport and his meeting with Coubertin when he wrote that 'Increasingly the English athletic games find more support. The goodness of these games is praised by Mr. Pierre de Coubertin … Cricket, football, rowing, equestrianism, fencing and the whole series of virile exercises and games, tending to form the robust man, are acquiring recognition, as it were citizenship, in the French schools.'[12]

In spite of their shared interest in Coubertin's fascination with Anglo-American sports only Zubiaur would refer to the writing and thoughts of Coubertin, albeit rarely, during his career. When he did, Zubiaur mentioned Coubertin not in association with the establishment of the modern Olympic Games but exclusively as a progressive thinker who publicly recommended sport as a valuable subject to be included in the school curriculum. After the 1889 Universal Exposition, both Coubertin and Zubiaur would became famous in their respective countries for their articulation and promotion of educational reform.[13]

In all probability, the only personal encounter between Zubiaur and Coubertin took place during the Universal Exposition. A 1907 letter from Zubiaur to Coubertin, in which the Argentine noted that 'since 1889 I can recall that I have received only one note inviting me to the Athens athletic meeting',[14] would seem to corroborate this fact. A few years after Zubiaur's experience in Paris, while he was introducing outdoor sport to replace the 'dangerous, ancient and monotonous indoor gymnastics'[15] as headmaster of the Colegio Nacional de Concepción del Uruguay, Coubertin revived the idea of organizing a modern international version of the ancient Olympic Games. At the 1894 Sorbonne planning meeting, Coubertin established the IOC and included Zubiaur as a founding member, probably without Zubiaur's knowledge or permission. For a brief period, as illustrated by the 1889 Congress in Paris, Zubiaur's and Coubertin's passions overlapped. Both were intrigued by the prospect of reforming their nations' educational systems by implementing Anglo-American programmes of physical education and sport. However, Coubertin promoted his Olympic idea as an international endeavour while Zubiaur remained attached to the establishment of the foundation of a stable nation in Argentina.[16]

Although Zubiaur devoted a significant amount of time and energy to the promotion of sport and physical education, he never wrote a word in promotion of the modern Olympic Games. In spite of being an IOC member, Zubiaur never attended a committee meeting, nor did he make any effort to form an Argentine Olympic Committee. These facts and the lack of communication with Coubertin lead to his dismissal from the IOC in 1907. Zubiaur was not pleased with his exclusion and argued that he deserved to remain in the IOC because he had done more, maybe more than anyone else in Argentina, to foster education through sports in the school system. However, Zubiaur had failed to promote what Coubertin desired most – the Olympic ideal. Ironically, the first Argentine to take part in the Games did so when Zubiaur was still an IOC member. Eduardo Camet, a fencer, participated in the 1900 Paris Games.[17] Zubiaur evidently had no hand in Camet's participation, for in all probability he would have mentioned this in his letter responding to his dismissal as proof of his involvement.[18]

Zubiaur did not understand Coubertin's project because when he met the Baron, Coubertin himself had not yet conceived his Olympic concept. Thus Zubiaur had little chance to impress Coubertin. The static image of Coubertin that remained with Zubiaur resulted from their 1889 meeting. For Zubiaur, Coubertin remained the champion of the promotion of sport and physical education and not the Olympic advocate who sought to promote international understanding through an elitist competition.[19]

Although Zubiaur was not instrumental in promoting the Olympic ideology, his fascination with the English public school system and its sports ethic[20] stemmed from his historic encounter with the Baron and his acquaintance with Coubertin's early works. The result was that Zubiaur became an indefatigable devotee and promoter of English sport in Argentina until his death in 1921. His contribution to the popularization of modern sport was more complete than efforts of others. His success was due in no measure to the fact that it was the patrician Argentine elite, which at the height of the economic boom spent its time shuttling between Buenos Aires and Paris devotedly admiring European *haute culture*, that embraced Coubertin's Olympism.[21] There was an obvious paradox in this since Rugby School, a main source of inspiration for Coubertin, was not a French *école*!

TRIBULATIONS: ATTEMPTS AT INSTITUTIONALIZATION

At precisely the same time that Zubiaur, who was not a member of the social elite, advocated sport and its value within the formal schooling system, a group of upper class men were promoting sport outside of this educational system. Although there were several clubs that this group was involved in, there was one in particular that was crucial for the diffusion of Olympism in Argentina. This institution was the Sociedad Sportiva Argentina (Argentine Sporting Society).

The Sociedad Sportiva Argentina began as the Sociedad Hípica Argentina (Argentine Equestrian Society). Julio Argentino Roca, twice president of Argentina, and other affluent and influential members of Buenos Aires society established the Sociedad Hípica Argentina in September 1899. Its first president was Rodolfo Jiménez. The primary purpose of this upper class organization was the promotion of equestrian sports. However, soon after its creation Baron Antonio De Marchi, an Italian who imprinted his indelible mark on Argentine sport, extended the scope of the club.[22]

De Marchi had arrived in Argentina in the mid-1890s. A nobleman with elegant manners and pleasant personality, he rapidly eased his way into Buenos Aires' leading social, economic and political circles. De Marchi, who married one of Roca's daughters, won the goodwill of many prominent citizens, including his father-in-law. This approval, his own manners and his convictions propelled him to the upper echelons of Buenos Aires society and converted him into a typical *porteño*.[23] In 1902, he was named president of the Sociedad Hípica Argentina and immediately began to instil his own energy and industry in the club.[24]

De Marchi changed the name of the Sociedad Hípica Argentina to the more subsuming Sociedad Sportiva Argentina; a one-word modification that signified a radical alteration of the mission of the society. The Sportiva, as it would commonly be referred to, was transformed from a predominantly mono-sport to a multi-sport organization. Equestrian sports, which were seen as idiosyncratic practices of the elite, lost their privileged status and increasingly had to share their prominence with other sports. This created tensions within the membership of the Sportiva. It is probably no coincidence that in 1909, after a heated debate over the approval of the Memoria y Balance (Minutes and Budget) of the Sociedad Sportiva Argentina, a group of opponents to De Marchi's ideas deserted the institution to create the Club Hípico Argentino (Argentine Equestrian Club). The Club Hípico Argentino, self-evidently, was to be devoted exclusively to equestrian sports.[25]

Despite internal confrontations, De Marchi expanded the sports of the Sportiva. Conventional sports such as athletics (track and field), fencing, boxing, polo, rugby, football, weightlifting, cycling, shooting and hockey, among others, now constituted the activities of the club. Other cultural activities such as tango contests were organized and activities which at that time had a thrilling and adventurous flavour were also available. Motorcycle and automobile races as well as airplane and aerostat flights help fill the calendar. In addition, the Sportiva supported contests and exhibitions of traditional rural practices such as *doma de potro* (horse breaking).[26] *Batallones escolares* (school battalions) provided opportunities for children. This considerable range of activities took place at several venues, the most prominent of which was the Palermo Stadium. The massively attended *fiestas deportivas* (sporting festivals) organized by the Sportiva in the Stadium were a means of stimulating general interest in sport. However, although participation in the events organized by the Sportiva was frequently open to the general public, some events remained exclusively reserved for members and membership of Sportiva was not easily available.[27]

FIGURE 3.1

Aerial view of the Sociedad Sportiva Argentina's Palermo Stadium *c.*1910.

Courtesy: Archivo General de la Nación, Buenos Aires.

De Marchi's confident leadership transformed the Sportiva and helped the spread of sport. During the first decade of the twentieth century, the Sportiva became the leading Argentine sports organization. Unlike Zubiaur's, the Sportiva's primary view of sport was recreational rather than educational. For the members of the Sportiva, sports were synonymous with pleasant amusement, aristocratic pastimes and social entertainment. In their view, sport was a necessary part of the lifestyle of the gentleman. The De Marchi/Sportiva view of sport ensured that they were comfortable with Coubertin's elitist idealism.

Manuel Quintana,[28] one of the Argentine patricians in the Sportiva, had been appointed to the IOC in May 1907 in order to replace Zubiaur whom Coubertin considered to be inefficient. Coubertin hoped that Quintana would push back the South American Olympic frontiers, but he was again to be disappointed. In 1907 it appears that Quintana, who was living in France, received a letter from Count Eugenio Brunetta d'Usseaux on behalf of Lord Desborough in which the Italian stated that the British Olympic Association and the IOC wished for Argentine participation in the forthcoming 1908 London Olympic Games. The letter also expressed the wish that Quintana accept the challenge to organize an Argentine Committee for the Games.[29] Although the letter has since been lost, there was certainly an English invitation to the Argentines.[30] In June 1907 the Argentine newspapers were favourably reporting the work of the 'commission in charge of organizing the Argentine teams that will act in the Olympic Games that will be held in London next year'.[31] This commission, which was known as the Comisión de Juegos Olímpicos (Commission of Olympic Games), was formed within the genteel confines of the Sociedad Sportiva Argentina. Newspaper reports recognized the important role of the Sportiva in the arrangements and stated that this was an excellent opportunity for it to become the leader of a grand sporting movement.[32]

The Sportiva's commission established two working groups to realize the Olympic project, one group was to work in Argentina and the other in Europe. De Marchi led the former, Quintana the latter.[33] The commission solicited support from the president of Argentina, José Figueroa Alcorta. On 18 June 1907, the president sent a scheme to the Chamber of Deputies that would allocate to the commission a considerable amount of money in order to send the first Argentine Olympic delegation to London. The presidential note proclaimed that it constituted an act of good government to stimulate sport and that Argentine participation in the London Games would allow the country to progress to modernity. The project was debated intensely on 17 and 19 July. Carlos Delcasse, a deputy, assiduous Sportiva collaborator and also well-known for his patronage of sport, and Julio Argentino Roca Jr., were among the most passionate defenders of the scheme. The former, in order to justify sending a team to London, emphasized the moral benefits that sport brings to a country by quoting a rather cavalier version of a famous saying attributed to the Duke of Wellington. Delcasse, whose command of English sporting traditions was better than his European geography, argued that 'Napoleon had been defeated on the [playing] fields of England'.[34]

Besides character building, the advocates advanced additional reasons to support the project. Olympic proponents argued that if England's polite invitation was ignored, it could easily be interpreted as an insult. In addition, Olympic involvement provided a chance to measure, and prove the worth of, the national athletic talent against the world's elite. The assumed athletic success would in return boost sport within Argentina. Finally, the London Games, Olympic supporters opined, could provide a unique international showcase in which to display what they considered the most civilized and the foremost nation in South America, their own Argentina.

The Olympic scheme attracted enemies in Congress as well as friends. Opponents of government funding of the Olympics argued that the promotion of physical education at all levels should take priority over elite sport, that Argentine sportsmen were not qualified to compete in Europe and, above all, that the amount of money requested was excessive considering that at that precise moment the Chamber of Deputies was required to exercise fiscal austerity. After a vigorous debate, the project was approved by a narrow margin. Unfortunately, after the commission had scheduled a series of trials to select a team that would consist of one hundred athletes, it was informed on 12 August that the Senate had aborted the ambitious Olympic enterprise.[35] The Senate had not been persuaded by the argument held by some deputies that sport bolstered national identity and international status – a view that was novel at the time though one rapidly attracting adherents in numbers all-over the world. More familiar arguments, such as the desirability of fiscal restraint and economic austerity, prevailed over the desires of the Europeanized Olympic enthusiasts. However, sport in general, and Olympic participation in particular, was to become increasingly accepted in Argentina and elsewhere as an arena in which societies or nations could create, recreate and express ideals of common identity, progress and modernity.[36]

In spite of the denial of government subsidy, Argentina was represented in the 1908 London Games by Henri Torromé, a figure skater who was mentioned by Quintana in a letter to Coubertin sent in October 1908.[37] Quintana wrote that he had believed that Argentina would be represented in the London Games and that he was thoroughly disappointed with the government's lack of support. Undoubtedly referring to the termination of the Olympic plan by the Senate, Quintana feared he had become a forlorn figure in the eyes of IOC. Quintana's message to Coubertin about the Senate decision came more than a year after it had been taken indicating lack of communication between the two men. In an attempt to demonstrate his involvement in Olympic matters, Quintana promised Coubertin that he would do everything possible to create the 'Comité Olympic Argentin'.[38]

Perhaps Quintana was aware that officials from the Sportiva were committed to putting the country on the Olympic map. The centennial celebration of Argentina's revolution in pursuit of national independence in May of 1910 was selected as the next appropriate occasion to promote the Olympics. The Comisión Nacional del Centenario (Centennial National Commission), established in February 1909, created a number

FIGURE 3.2

Banquet sponsored by Baron Antonio De Marchi, president of the Sociedad Sportiva Argentina, for the members of the Comisión Nacional del Centenario, 1910. De Marchi is the sixth from the left in the forefront.

Courtesy: Archivo General de la Nación, Buenos Aires.

of special commissions including the Comisión de Juegos Olímpicos.[39] The omnipresent De Marchi chaired the latter commission, which bore the same name as the earlier one established to organize representation at the 1908 London Games. This fact can be seen as a sign of purposeful continuity. When the Chamber of Deputies discussed how the centennial celebrations should be conducted, it stressed its belief in the Olympic ideal. Deputy Joaquín V. Gonzalez proclaimed that 'someday they [the Olympic Games] must take place in the city of Buenos Aires'.[40] In fact, an international competition resembling the Olympics occurred a year and a half later in Buenos Aires.

The Comisión de Juegos Olímpicos prepared an extensive programme of international competitions. The spectacle was commonly regarded as the Juegos Olímpicos del Centenario (Centennial Olympic Games). As expected, De Marchi's Sportiva was given the responsibility for organizing the activities[41] but the Club Hípico Argentino continued to question De Marchi's power. After a bitter quarrel over which club should prepare the equestrian events, the Comisión Nacional del Centenario intervened and transferred the events to the Club Hípico Argentino.[42] President José Figueroa Alcorta diplomatically declared at the opening of the 1910 congressional sessions that 'physical prowess, a subject of the artistic cult in Ancient Greece, appears as special events [in the celebrations] under the names of Olympic Games and International Equestrian Contests'.[43]

The presidential remarks not only implicitly referred to the confrontation but also indicated the status now bestowed upon sport. According to the mainstream press, the Juegos Olímpicos del Centenario were a complete success.[44] One of its glorious moments occurred in the Sportiva's Stadium when the Italian Dorando Pietri, a legend of the 1908 London Games, won the marathon in a unique display of athletic endurance. This would be the last marathon of Pietri's career.[45]

According to one journalist, the Juegos Olímpicos del Centenario were 'undoubtedly unique and without precedent in South America, a definition that is clear proof of its beauty'.[46] It seems that at last, Argentina was at the forefront of the promotion of the Olympic ideal in South America. However, Coubertin was infuriated by the Centennial Olympics. In June 1910, less than a month after the Games in Buenos Aires, Quintana was expelled from the IOC. Coubertin argued that Quintana 'had used the term "Olympic Games" improperly for personal publicity'.[47] This may have been a harsh judgement as Quintana did not have a prominent role in the Juegos Olímpicos del Centenario. Nevertheless, Coubertin was clearly upset by the misuse of the sacred term and took the opportunity to make a clear statement: the appropriation of his 'Olympic Games' was not a frivolous matter. Thus the sweet taste of Olympic glory did not last long for the Argentines. With the expulsion of Quintana, Argentina entered into a twelve-year interregnum without an IOC member. In Olympic matters, both inactivity and proactivity had their price.[48]

Not having an IOC member did not mean that a country could not send a team to the 'true' Olympic Games. Early in January 1912, the organizing committee of the Stockholm Games wrote to the Sportiva asking it to arrange and send an Argentine team to Stockholm.[49] Surprisingly, and despite the fact that the Sportiva had its own headquarters, the address of the Comisión de Juegos Olímpicos published by the Stockholm Organizing Committee was De Marchi's home address.[50] But De Marchi represented the Sportiva. Interestingly, neither the Sportiva nor the Argentine newspapers used the label Comisión de Juegos Olímpicos when referring to the effort to comply with the Swedish request. It may well have been implicitly understood that the Comisión de Juegos Olímpicos was the Sportiva. Be that as it may, the invitation was well received by all involved and De Marchi activated his connections immediately.

On 13 January 1912, De Marchi and Jorge Newbery, an upper-class sportsman and aeronautics pioneer, were received by Roque Saenz Peña, then president of Argentina. As expected, the pair asked for Saenz Peña's material support in order to send the best of the Argentine sportsmen to the Games. The president showed sympathy for the enterprise and promised to take steps to make it a reality. With this favourable news, the Sportiva declared April as a tentative date for trials. In the meantime, the rival Club Hípico Argentino had received the programme of the forthcoming Games from the Swedish ambassador to Argentina.[51] All this was to prove unimportant; the Argentine Olympic project once again failed to materialize. According to Sportiva's 1911–13 records, although the government supported its initiative, the economic climate did not allow for exceptional subsidies for an Olympic expedition. Once more, cherished Argentine Olympic ambitions were put on hold until more propitious times.[52]

Once again politicians chose to maintain orthodox economic austerity rather than incur the cost of sending an Olympic delegation. Other recently settled nations such as Australia or Canada, which experienced economic development analogous to Argentina's in the early twentieth century, considered the Olympics a powerful means of integration into the international community and an affirmation of their national identities. For Australia and Canada participation was an affair of national interest and concern.[53] In Argentina, however, the elite minority that saw sport as a tool to foster national pride and was unable to make it a national cause. However, by the 1920s, the majority of the elite considered athletic nationalism as a real opportunity to construct the image of a westernized Argentina and to present the nation to the world as a devotee of the cherished principles and practices of European civilization.

UPHEAVAL AND SUCCESS

Argentina was not represented in the 1912 Stockholm Games and the roar of cannons in Europe dashed any hopes of a team for the next Olympics. The First World War was a globally devastating shock which prevented the 1916 Olympic Games that had been awarded to Berlin. The calamitous times were not auspicious for the effective diffusion of the Olympic ideal. From 1914 to 1919 there were no IOC sessions; for Coubertin 1912–20 'must have seemed like an interminable period of waiting'.[54]

In Argentina, which maintained a policy of neutrality throughout the war, attempts to promote Olympism dissolved. De Marchi, the leader of the Olympic effort before the war, felt the patriotic call of duty in 1915 and travelled to Italy in order to serve his homeland.

Before De Marchi's departure, the Sociedad Sportiva Argentina had entered into a serious struggle with the authorities over an effort to obtain an extension of the right to use the land where the Sportiva had built its main venue, the Palermo Stadium. The Ministerio de Guerra (Ministry of War) and the Municipalidad de Buenos Aires (Municipality of Buenos Aires) claimed ownership of the land. There were interminable rounds of negotiations to settle the issue. In the end the Sportiva lost its Stadium. This development, which deprived the Sportiva of its main source of income, together with De Marchi's absence, brought about the dissolution of Argentina's most influential sports club.[55]

Although the Sportiva had been unable to send a team to the Olympic Games, it had had a great impact on Argentine sport. Sportiva's struggles to send teams to the 1908 and 1912 Olympic Games as well as its role in the Juegos Olímpicos del Centenario, had made the term

'Olympic Games' known to government officials, deputies and senators and, more importantly, to athletes and coaches, clubs and the general public. With this publicity, and with the expansion of sport in the country after the First World War, it was only a matter of time until the pioneering Argentine Olympic experiments led to the creation of an Argentine Olympic Committee and the first official Argentine participation in the Games.

Early in 1920 a group of representatives, led by Eugenio Pini,[56] from sport clubs, sport federations and a government agency, many of whom had previously had connections with the Sportiva, assembled to discuss the 'possibility that the Argentine Republic be represented in the Universal Olympiad to be held in July of this year [1920] in Antwerp'.[57] De Marchi, who had returned to Argentina in 1919, was part of this group.[58] In the meeting, the delegates expeditiously approved a 'patriotic idea' that 'would be the basis of a vigorous impulse for the diffusion of all sports in the country'.[59] On 10 January the 'provisional commission' constituted at the previous gathering, which had already decided to send the renewed project for Olympic participation to the Congress and invite all clubs from Buenos Aires to attend the ongoing meeting, regenerated itself as the Comité Pro–Juegos Olímpicos (Pro-Olympic Games Committee).[60]

Unlike its predecessors, which had a tendency to favour a single institution which claimed a monopoly on representation, this Comité Pro–Juegos Olímpicos was the first serious attempt to bring together a number of sport-related institutions with the intention of multiple representation. After its creation, the Comité Pro–Juegos Olímpicos immediately set up a plan to gain support. The plan included petitioning the National Congress for a subsidy in order to send a team to the Antwerp Olympics.[61] On 20 January, César Viale, who had been named vice-president of the Comité, wrote a long article for the Buenos Aires newspaper *La Nación* explaining the aims of the petition since the request had resulted in what Viale termed 'inadequate judgments' on the part of the public. The article explained the benefits that an Argentine Olympic team in Antwerp would bring to the country. As expected, Viale advanced the positive moral and patriotic benefits of participating in the Olympics. He also mentioned that Argentina could not be inactive knowing that its 'northern and western' neighbours were off to Antwerp.[62]

Far from appeasing the critics, Viale's article prompted a caustic response from Augusto De Muro, who had been president of Club Atlanta and was member of the Círculo de la Prensa (Circle of the Press).

De Muro resolutely argued that Argentine Olympic participation would be a debacle due to insufficient preparation and the lack of athletic progress in the country and that the amount of money requested from the National Congress would be better invested in the improvement of the meagre promotion of physical education.[63] He disapproved of the composition of the Comité claiming that it had ignored national federations in favour of clubs and that it had welcomed a federation that was not recognized by its international counterparts when one with that status already existed.[64] De Muro questioned the patrician composition of the Comité and its earlier policies by stating that 'it is crucial to put an end to the improvisations that we have been unfortunately suffering during the last fifteen years – improvisations based on the excessive advertising of great projects that lack a central concept of the educational movement that is indispensable for the country to reach, once and for all, what it deserves for the benefit of its sons'.[65] Undoubtedly, De Muro was a sharp critic and careful observer of Argentine Olympic history. The debate surrounding the 1920 Olympic participation echoed the debate of 1908. Indeed, the tension between the advocates of elite sport and the proponents of democratization of sport was now even stronger. This might be interpreted as an indirect outcome of the political and social climate created by the Saenz Peña Law of 1912 establishing universal male suffrage for Argentine natives over 18 years of age. During the early years of the twentieth century there had been a pressing demand for the introduction of democracy in Argentina. The progressive movements that fought for reforms began to win their battles and the nation soon experienced a significant change in political intentions. Wider participation in all areas of life by all classes was fostered by the new legislation and sport was no exception.[66] In 1920 the debate on Olympic elite sport versus sport for the masses reached a broader public and new heights.

De Muro's accusations touched a nerve and brought a reply from the Comité. Viale recognized that Argentine athletes were not among the world's elite but pointed out that nothing would be more educational than seeking new challenges. He agreed with his critic that physical education needed rejuvenation. However, Viale was emphatic about the composition of the Comité. He declared that 'our Comité is not one of the many oligarchic and exclusivist expressions that have marked the Argentine milieu ... Our origins and composition are genuinely democratic'.[67] Viale emphasized that the Comité could not be blamed for those absent from it because the group had invited everyone interested to join the Comité through the press. Viale accused De Muro of segregating himself from the Comité and reaffirmed that it 'admits every citizen of good will who sympathizes with ... the goal: the strengthening and virilization of the race'.[68] Viale, who was a man of remarkable finesse and *spirit diplomatique*, ended his letter by inviting De Muro to be part of the Olympic campaign.[69]

Despite the controversy, the Comité Pro-Juegos Olímpicos, which was usually referred to as Comité Pro-Juegos Olímpicos de Amberes (Pro-Antwerp Olympic Games Committee) or simply as Comité Olímpico Argentino (Argentine Olympic Committee), continued its work. March and April of 1920 were busy months for the Comité. It sought support for the Antwerp Games as well as for the April's Santiago de Chile Olimpíadas Sudamericanas (South American Olympics), which was the title given to the South American athletics (track and field) championships. Coubertin would later make it clear that the IOC had not given the Chilean organizers of the Olimpíadas Sudamericanas the right to name the event an Olympic Games.[70] Viale's efforts to help the delegation set up by the Federación Atlética Argentina (Argentine Athletics [Track and Field] Federation) paid off. The Comité obtained funds from the aristocratic Jockey Club, the Buenos Aires' Consejo Deliberante (Buenos Aires Legislative Body), a sport association and various illustrious citizens.[71]

The Argentine participation in the Olimpíadas Sudamericanas was a valuable experience. Viale publicized the work of the Comité at the Chilean contest. Things went so well for Viale in Chile that in consideration of 'the incontestable material and moral necessity that South America present itself at the seventh Universal Olympiad', he signed an agreement *ad referendum* with the Chilean Federación Sportiva Nacional (National Sporting Federation) 'to undertake together as a single and fraternal block the round trip to Antwerp'.[72] The Comité's support of the Argentine delegation's participation in the athletic events was seen as a sign of true commitment to and leadership of national athletic and Olympic affairs.[73]

On the back of its first success and with a new confidence in itself, the Comité charged forward again for support of its Antwerp project. A few days after returning from Chile, Viale repeated the request for a subsidy to the National Congress.[74] The petition officially came before the Senate on 20 May 1920.[75] The Comité gained even more visibility when, also in

May, the news came that Marcelo Torcuato de Alvear had accepted the position of Comité president.[76] Alvear, a member of one of the country's wealthiest families, was then serving as Argentina's ambassador to France. In 1922 he became both an IOC member and President of the Argentine Republic. In the 1890s, Alvear had belonged to the patrician group that founded the Unión Cívica Radical (Radical Civic Union) – a party that pushed forward political reform at the turn of the century. Alvear was Janus-headed. In addition to his links to the reformers, he was a symbol of reassurance to the elites who had historically controlled Argentina. He successfully bridged two worlds. Furthermore, Alvear was not only a politician but also a dedicated sportsman; he frequented the Sportiva and knew many of its distinguished members. With Alvear's prestige, the Comité was in a uniquely fortunate situation. It seemed as if Argentina would finally have an Olympic Delegation.[77]

On 22 June 1920, the Senate discussed the Comité Olímpico Argentino's petition. Julio A. Roca Jr., now a senator, mounted a defence of the Olympic project. He invoked the Argentine achievements at the recent Olimpíadas Sudamericanas, the fact that Chile, Brazil and Uruguay would send representatives to the Antwerp Olympic Games and claimed that Argentina's athletes were good enough to participate in the Games with dignity. The Senate approved the subsidy. If the Chamber of Deputies endorsed the Senate decision, the subsidy would be sanctioned as law. The Olympic dream was only one step from reality.[78]

The next day, 23 June, the Chamber of Deputies took up the matter of the subsidy. Deputy Mariano Demaría Jr. referred to the potential successes of the Argentine rowers, fencers and shooters in Antwerp and spoke of the Comité's eminent leaders, Alvear and Viale, as guarantors of the good faith of the petition. It was a powerful speech. Demaría also requested that the chamber should make a prompt decision since the Argentine delegation would have to depart within a week. To comply with the Chamber of Deputies procedures, a prompt decision meant either that day, which ironically was the twenty-sixth anniversary of the foundation of the IOC, or the day after. Disappointingly for the Comité the deputies failed to discuss the project again.[79] Money may have been an issue or, more realistically, the deputies may have thought that there was not enough time to fully debate the demands of such an important enterprise. Probably, the deputies considered that it was more suitable to calmly analyse and efficiently organize arrangements rather than endorse any trip overnight. After all it was not an urgent issue of national security. The upshot of this pragmatic reasoning was that the Argentine Olympic dream failed to be realized once again. Argentina had one unofficial entry in the 1920 Olympic Games – a mysterious boxer whose last name was Rodríguez.[80]

The misfortune of the Comité Olímpico Argentino caused despondency in the Argentine sport community. A year went by without much activity. Viale, who had written to Coubertin to put him in the picture, heard back in January 1921. Coubertin's response was not encouraging; he told Viale emphatically that his letter revealed lack of knowledge of the IOC organization.[81] The internal stalemate exasperated some sports leaders. The silence was broken on 4 July 1921 when Tito Arata, president of the Círculo de la Prensa, invited all the presidents of sport federations to meet and discuss the formation of an alternative superior sport organization that would assemble the federations in order to provide support for Argentine sport. Coincidentally, Rafael Cullen, president of the Federación Atlética Argentina, arrived at the gathering with a proposal to create the Confederación Argentina de Deportes (Argentine Confederation of Sports).[82] Viale, foreseeing the consequences for his Comité, stated that 'it seems to me that the new institution could not be other than the same Comité under a different or a modified name'.[83] Despite Viale's observation, after a brief discussion, 'the idea of constituting that superior entity was accepted'[84] by the delegates of the sports federations. The intention to oppose the Comité was clear.

On 12 July 1921, eight days after the first meeting, under the presidency of Augusto De Muro on behalf of the Círculo de la Prensa, there was a second gathering in which the majority of the delegates gave their support to the establishment of the Confederación Argentina de Deportes. Viale said that the Federación Argentina de Box (Argentine Boxing Federation), over which he himself presided, was not in a position to give a definite answer before consulting the position of its affiliates. Viale declared that as the delegate of the Comité Olímpico Argentino he had to wait until its next meeting to make a decision. He also suggested waiting for the position of the Comité's president, Alvear, on this issue. However, Cullen proposed to immediately create the Confederación Argentina de Deportes *ad referendum*. Everyone but Viale voted in the affirmative.[85]

The Comité Olímpico Argentino met on 15 July under Viale's leadership. The Comité designated Viale and Juan Gibson to mediate in any problems that might arise with the Confederación.[86] Viale recognized that the Confederación had to be accepted 'if it saved harmony – the ideal goal – of the institutions'.[87] He renounced his position in the Federación Argentina de Box but not without first registering his objections.[88] Viale said that 'it was not his will to "drag" the institution down a road contrary to its sympathies'[89] and commented that he had not voted during the last meeting of the Confederación, because he had no mandate to do so.[90] Viale also declared that as acting president of the Comité he had to wait for an answer from Alvear, who was negotiating its affiliation with the IOC, before making any move.[91]

Alvear's response came after the Confederación met again on 19 September. This was precisely the day, after the proposed constitution was approved, on which the Confederación was officially established.[92] Apparently, Viale had written to Alvear as early as April 1921 asking Alvear to seek the admission of the Comité Olímpico Argentino to the IOC. Alvear revealed that Coubertin 'reproached some mistakes of the Comité Argentino, among them the sad memories left by the previous delegates'.[93] Coubertin later recollected that some Argentine members 'had been of no help at all, and either a complete lack of understanding or attempts at independence that were carried to the extreme ... were exceedingly annoying for us'.[94] Evidently Coubertin was referring to the 'inactive' Zubiaur and the 'hyperactive' Quintana.

In order to erase those regrettable memories, Alvear, the sophisticated Argentine ambassador, must have seemed an appealing choice to Coubertin. Alvear was formally installed in the IOC in June 1922 although Coubertin informed him as early as October 1921 that the decision regarding his membership had already been taken.[95] However, Viale only learned about Alvear's position after it was too late to make a case for the Comité to the Confederación. Finally, on 31 January 1922, Alvear wrote Viale about the conflict between the Comité and the Confederación. Each institution claimed to legitimately represent Argentine sports. Alvear stressed 'the urgent need for harmony and cooperation, among all the existing institutions in the Republic, for the purpose of reaching a definitive organization to develop even more, if it is possible, sport in our country'. He added that 'nothing would hinder [,] and on the contrary [,] it would produce the indispensable cooperation, if the members of the Comité Nacional Deportivo Argentino [Argentine National Sporting Committee – although he actually meant the Confederación Argentina de Deportes] to be created or already existing, were members of the Comité Olímpico Argentino'.[96]

The Confederación, which had received an invitation to participate in the Brazilian Olimpíadas Latinoamericanas (Latin American Olympics) – an event similar to Argentina's 1910 Juegos Olímpicos del Centenario – arranged to celebrate Brazil's centennial, met on 18 March and explicitly challenged the Comité's claim to direction of sports matters.[97] At the same time, De Marchi, surprisingly signing himself as president of the Comité, solicited Alvear to ask for IOC support so the Comité would be recognized as the sole Argentine authority to send a team to Brazil. In turn, Alvear asked Comte Melchior de Polignac, a French IOC member, for advice. Polignac simply recommended that Alvear contact the Brazilian IOC member.[98] Late in March, Viale and De Marchi, who had not heard from Alvear regarding the required IOC support, were still wondering which institution was going to have responsibility for the representation in Brazil. Rather than risk confrontation, Viale and De Marchi advocated peaceful conciliation.[99] Alvear's silence on this issue, and his January suggestion of cooperation, were messages that could not be ignored.

On 28 March 1922, five days after Alvear won the Argentine elections, the Comité Olímpico Argentino held a meeting to which they invited the Confederación Argentina de Deportes. Alvear's position prevailed during the meeting. According to Viale, those assembled, taking into account Alvear's letter, decided that there was agreement between the two institutions and that their respective executive boards would resign. During the meeting it was also agreed that participation in the forthcoming Olimpíadas Latinoamericanas would be determined by the authorities of the soon to be created new and inclusive committee.[100]

The same day Viale wrote a letter to Alvear, which was later published in *La Nación*, with a full report of the meeting. The next day, 29 March, Viale also telegraphed Alvear with the 'patriotic' news.[101] However, Cullen, who had attended the meeting as president of the Confederación, disagreed with Viale's interpretation of events. Cullen recollected that the gathering had decided that the Comité agreed with the Confederación, that the Comité's executive board would resign because the Confederación did not have one and that the executive board of the Confederación would be elected in an assembly made up of the federations from the two organizations.[102] Cullen's account would seem to be correct because Viale sent Alvear details of the corrections.[103] The Confederación Argentina de Deportes had established itself as the supreme sport authority in Argentina.

On 7 April 1922, Cullen informed the Confederación that he had attended a meeting of the Comité. According to Cullen, its members decided to dissolve the Comité and free its affiliated federations.[104] A month later, Alvear was named honorary president of the Confederación. The year passed in preparation of the delegation for the Olimpíadas Latinoamericanas. Unlike Argentina's 1910 Juegos Olímpicos del Centenario, the Olimpíadas Latinoamericanas had been placed under the patronage of the IOC.[105] The Confederación sent a team to the Brazilian Games. Alvear, on way back from France to Argentina to take office as president of the republic, was given a warm reception in Río de Janeiro. The Brazilian government had sent an invitation for Coubertin to preside over the Games. Although Coubertin could not attend the festival, Count Henri de Baillet Latour, a future IOC president, replaced him.[106] Baillet Latour not only attended the Games but also travelled throughout the Americas promoting Olympism. On 23 November the Confederación welcomed him in Buenos Aires – a pleasant end to a fractious year.[107]

The good times did not last. In 1923 the Confederación sought international recognition and domestic support. In April 1923 Cullen reported that he had discussed the 1924 Olympic Games with Alvear and found the president well-disposed to a request for congressional support so Argentina could be represented in Paris. Significantly, it was not at all clear who would be the beneficiary of that support.[108] Word that Alvear desired to form a Comité Olímpico Argentino spread rapidly and the Confederación panicked. The accusations and counter-accusations among members only consolidated the shock.[109] However, the Confederación tried to continue with its business. On 25 August, Alvear sent a note to Congress promoting the value of participating in the Olympics and indicating that the Comité Olímpico Argentino, the institution that would be in charge of participation, had not yet been formed. Finally, Alvear stated that the government considered it an appropriate action to create such a Comité.[110] Undoubtedly, Alvear was loyal to the past Olympic cause. He would forget neither his patrician sporting colleagues nor their previous Olympic efforts. His elitist loyalties were hardly surprising since he was a man who believed that only one of his class could understand Coubertin's Olympic language and vision.

The decisive blow to the Confederación came on 31 December 1923. That day Alvear signed a decree establishing the Comité Olímpico

Argentino. The rumour had become reality. Four days later the Comité was formed. Ricardo C. Aldao,[111] a member of Alvear's ruling party and long-time president of the prominent Club de Gimnasia y Esgrima de Buenos Aires (Buenos Aires Gymnastic and Fencing Club) – a club that had been led by Alvear in the year 1900 – was named president of the Comité. Prospero Alemandri, vice-president of that club,[112] Viale and Pini, who had introduced Alvear to the art of fencing, were asked to serve respectively as secretary, treasurer and general commissar. All accepted their posts except Viale. He declined, for personal reasons.[113]

The newly founded Comité Olímpico Argentino set up a programme intended to make the Argentine Olympic dream come true. After almost twenty years of struggle, Argentina sent its first official delegation to the 1924 Games. However, the arrangements for the Olympic debut were not without trouble. The formation of the team brought the underlying

FIGURE 3.3

Meeting held on the premises of the Club de Gimnasia y Esgrima de Buenos Aires, 1924.
Notice the presence among others of (1) Prospero Alemandri, (2) Carlos Martinez,
(3) Ricardo Aldao, and (7) César Viale, all prominent figures of the newly founded Comité
Olímpico Argentino. Although it is not clear whether the Club de Gimnasia y Esgrima de Buenos
Aires or the Comité Olímpico Argentino called the meeting, the connection
between the two institutions is evident.

Courtesy: Archivo General de la Nación, Buenos Aires.

tensions between the Comité and the Confederación to the surface. The Comité declared that in order to have the most competitive team, any athlete, regardless of sport affiliation, would be eligible for the trials. This was not accepted by the Confederación, which perceived it as an intrusion into its functions. The controversy was resolved by transferring the trials to the individual sports federations. At last, the Argentine Olympic delegation was formed with representatives from eleven sports with one remarkable absence – there was no football team.[114]

Late in 1919, the Asociación Argentina de Football (Argentine Football Association) was accused of arbitrariness in the management of the several leagues under its control by many of its member clubs. As protests escalated, a group of clubs decided to disaffiliate themselves from the Asociación Argentina de Football and created their own Asociación Amateur de Football (Amateur Football Association). This breakaway was led by Aldao, among others. The Confederación recognized the Asociación Argentina de Football, which was affiliated with the Fédération Internationale de Football Association (FIFA), football's international governing body, while the Comité welcomed the rebel Asociación Amateur de Football. There was a bitter dispute over whether footballers from the latter could be chosen for the Argentine Olympic squad. According to the Comité any footballer was eligible but the Confederación maintained that the selection had to be limited to footballers affiliated to the association recognized by FIFA. The French Olympic Committee solved the problem by insisting that all members of the Argentine Olympic football team needed to be members of clubs recognized by the international governing body. Although the squabble was ended in principle, continuing hostility between the Comité and the Confederación prevented Argentina from fielding a football team for the Paris Games. The two organizations were incapable of reaching an agreement even after mediation by the Minister of Justice and Public Instruction.[115]

In spite of the absence of a team representing Argentina's most popular sport, the nation's participation in Paris was an achievement in itself. The 1924 Argentine Olympic expedition generated attention beyond sporting circles – as confirmed by a dispatch from the United States Embassy in Buenos Aires to the State Department in Washington, DC which discussed the Argentine Olympic developments.[116] Argentina won six medals in three sports – polo, athletics and boxing. It also won its first gold. In addition to these athletic accomplishments there was more to come. Aldao, who had been

FIGURE 3.4

Ricardo Aldao and the first Argentine Olympic delegation, 1924.
Aldao is in the middle of the front row.

Courtesy: Archivo General de la Nación, Buenos Aires.

co-opted in 1923 as a member of the IOC, presided over the delegation. While leading the Argentine team to the Paris Games, Aldao outlined some of the circumstances associated with the creation of the Comité. He mentioned that the Argentine government, after having considered all relevant aspects of the matter and having detected problems in the national sport organizations, had decided to create the Comité and confer on it the exclusive authority to represent Argentina in the Olympics. Aldao added that because of this unusual contingency the Comité did not, as the IOC bylaws stipulated, have the mandate from the sport federations existing in the country. However, Aldao went on, the governmental decree specified that as soon as the national sport federations regularized their functions and created the Confederación, the Comité's functions would cease. Indeed, this happened a few years later. Nonetheless, the creation of the Comité Olímpico Argentino in 1923 clarified the distribution of power in Argentine Olympic matters: the progressive wing of the aristocracy and its sport-minded affiliates controlled Olympic endeavours. In those early years of inchoate sport organization when there was no government agency involved in regulating sports matters, those who had the right connections to manipulate the state apparatus for the advancement of their interests and projects dominated Argentine Olympic activities. The government's blessing in the form of subsidies and patronage was a means of consolidating and legitimating this manipulation.

CONCLUSION

Although it took Argentina almost three decades to form its own National Olympic Committee after Coubertin named José B. Zubiaur as a founding member of the IOC in 1894; interest in Olympism arose in elite Argentine sporting circles little more than a decade after the Baron's successful recreation of the Olympics. In spite of Coubertin's limited patience with those who did not stay in line with his aspirations, these early contacts constituted the early stage of the diffusion of Olympism in Argentina. However, it was not Zubiaur, for whom sport was an educational tool, but the aristocratic *porteños*, with their view of sport as a distinctive trait of a gentleman and as a component of the leisured class, who would bring the Olympic project to fruition.

As soon as this exclusive group, which had strong ties with, and devotion to, Europe, discovered Coubertin's cosmopolitan vision, they were captivated by the idealistic Olympic rhetoric but not before carefully noticing the pragmatic potential that such an endeavour held for the advancement of their own agendas. However, matters were more complex than this. The *porteños* early struggles to establish a National Olympic Committee were also a response to the early twentieth century enthusiasm for sport that was blossoming in Argentina. They believed that nothing could be better to incorporate their young and progressive nation into the Western-defined international scene than a project that blended the gentlemanly pastimes of the British investors, the mythical aura of Greek classicism and the French flavour of Coubertin's cosmopolitanism. It was a seductive combination: sports were seen as modern and chivalrous practices and the Olympics were perceived as a stage upon which the 'moral' progress of the growing nation could be displayed. As Deputy Carlos Delcasse pompously declared in 1907, 'An Argentine triumph in the fields of England would mean something more than the fact of having had more strength or endurance than the English: it would mean that we are at the top of the South American nations'.[117] During the first two decades of the twentieth century there was a sense of pride in the confident Argentine elite. This pride not only stimulated a desire to advertise the country's prowess but also to demonstrate that there was no other country in the region as modern and westernized as Argentina. This elite considered devotion to athletics as a tool with which to demonstrate the benefits of imitating the practices of the hegemonic powers.

However, the view that Olympic arenas provided unique opportunities for the display of national achievements did not enjoy a clear consensus. Indeed, it generated resistance. This opposition was revealed in 1907 when Deputy Andrónico Castro disapprovingly exclaimed, after the Chamber of Deputies approved the subsidy (later aborted by the Senate) to send an Argentine delegation to the 1908 London Olympic Games, 'What a way to spend the money of the nation!'[118] For some it was not only a matter of misusing funds but of equality. That same year Deputy Aureliano Gigena claimed that the nation lacked democratic sporting societies.[119]

Whatever the divergent political views on sport, the Olympic advocates had the connections and the power to force one congressional debate and several governmental deliberations on Olympic participation before the First World War. However, there was no room in this era for economic 'irresponsibility' such as the expansion of public spending for Olympic excursions. As the critics noted, Argentina had other priorities, such as supporting education in general and physical education in particular, before taking up grandiose athletic projects for which local athletes were supposedly not yet ready. Unlike other early twentieth century second-tier industrialized nations, Argentine Olympic participation faced substantial internal opposition. Even when their early adoption of modern sport afforded them a significant position in Argentina as well as in South America and beyond, internal disagreements about the role of sport reflecting the class dynamics of Argentine society, international misunderstandings by Argentine IOC members and failed attempts at institutionalization delayed the Olympic representation.

The situation changed after the First World War. The 1920s brought a new economic bonanza and participation in sport continued to grow. Even more importantly, the view that sport was an important aspect of western-style modernization gained momentum among the elite. Once again, long-time aristocratic Olympic promoters sought state support for their Olympic enterprise. This time they benefited from having one of their own as President of Argentina. President Marcelo T. de Alvear, distinguished aristocrat, politician and sportsman, sought to promote an alliance between the aristocracy and the other social classes whilst remaining faithful to his upper-class origins. With Alvear in office the power was in the hands of aristocrats whom the elite trusted to protect their interests. However, maintaining the alliance meant the increase of public spending for, in most cases, patronage purposes. In this context, Alvear inaugurated a state policy of financial support for the Comité Olímpico Argentino. Moreover, Alvear decreed the establishment of the Comité. It was Alvear who ensured that Argentina's Olympic dreams finally came true. His awareness of the critical role that Argentina's international image played in the nation's ability to attract foreign investment, which greatly increased after the post-war revival of the European economies, might well have influenced his decision to put Argentina on the Olympic map. Coubertin expressed his gratitude for Alvear's support, writing that the Argentine greatly honoured the IOC by remaining in the organization while serving as president of the nation.[120]

The search for subsidies became a distinguishing element in the Comité's *modus operandi* although this practice was not exclusive to the Comité. For many decades, social actors in Argentina had relied upon the state for the realization of their demands and aspirations. In return, the state needed the support of these actors for legitimacy. This configuration created a state–society relationship that the Argentine political scientist Marcelo Cavarozzi has called a 'state-centered matrix'.[121] This matrix illustrates the central role that the state has played in Argentine society and economy. Argentina's Olympic dreams were not exempt from this matrix.

The diffusion of Olympism in Argentina was not as late an occurrence as it might appear as first glance. Olympism originally disembarked on the Argentine shores of the Río de la Plata just a few years after Coubertin's creation of the IOC. However, the story of Olympism in Argentina is one of the gradual adoption of the idea that the Olympic Games would serve the national interests. The pattern that the diffusion of Olympism followed in Argentina included several unnerving periods of procrastination. The fact that Argentina was in an extraordinarily advantageous position to lead the Olympic movement in South America yet only managed to send its first official team at almost the same time as many of the other South American republics is better understood when set against the larger forces that shaped the nation's sporting culture. Argentine Olympic prospects marched to the drum of the state; when the

Olympic promoters convinced the politicians of the national benefits of Olympism, or perhaps when the politicians themselves were convinced of these benefits, the promoters received state assistance for their project and Argentina sent a team to the Olympic Games.

Undoubtedly, events such as Count Henri de Baillet Latour's 1923 South American tour explains, to some extent, the 1920s 'Olympic explosion' in the region. However, such events do not account for the intensity and depth of the Olympic struggle in Argentina. The process of Olympic expansion began when pioneers such as Zubiaur, Alejo Peyret and Antonio De Marchi either met Coubertin or encountered his ideology. This process gained strength through the establishment of social structures such as the Comité Olímpico Argentino. The Olympic movement was incorporated into the fabric of the nation through the systematization of social endeavours such as the attempted Olympic expeditions. The diffusion of Olympism in Argentina is a series of expectations, tribulations and failures that reflect an ongoing unfulfilled hope – a hope that sharply revealed the intersection of social, political and economic interests that were finally realized in 1924 when Argentina sent its first team to the Paris Olympics. Those Games, which were the climax of a long struggle, inaugurated the country's thirty 'golden' Olympic years. From 1924 to 1952, Argentina became the most successful Latin American country in the Olympic Games. Argentine athletes stood on the victory podium 36 times during that time, 13 times to receive gold medals.[122]

The 1924 Argentine Olympic participation proved to be a success for De Marchi, César Viale, Ricardo C. Aldao, Eugenio Pini and the rest of the Olympic promoters. Argentina obtained six medals, including its first gold. To some degree the Olympic advocates were correct in affirming that Argentine athletes could be serious contenders in Olympic arenas. More importantly, this was the progress of the nation that at last had been fully displayed in Europe. Tom Keane, a journalist with the *Atlanta Constitution*, proved this point when he noted, of Luis Bruneto's silver medal in the triple jump, that 'it was [a] strange thing to see a man from South America smashing an Olympic record, because in the past we didn't look to Latin-America for startling athletic work'.[123]

Pini, proud of his incessant work in favour of Olympism in Argentina recollected, several years after the 1924 Olympic Games, that the Argentine participation in Paris was glorious.[124] Those Games and the establishment of the Comité Olímpico Argentino the year before constitute the closure of a period in Argentine Olympic history. The late institutionalization of

Olympism in Argentina and the athletic success of the first Argentine Olympic delegations represent the tribulations and achievements of a sporting community searching for its identity. Unfortunately, the achievements would soon disappear and the tribulations would reappear.

ACKNOWLEDGEMENT

I would like to express my gratitude to Professor Mark Dyreson for his assistance. I would also like to thank the Centro de Documentación Histórica IEF No. 1 'Dr. Enrique R. Brest' in Buenos Aires, Argentina and the Olympic Museum in Lausanne, Switzerland for their invaluable co-operation. I would like also to express my appreciation to Professor J.A. Mangan for his editorial assistance with this essay.

NOTES

1. For a discussion of the diffusion of modern sports, see Allen Guttmann, *Games and Empires* (New York: Columbia University Press, 1994) and J.A. Mangan, *The Games Ethic and Imperialism: Aspects of the Diffusion of an Ideal* (London and Portland, OR: Frank Cass, 1999). For additional insights into this process, see J.A. Mangan (ed.), *The Cultural Bond: Sport, Empire, Society* (London and Portland, OR: Frank Cass, 1992), William J. Baker and James A. Mangan, *Sport in Africa: Essays in Social History* (New York: Holmes and Meier, 1987). See also the chapters by J.A. Mangan and Vic Duke and Liz Crolley in this volume.
2. See Eduardo Olivera, *Orígenes de los Deportes Británicos en el Río de la Plata* (Buenos Aires: L. J. Rosso, 1932) and Ricardo Hogg, *Yerba Vieja* (Buenos Aires: Julio Suarez, 1945).
3. Thomas Turner, *Argentina and the Argentines* (London: Swan Sonnenschein, 1892), pp.59–60.
4. Detailed accounts of Coubertin's life and ideas can be found in Yves-Pierre Boulonge, *La Vie et L'ouvre Pèdagogique de Pierre de Coubertin, 1863–1937* (Ottawa: Lemeac, 1975); John MacAloon, *This Great Symbol* (Chicago: The University of Chicago Press, 1981) and David Young, *The Modern Olympics* (Baltimore: The Johns Hopkins University Press, 1996).
5. For a complete account of this period of Argentine economic development, see Carlos Diaz Alejandro, *Essays on the Economic History of the Argentine Republic* (New Haven, CT: Yale University Press, 1970). An analysis of the composition of the Argentine elite can be found in David Rock, *Politics in Argentina, 1890–1930* (London: Cambridge University Press, 1975).
6. See Young, *The Modern Olympics*, p.75.
7. See ibid., pp.73–6; MacAloon, *This Great Symbol*, pp.136–38 and *La República Argentina en la Exposición Universal de Paris de 1889* (Paris: P. Moullot, 1890), tomo 1.
8. Fermín Chavez, *Civilización y Barbarie* (Buenos Aires: Trafac, 1956); Rodolfo A. Seró Mantero, *Carta sobre Misiones del Profesor Alejo Peyret* (Buenos Aires: Ministerio de Educación de la Nación, 1949); Juan Antonio Solari, *Pensamiento y Acción de Alejo Peyret* (Buenos Aires: Bases, 1972); Diego A. de Santillan, *Gran Enciclopedia Argentina* (Buenos Aires: Ediar, 1960), tomo 6, 357; *La Prensa* (Buenos Aires), 28 Aug. 1902, 5, 5.
9. Godofredo Daireaux in Alejo Peyret, *La Evolución del Cristianismo* (Buenos Aires: La Cultura Argentina, 1917), p.7. For a brief biography of Daireaux, see de Santillan, *Gran Enciclopedia Argentina*, tomo 2, 360.
10. For a full account of Zubiaur's life, see Cesar R. Torres, 'Mass Sport Through Education or Elite Olympic Sport? José Benjamín Zubiaur's Dilemma and Argentina's Olympic Sports Legacy', *Olympika: The International Journal of Olympic Studies*, 7 (1998), 61–88.
11. Alejo Peyret, 'Informe sobre el Congreso de Ejercicios Físicos', *La República Argentina en la Exposición Universal de Paris de 1889*, 263.
12. José B. Zubiaur, 'La Sección Escolar Francesa de Instrucción Primaria en la Exposición Universal de Paris de 1889', ibid., 407.
13. See José B. Zubiaur, *La Enseñanza Práctica e Industrial en la República Argentina* (Buenos Aires: Felix Lajouane, 1900), p.351 and idem., 'Una Nueva Institucion Escolar', *Tribuna Libre*, n.s., 58 (1919), 208.

14. José B. Zubiaur to Pierre de Coubertin, 22 June 1907, International Olympic Committee Archives, Lausanne, Switzerland.
15. José B. Zubiaur, *Labor Dispersa e Inédita* (Buenos Aires: Perrotti, 1916), p.11.
16. See Torres, 'Mass Sport Through Education or Elite Olympic Sport?', 65–71.
17. Bill Mallon, *The 1900 Olympic Games* (Jefferson: McFarland, 1998), p.124.
18. See Torres, 'Mass Sport Through Education or Elite Olympic Sport?', 65–71.
19. Ibid., 78–81.
20. The standard work on the English public schools games ethic is J.A. Mangan, *Athleticism in the Victorian and Edwardian Public School: The Emergence and Consolidation of an Educational Ideology* (London and Portland, OR: Frank Cass, 2000).
21. Torres, 'Mass Sport Through Education or Elite Olympic Sport?', 78–81.
22. Jorge Saraví Riviere, *Aportes para una Historia de la Educación Física, 1900 a 1945* (Buenos Aires: IEF No. 1 'Dr. Enrique R. Brest', 1998), pp.7–8.
23. *Porteño* is the term that designates someone from Buenos Aires.
24. Saraví Riviere, *Aportes para una Historia de la Educación Física, 1900 a 1945*, 9; Felix Luna, *Soy Roca* (Buenos Aires: Sudamericana, 1989), p.343; *La Nación* (Buenos Aires), 21 Feb. 1934, 5, 5 and 22 Feb. 1934, 7, 6.
25. Saraví Riviere, *Aportes para una Historia de la Educación Física, 1900 a 1945*, 14. See also *La Nación* (Buenos Aires), 1 June 1909, 8, 2–3, 2 June 1909, 12, 4, 3 June 1909, 10, 3–4 and 12 Aug. 1909, 12, 4–5; *La Prensa* (Buenos Aires) 2 June 1909, 10, 7, 14 Aug. 1909, 6, 7 and 15 Aug. 1909, 7, 5–5.
26. People from rural areas spent a great deal of time moving about on horseback. An important aspect of their tasks and diversions revolved around horse related activities such as horse-racing, horse-breaking and lassoing. Many of these activities have been associated with the romanticized *gaucho* figure of the Argentine pampas. For details of these traditional physical practices and their transformation, see Richard W. Slatta, 'The Demise of the Gaucho and the Rise of Equestrian Sport in Argentina', *Journal of Sport History*, 13, 2 (1986), 97–110.
27. Saraví Riviere, *Aportes para una Historia de la Educación Física, 1900 a 1945*, 8 and 15–16. For accounts of the aeronautics activities, see Roberto C. Castelli and Vicente Bonvissuto, *Jorge Newbery y el Legado de su Genio Luminoso* (Buenos Aires: n.p., 1988) and Raúl Larra, *Jorge Newbery* (Buenos Aires: Schapire, 1975). The ambiance of the 'fiestas deportivas' can be perceived in, for example, *La Prensa* (Buenos Aires), 11 and 18 Sept. 1911.
28. Manuel Quintana has been an elusive figure for Olympic historians. Several publications have mentioned Quintana as a former president of Argentina. For example, the *Olympic Review*, 87–88 (Jan.–Feb. 1975), 23–4 says that 'Dr. Zubiaur was replaced by Mr. Manuel Quintana, future president of the Republic'. Similarly, Wolf Kraemer-Mandeau, in his article 'National and International Olympic Movements in Latin America' in Roland Naul (ed.), *Contemporary Studies in the National Olympic Games Movement* (Frankfurt am Main: Peter Lang, 1997), p.183, described Quintana as 'a former president of Argentina'. These remarks are obviously incorrect since Quintana the president took office in 1904 and died while serving as president of the nation in 1906. On the other hand, Quintana the IOC member became so in 1907. Quintana the IOC member was the son of Quintana the president and Susana Rodríguez. Manuel Quintana, the younger, was married to Mercedes Unzué. The couple had four children. Quintana, the younger, was a lawyer and a landowner, and a promoter of sports with a special bent for yachting. He was associated with and active in several aristocratic sports institutions including: Jockey Club, Yacht Club Argentino (Argentine Yacht Club,) Sociedad Sportiva Argentina and Círculo de Armas (Circle of Arms). He also belonged to the Liga Patriótica Argentina (Argentine Patriotic League). Quintana, the younger, died on 9 May 1920 in Buenos Aires. At the time of writing, his date of birth had not yet been confirmed (it was probably 1867). See *La Prensa* (Buenos Aires) 10 May 1920, 5, 4.
29. Luis A. Martín, *La Argentina en el Movimiento Olímpico*. Unpublished article, Buenos Aires (1975), 8.
30. Several references to the invitation can be found in *Diario de Sesiones de la Cámara de Diputados – Año 1907* (Buenos Aires: La Patria degli Italiani, 1907), tomo 1.
31. *La Prensa* (Buenos Aires), 25 June 1907, 8, 7.
32. Ibid. and *La Prensa* (Buenos Aires), 26 June 1907, 10, 3.

33. Martín, *La Argentina en el Movimiento Olímpico*, 8–9.
34. *Diario de Sesiones de la Cámara de Diputados – Año 1907*, 488.
35. Ibid., 486–99, 511–13, 524–7, 722; *La Prensa* (Buenos Aires), 18 July 1907, 6, 1–3 and 20 July 1907, 4, 6–7.
36. For discussions of the historical development of the relationship between sport and nationalism, see, for example, Mike Cronin, *Sport and Nationalism in Ireland* (Dublin: Four Court Press, 1999) and Mark Dyreson, *Making the American Team* (Urbana: University of Illinois Press, 1998).
37. Manuel Quintana to Pierre de Coubertin, 16 Oct. 1908, International Olympic Committee Archives, Lausanne, Switzerland.
38. Ibid.
39. *Memoria de la Comisión del Centenario al Poder Ejecutivo Nacional* (Buenos Aires: Coni, 1910); *Guía-Programa de los Festejos del Centenario, 1810–1910* (Buenos Aires: Talleres Heliográficos de Ortega y Radaelli, 1910).
40. Joaquín V. Gonzalez, *Obras Completas* (Buenos Aires: Universidad Nacional de La Plata, 1935), pp.9, 344.
41. See *La Nación* (Buenos Aires), 3 July 1909, 11, 6 and 7 Aug. 1909, 11, 1.
42. *Memoria de la Comisión del Centenario al Poder Ejecutivo Nacional*, 76.
43. Heraclio Mabragaña, *Los Mensajes* (Buenos Aires: Talleres Gráficos de la Compañia General de Fósforos, 1910), tomo 6, 412.
44. During the 1900s the Argentine labour movement carried out demonstrations and strikes culminating during the centennial celebrations. The choice and timing of these activities frightened and infuriated the upper classes. Civilian groups arose to counter the workers' actions. For example, members of the Sociedad Sportiva Argentina, including president De Marchi, and other groups took part in attacks on three worker newspapers and the headquarters of the Socialist party on 14 May 1910. For a full account of the incidents, see Sandra McGee Deutsch, *Counterrevolution in Argentina, 1900–1932* (Lincoln: University of Nebraska Press, 1986) and idem, *Las Derechas. The Extreme Right in Argentina, Brazil, and Chile, 1890–1939* (Stanford: Stanford University Press, 1999).
45. See *Caras y Caretas* (Buenos Aires), 7, 14 May 1910 and 4, 11 and 25 June 1910; *La Prensa* (Buenos Aires), 29, 30 and 31 May 1910; *El Nacional* (Buenos Aires), 28 May 1910; *El Pueblo* (Buenos Aires), 23 and 24 May 1910; *O Estado de São Paulo* (São Paulo), 26 and 29 May 1910, and Alain Lunzenfichter, *Le Roman de Marathon* (Lausanne: International Olympic Committee, 1997), p.47.
46. *El Pueblo* (Buenos Aires), 23 May 1910, 1.
47. *The International Olympic Committee – One Hundred Years* (Lausanne: International Olympic Committee, 1996), 1, 105; Otto Mayer, *A Travers les Anneaux Olympiques* (Geneva: Pierre Cailler, 1960), p.61.
48. Quintana is not listed in the many working groups formed within the *Sportiva* to organize the events of the *Juegos Olímpicos del Centenario*. See *La Nación* (Buenos Aires), 3 July 1909, 11, 6.
49. *La Nación* (Buenos Aires), 4 Jan. 1912, 14:5, *La Prensa* (Buenos Aires), 4 Jan. 1912, 16, 1.
50. *The International Olympic Committee – One Hundred Years*, 2, 246. See also Luna, *Soy Roca*, 235 and 392.
51. *La Nación* (Buenos Aires), 11 Jan. 1912, 15, 7; *La Prensa* (Buenos Aires), 14 Jan. 1912, 16, 2–3, 15 Jan. 1912, 12, 5.
52. Sociedad Sportiva Argentina, 'Memoria y Ejercicio Económico, Junio 1911–Junio 1913', quoted in Martín, *La Argentina en el Movimiento Olímpico*, 10.
53. For details of the development of Olympic sport in those countries, see Bruce Kidd, *The Struggle of Canadian Sport* (Toronto: University of Toronto Press, 1996) and *The Oxford Companion to Australian Sport* (Melbourne: Oxford University Press, 1994).
54. John A. Lucas, *The Modern Olympic Games* (New York: Barnes, 1980), p.95.
55. Riviere, *Aportes para una Historia de la Educación Física, 1900 a 1945*, pp.33–4.
56. See César Viale, *El Deporte Argentino* (Buenos Aires: García Santos, 1922), p.181.
57. *La Prensa* (Buenos Aires), 4 Jan. 1920, 12, 7.
58. See Viale, *El Deporte Argentino*, pp.176–7.
59. Ibid.

60. *La Prensa* (Buenos Aires), 13 Jan. 1920, 12, 7.
61. The petition can be found in Viale, *El Deporte Argentino*, p.13.
62. Ibid., pp.17–23.
63. Viale, *El Deporte Argentino*, pp.24–35. Even the United States, which had become the world's industrial giant after the First World War, had a hard time sending a team to Antwerp. See Mark Dyreson, 'Selling American Civilization: The Olympic Games of 1920 and American Culture', *Olympika: The International Journal of Olympic Studies*, 8 (1999) and John A. Lucas, 'American Preparation for the First Post World War Olympic Games, 1919–1920', *Journal of Sport History*, 10 (1983).
64. At that time there were two football federations, the Asociación Argentina de Football and the Asociación Amateur de Football. The *Comité* recognized the latter.
65. Viale, *El Deporte Argentino*, p.29.
66. For an account of the influences of the Saenz Peña Law, see David Rock, *Argentina 1516–1987* (Berkeley: University of California Press, 1987).
67. Viale, *El Deporte Argentino*, p.37.
68. Ibid.
69. Ibid., pp.35–9.
70. Pierre de Coubertin to César Viale, 29 Dec. 1920, in ibid., pp.139–40.
71. Ibid., pp.42 and 55–62.
72. Ibid., pp.65–6.
73. The *Olimpíadas Sudamericanas* were held in Santiago de Chile from 23–25 April 1920. Reports of the preparations and events can be found in *La Prensa* (Buenos Aires), 1, 9, 13, 14, 17, 18 and 22–26 April 1920; *El Mercurio* (Santiago de Chile), 1–30 April 1920.
74. Viale, *El Deporte Argentino*, pp.75–6.
75. *Diario de Sesiones de la Cámara de Senadores – Año 1920* (Buenos Aires: Establecimiento Gráfico A. de Martino, 1920), tomo 1, 32.
76. Although Alvear confirmed his acceptance through a letter to Viale in June, Viale may have received a telegram in May with the news. See Viale, *El Deporte Argentino*, pp.77–8 and *La Prensa* (Buenos Aires), 9 May 1920, 11, 7.
77. For a complete biography of Alvear, see Felix Luna, *Alvear* (Buenos Aires: Hyspamerica, 1986).
78. *Diario de Sesiones de la Cámara de Senadores – Año 1920*, pp.375–6.
79. *Diario de Sesiones de la Cámara de Diputados – Año 1920* (Buenos Aires: Imprenta y encuadernacion de la H. Camara de Diputados, 1920), tomo 2, pp.215–16; Viale, *El Deporte Argentino*, pp.80–86. On 8 Sept. 1920 the Chamber of Deputies archived the project because the Antwerp Olympic Games had already taken place. Finally, on 9 Sept. 1920, the Chamber of Deputies informed the Senate that the project had been rejected. See *Diario de Sesiones de la Cámara de Diputados – Año 1920*, tomo 4, 900 and *Diario de Sesiones de la Cámara de Senadores – Año 1920*, 746.
80. See Bill Mallon, *The Olympic Record Book* (New York: Garland, 1988), p.327.
81. Pierre de Coubertin to César Viale, 29 Dec. 1920 in Viale, *El Deporte Argentino*, pp.139–40.
82. Copy of the *Libro de Actas de la Confederación Argentina de Deportes*, Centro de Documentación Histórica IEF No. 1 'Dr. Enrique R. Brest', Buenos Aires, 1–3.
83. *La Nación* (Buenos Aires), 6 July 1921, 8, 1–2 and *La Prensa* (Buenos Aires), 6 July 1921, 12, 7.
84. *Libro de Actas de la Confederación Argentina de Deportes*.
85. *Libro de Actas de la Confederación Argentina de Deportes*, 4–5; *La Nación* (Buenos Aires), 15 July 1921, 7, 2 and *La Prensa* (Buenos Aires), 15 July 1921, 11, 7.
86. *La Nación* (Buenos Aires), 16 July 1921, 8, 1 and *La Prensa* (Buenos Aires), 17 July 1921, 14, 2.
87. Viale, *El Deporte Argentino*, p.134.
88. Ibid., pp.131–8.
89. Ibid., p.131.
90. Ibid., p.133.
91. Ibid., pp.133–4 and *La Nación* (Buenos Aires), 22 July 1921, 7, 3.
92. *Libro de Actas de la Confederación Argentina de Deportes*, 6–7. In 1925 the *Confederación* decided to establish 1 Sep. 1921 as its official date of creation. I have been unable to find a justification for this change. See copy of the *Actas del Congreso Extraordinario del 19 de Enero*

de 1925 *(Confederación Argentina de Deportes)*, Centro de Documentación Histórica IEF No. 1 'Dr. Enrique R. Brest', Buenos Aires, 1 and 10.

93. Marcelo T. de Alvear to César Viale, 26 Oct. 1921 in Viale, *El Deporte Argentino*, pp.161–2.
94. Pierre de Coubertin, *Olympic Memoirs* (Lausanne: International Olympic Committee, 1997), p.170.
95. Pierre de Coubertin to Marcelo T. de Alvear, 20 Oct. 1921 in Viale, *El Deporte Argentino*, p.163.
96. Marcelo T. de Alvear to César Viale, 31 Jan. 1922 in ibid., pp.169–70.
97. *Libro de Actas de la Confederación Argentina de Deportes*, 13–15.
98. Melchior de Polignac to Pierre de Coubertin, 24 Feb. 1922, International Olympic Committee Archives, Lausanne, Switzerland.
99. Antonio De Marchi to César Viale, 24 March 1922 and César Viale to Antonio De Marchi, 25 March 1922 in Viale, *El Deporte Argentino*, pp.167–77.
100. Ibid., pp.179–82.
101. Ibid., p.178.
102. Ibid., pp.183–4.
103. Ibid., pp.182–3.
104. *Libro de Actas de la Confederación Argentina de Deportes*, 19–20.
105. Coubertin, *Olympic Memoirs*, 203; *The International Olympic Committee – One Hundred Years*, 1, 285; Mayer, *A Travers les Anneaux Olympiques*, p.96.
106. Coubertin, *Olympic Memoirs*, 203; Mayer, *A Travers les Anneaux Olympiques*, p.96; *O Estado de São Paulo* (São Paulo), 12 Sept. 1922, 2, 5.
107. *Libro de Actas de la Confederación Argentina de Deportes*, 35–7.
108. Ibid., 48.
109. Ibid., 61–6.
110. Marcelo T. de Alvear to Argentine Congress, 25 Aug. 1923, International Olympic Committee Archives, Lausanne, Switzerland.
111. At the end of 1918 and the beginning of 1919, the Federación Obrera Marítima (Maritime Workers Federation) made a series of demands to the coastal shipping companies. Aldao was the chief lawyer representing the shipowners. Aldao opposed party leader and twice elected president of Argentina, Hipólito Yrigoyen, because of Yrigoyen's lenient policy toward workers. For an account of this dispute, see Rock, *Politics in Argentina, 1890–1930*, pp.180–200.
112. Alemandri had served in the *Comisión de Juegos Olímpicos* that organized the *Juegos Olímpicos del Centenario* in 1910.
113. *La Participación de los Atletas Argentinos en los Torneos de la VIII Olimpiada* (Buenos Aires: Comité Olímpico Argentino, 1924), p.7.
114. Ibid., pp.7–9
115. Ibid. See also Tony Mason, *Passion of the People? Football in South America* (London: Verso, 1995), pp.46–7 and *The New York Times*, 27 March 1924, 14, 2. Aldao was also involved in 1912 in a previous rift in Argentine football.
116. United States Embassy in Argentina to US State Department, 11 Feb. 1924, State Department Records Division, Record Group 59, Foreign Relations Microfilm Files, National Archives and Record Administration II, College Park, Maryland.
117. *Diario de Sesiones de la Cámara de Diputados – Año 1907*, 488.
118. Ibid., 496.
119. Ibid., 491.
120. Coubertin, *Olympic Memoirs*, p.198.
121. See Marcelo Cavarozzi, 'Beyond Transitions to Democracy in Latin America', *Journal of Latin American Studies*, 24 (1992), 665–84.
122. The 36 medals won by Argentine athletes 1924–52 were an impressive achievement when compared to the rest of Latin America. Mexican athletes, the second most successful Latin Americans during that period, obtained 11 medals. See David Wallechinsky, *The Complete Book of the Summer Olympics* (New York: Overlook, 2000).
123. *Atlanta Constitution*, 13 July 1924, A13.
124. Eugenio Pini, *La Historia de la Esgrima Argentina en la X Olimpiada de Los Angeles* (Buenos Aires: Gadola, 1932), p.25.

Fútbol, Politicians and the People: Populism and Politics in Argentina

VIC DUKE and LIZ CROLLEY

Association football is undoubtedly the leading spectator sport in the world and this role is confirmed throughout most of Latin America. On mainland South America, only in Venezuela is *fútbol* less popular than imported North American sports such as baseball (it is only North Americans who insist on calling the game soccer in order to distinguish it from their own brand of American football). Notwithstanding the world dominance of the sport, football culture varies markedly according to the economic, social, political and historical characteristics of a society.[1] What is distinctive about Argentina is that sport and politics are inextricably linked. *Fútbol* is an extension of politics; it is part of the political system and anything that begins as a sports issue rapidly becomes politicised.[2] Historically, there are grounds to claim that *fútbol* is the social model around which the political system has been constructed.

This essay will outline how the ties between *fútbol* and politics were established, the form in which these links are maintained and comments briefly on whether the relationship is likely to continue.[3] At the infancy stage of football in Argentina, the game was established and dominated by the English population of Buenos Aires.[4] During the period of adolescence, the Argentines took-over both off and on the pitch, football became *fútbol* and the links between politics, the people and *fútbol* were established. Maturity brought the institutionalization of these relationships and the appearance of politically organized fan groups, the *barras bravas*. Towards the end of the twentieth century, pressures emanating from the globalization of sport began to challenge the traditional *fútbol* culture.

THE INFANT PERIOD OF ENGLISH DOMINANCE OF
ARGENTINE FOOTBALL

Britain was Argentina's leading trade partner in the second half of the nineteenth century and there were a significant population of British nationals, mostly English, living in Buenos Aires. The first football in Argentina was played by visiting seamen in the port area of Buenos Aires; they were known locally as *los ingleses locos*.[5] Expatriate railway workers helped to spread the game further inland during a period of extensive railway construction. Educationalists also played their part.[6] The English made the physical space in which to play and were encouraged by employers and educationalists. Two of the oldest surviving football clubs were started by railway workers – Quilmes Athletic Club in 1887 and Rosario Central in 1889. As the suburbs of Buenos Aires spread outwards with the railway lines, a football club was formed at every settlement along the line. This historical pattern remains clearly visible today. Further afield in the provinces, football clubs were also formed by, and named after, railway companies, e.g. Central Norte in Mendoza, Pacifico in Bahia Blanca and Andes Talleres in Mendoza.

Games involving a mixture of what are now association football and rugby rules took place from the early 1860s onwards. The first official club in Argentina was Buenos Aires Football Club which formed in 1867 as a spin-off from Buenos Aires Cricket Club (founded in 1862). On 20 June 1867, the first recorded match took place: the Colorados defeated the Blancos 4–0. By 1890 there were around 45,000 British nationals living in Greater Buenos Aires and they were instrumental in the formation of several other football clubs. In 1891, Saint Andrews School won a tournament in Buenos Aires and the Argentine Association Football League was established in 1893.

A Scot, Alexander Watson Hutton is regarded as the *padre* (father) of Argentine football. He founded the English High School in 1884 where football was an essential part of the curriculum. Hutton became the first president of the Argentine Association Football League and the old boys of the High School formed Alumni who became the most successful club during the period of mainly English dominance.[7] The founding clubs of the Argentine Association Football League reflected the twin influences of school (e.g. English High School and Lomas Athletic Club) and railway (e.g. Buenos Aires–Rosario Railway and Quilmes Athletic Club).

Football developed very early in Buenos Aires. Indeed, in terms of development it was second only to Britain. The first club, Buenos Aires Football Club, was formed in 1867, only ten years after the first English club (Sheffield FC) and in the same year as the first Scottish club (Queen's Park). The establishment of a league championship in 1893 was preceded only by The (English) Football League in 1888 and the Scottish and Irish Leagues in 1890. Mainland Europe did not develop any leagues until 1895 (Belgium) and then 1896 (Sweden).

Evidence for essentially English dominance in the early period is available in many forms. On the pitch the league was won by clubs with overwhelmingly British players until 1912. In the 1990s, Lomas Athletic Club won the championship six times, and Alumni were undoubtedly the team of the first decade of the twentieth century. Between 1901 and 1911, Alumni won the league nine times. Furthermore, they acquired immortal fame in Argentina by defeating a visiting South African side in 1906. The Alumni team that day included five Brown brothers and four other British surnames, plus Weiss and Laforia. Visiting English professional teams provided the yardstick by which local players could judge their own progress (or lack of it). Notable examples were Southampton in 1904, Nottingham Forest in 1905 and both Everton and Tottenham Hotspur in 1909.

The earliest clubs consisted of predominantly, and usually exclusively, 'Anglo-Saxon' members. These clubs were unsurprisingly given English names and some clubs still carry this legacy today as a revelation of the roots of Argentine football. Examples among current leading clubs are River Plate, Newells Old Boys and Quilmes Athletic Club. Early English dominance is exemplified by the nomenclature of the football organizations in this period – consider the Argentine Association Football League in 1893, which became the Argentine Football Association in 1903. In the early days of these organizations the officials all had English surnames; the first four presidents were Hutton, Boyd, Wibberley and Boutell.[8]

Another indicator of English dominance lies in the fact that the official language for association business remained English until 1906. In 1905, a pamphlet on the rules of the game was printed in both English and Spanish. Only in 1912, following a split in the association, was there a partial change to Spanish wording in the title of what was now two organizations: the original and traditional Argentine Football Association became the Asociación Argentina de Football whereas the breakaway group was entitled the Federación Argentina de Football. Interestingly both switched to Spanish for the organizational description (Asociación and Federación), both employed 'Argentina' rather than 'Argentine' (which is English), yet the name of the game remained 'football'. Only in 1934 with the official acceptance of professionalism did the governing body become the Asociación de Fútbol Argentino.

Given that many of the early clubs emanated from English schools or were formed by English (or occasionally Scottish) middle-class professionals with a university education, involvement of the social elite was evident from the very beginning (although this is not to deny the role of the railway workers). For instance Hugo Wilson[9] was not only president of the Argentine Football Association 1909–12 and president of the Asociación Argentina de Football 1912–15, he was also president of the Jockey Club; a highly prestigious institution to this day. Incidentally, Wilson was the last president of any of the Argentine football organizations to bear an English surname. Evidence of interest in football from the Argentine elite at this time is clearly furnished by the visit of the President of the Republic to the Alumni–Southampton match in June 1904.

1912 is usually cited as the last year of the period of English dominance in Argentine football. In that year Quilmes Athletic Club won the Asociación championship; they were the last predominantly English team to do so. The following year, Racing Club won the first of seven consecutive titles with a team including only three players of English origin. Racing Club are regarded as the first *criollo* champions of Argentina. A symbolic indication of the approaching end of an era occurred in 1910 when Argentinos beat Británicos 5–1 in the annual challenge match.

Although popular histories of Argentine football convey a discontinuity between 1912 and 1913, in reality the 'creolization'[10] of football was a more gradual process. As football became accepted and adopted by the Argentine population of predominantly Italian and Spanish immigrants, friction arose as the integration of other Argentines into some traditionally English/Anglo-Argentine clubs was resisted. This led to the establishment of new clubs where Argentines were welcome. Such clubs included Argentino de Quilmes (formed in 1899 as an Argentine-friendly counterpart to Quilmes Athletic Club), Estudiantes de Buenos Aires (established 1898) and Independiente Football Club (formed in 1905). Later Independiente made its name fully Spanish and became Club Atlético Independiente.

By the beginning of the twentieth century most of the major clubs we recognise today were established. All of the big five clubs in Argentine football were founded over a four-year period; River Plate in 1901, Racing Club in 1903 and Boca Juniors, Independiente and San Lorenzo in 1905. Boca Juniors were, and still are, based in the Genovese *barrio* alongside the port in Buenos Aires. The name chosen for the club is instructive, legend tells us they rejected other names such as Italian Stars and Children of Italy because they felt a strong identity with their *barrio*. 'Boca', meaning mouth of the river, establishes their identification with their port on the River Plate and 'Juniors' reflects the fact that they now considered themselves to be children of that place, rather than immigrants. In football's formative years, the clubs developed a close association with the roots of their local communities.

At the very same time as football was imported into Argentina, Buenos Aires experienced a population explosion from 90,000 in 1854, to 670,000 in 1895, to 1,576,000 in 1914. By the early twentieth century there were over a million immigrants in the city. An accelerated process of suburbanization and a marked expansion in the transport infrastructure accompanied the rapid increase in population. An electric tramway was opened in 1897 and suburban railways developed in the latter part of the century.

This combination of urban elements rendered the *barrio*, or neighbourhood, central to life experience for the inhabitants of Buenos Aires. The *barrios* were crystallized as political and cultural creations in the 1910s. Those new football clubs that were established in the late nineteenth and early twentieth centuries played an important role in the social and political life of the *barrio* where they were based. The football club came to represent the locality and contributed to the integration of a young immigrant population into Argentine society.

From 1905 to 1910 hundreds of local football clubs were established as part of a genuine social and democratic movement. The new immigrants adopted the game played by the English workers and established their clubs in the new *barrios*. New identities emerged based on the *barrio* rather than the origins of immigrants. Local rivalries were central from the very beginning. Whereas the English learned their football in the schools, the *criollos* learned to play in the streets and on the patches of wasteland (*potreros*) on the edge of *barrios*. These very different 'classrooms' led inevitably to very different values on and off the pitch. Fair play and the amateur ethos of the gentleman were favoured by the bourgeois English clubs. These clubs monopolized official football, where requirements included a proper ground and decent changing rooms. In contrast, the *criollos* played to win and many of their clubs could not afford proper facilities. Local rivalries were intense.

By 1907 there were over 300 football clubs in Buenos Aires playing outside the official championship. Most of these were either workplace or neighbourhood based. Appropriation of football by the Argentine working class led not only to conflicting values but also to disputes over behaviour, both on and off the pitch. Many of the upper-class English clubs would shortly abandon the unruly working class game of football and switch to the more elite game of rugby (e.g. San Isidro and Belgrano). The traditional ritual of 'the third half', a convivial social gathering between the players of both sides after the match, soon disappeared from football but it remains to this day in Argentine rugby.

Tension between the English and *criollos* erupted in 1912 in the form of a split into two rival organizations. Those sticking with the traditional official organization joined the Asociación Argentina de Football, which had 52 member clubs;[11] the breakaway Federación Argentina de Football had 152 adherents. At the same time there were a further 280 clubs playing in *ligas independientes* (leagues independent of both organizations). The end result of all this was the entry of more non-English clubs from poorer social backgrounds into competitive football. The two organizations merged again in 1915 but by this time many of the traditional English clubs had abandoned football in favour of rugby. Alumni did not compete in 1912. The infancy stage was well and truly over.

ADOLESCENCE AND THE ARGENTINE TAKE-OVER OF *FÚTBOL*

From the very beginning of the adolescent period, native Argentines (excluding Anglo-Argentines) dominated the game that was becoming *fútbol* rather than football. This dominance was evident both on and off the pitch. On the pitch, all the championship winning teams from 1913 onwards were overwhelmingly composed of Argentines of Italian and Spanish origin. A debate ensued as to the superiority of the *criollo* style over the English style of play which was reinterpreted and romanticized by the sporting press in the 1930s and 1940s. The contrasting and conflicting styles of *criollo* football (characterized by individual flair, instinct, spontaneity) and English football (noted for its reliance on physical strength and hard work) complicated the search for a national football identity. Off the pitch, all the leading officials in the various governing bodies from 1915 onwards had non-English surnames. Moreover the names of the governing bodies became partially Spanish in 1912 and fully Spanish in 1934.

It is also during this period of adolescence that the structures that integrate *fútbol* and politics to this day were established. Of crucial importance to the subsequent development of *fútbol* in Argentina is that it preceded democratic politics. Universal male suffrage was not approved until 1912 and the first democratic election took place in 1916, by which time 46 of the leading professional clubs involved in the restructuring of *fútbol* in 1985 were already in existence. The newly formed political parties had no adequate organization of their own so they borrowed the infrastructure of *fútbol* and its neighbourhood-based clubs. Both football and politics were organized in a similar manner within the community. Football clubs in Argentina are private member associations, which means that the *socios* (members) elect the club officials. Party politics came to play a leading role in these club elections.

There are four main elements in the organization of Argentine *fútbol* and it is the relationships between them that determine the role of politics in sport and sport in politics. The state (represented by politicians), the football association – Asociación de Fútbol Argentino (AFA from 1934), the football clubs and the fans are the key players in the political network. Other elements such as businesses, local communities and the mass media have a part to play. The links between the four main elements are complex. However, sufficient motivation has been present on the part of all the players to ensure the continuation of the structure into the twenty-first century.

In theory, Argentine *fútbol* operates a hierarchical structure that is common to many other institutions. The AFA is responsible for the running of *fútbol* and is answerable only to the state. The clubs, whose chairmen and directors double as politicians, are governed by the AFA's structures and rules. Most of the club *presidentes* and *dirigentes* are associated with a political party. A well-known example from the adolescent period is that of Pedro Bidegain[12] at San Lorenzo de Almagro, who was also a leading figure in Unión Cívica Radical. In many countries, the fans traditionally have little power in the formal structures of football; they are merely the masses that constitute the crowd and provide the gate money. However, in Argentina, because of the unique ties between politics and *fútbol*, the role of the fans is of utmost importance in the running of a club and to a politician's career (to this day rival political lists appear in club elections).

The relationships between the four main elements of the *fútbol* hierarchy became established during the 1920s and 1930s. During this period, clubs were either financed by benefactors, received donations from supporters or sponsorship from local businesses. Football clubs became the sporting, social and political centre of the *barrio*. They provided much more for their members than watching a match. Racing Club and Sportivo Barracas were the first to develop advanced social facilities for their members and their *barrios*. For instance, Sportivo opened an enclosed *pelota* court in 1917, a new *fútbol* stadium in 1920 and a swimming pool in 1925.

The Unión Cívica Radical were in power from 1916 to 1930 until the government was overthrown by the first of Argentina's many military coups in the twentieth century. At the same time, rapid social and economic change resulted in the continued suburban expansion of Buenos Aires and industrialization heralded the rise of a significant working class. The workers were to be an important market for *fútbol* and *fútbol* was to become a useful medium by which the state could control the population since it could be used to distract the workers from everyday problems and political issues.

A breakaway professional league, the Liga Argentina de Football, was formed in 1931 and comprised 18 clubs from Buenos Aires and La Plata. P. Alabarces and M. Rodriguez recognize professionalization both as a key element and a watershed in the history of Argentine *fútbol* and also claim it provoked the definitive rupture between the upper classes and *fútbol*. While acknowledging the immense effects of the break away from amateurism, which was so central to the aristocratic ideals represented via football during its infancy, it is important to emphasize that this did not mean that the powerful and socially dominant abandoned *fútbol*. On the contrary, they continued to run the game, to use it as a political tool, to gain social status from it and, consciously or not, to exploit it as a vehicle of social control.

One of the main reasons behind the move to professionalism was a desire to stem the flow of top Argentine players to European clubs. Julio Libonatti was the first such player to move, from Newells Old Boys to Torino. More significant was the transfer of the outstanding Raimundo Orsi in 1928 from Independiente to Juventus. Orsi was later awarded Italian nationality and went on to make 35 international appearances for Italy; he was one of three Argentines (by birth) to play for Italy in the

1934 World Cup Final. By the end of 1934, the professional league had rejoined the official fold under the guise of the newly formed AFA.

The arrival of the professional league had a major impact on *fútbol*. Average attendance at matches increased significantly, competition between the clubs was intensified and the already fierce rivalry between supporters was heightened. The biggest of the club rivalries to this day, between Boca Juniors and River Plate, escalated during this period. Both clubs had become accustomed to success during the 1920s while they played in different leagues. In this period, *fútbol* experienced a short boom period of expansion and relative wealth, led by River, who were given their nickname of *Los Millonarios*.

Professionalization of *fútbol* increased its popularity even more. Fortuitously, this period coincided with the spread of the mass media. The press and radio contributed to the diffusion of the sport and to its exploitation in controlling and manipulating the masses during a period of political instability. The motivation for state involvement in the Liga Argentina de Football and in the running of clubs is clear. Government officials realized the potential of *fútbol* as political propaganda. It was advantageous to the state to establish a relationship, albeit indirect, between itself and football fans.

For individual politicians, football clubs provided a shop window, in which to display themselves and their 'wares' as they still do today. The motivation which helps explain the close links between *fútbol* and politics in Argentina in the 1930s remains the same today, thus enabling the continuation of the relationship. Directing a football club, supporting the club through some other activity, or simply attending a match provides politicians with the opportunity to become known to a large public. It facilitates networks for political canvassing and encouraging the loyalty of the local community. It is usual for the names of politicians to appear on lists of honorary *socios* for most clubs and it has gradually become a normal way of creating political propaganda. It is common practice during presidential elections at football clubs, for rival political opponents to stand as candidates and run campaigns against one another, thereby merging the structures of football and politics. In the past many businesses have decided to become involved in *fútbol*, not only for its potential for advertising but also so that businessmen (and the system involves exclusively men) could use *fútbol* as a stepping-stone to a political career. This remains true today. Involvement in the local club provided a positive image, shrewd politicians like to appear in touch with the people in this way.

Once *fútbol* was professionalized, its political function became more intense and more overt. Since its foundation in 1934, links between successive *presidentes* of the AFA and the state have been strong. During dictatorships, a state administrator has been appointed to run the AFA and at other times those officials who have been elected have usually had close relationships with the ruling government. Official links between state and *fútbol* are via the AFA. It is the AFA *presidente* who represents *fútbol* at a higher level.

The typical *presidente* of the AFA has three characteristics: links with politics, a business career and an apprenticeship in *fútbol* which often involves the running of a club. Of the 29 AFA *presidentes* from 1934 to the present day, one-third have been appointed as government officials during periods of state intervention. Many of the others who have been elected have either had links with political parties or held a position in government at some stage of their careers. Conversely, their political links meant that they held a relatively stable position as long as there was no change in the political power structure. Even when changes did take place, the ability to swap allegiance sometimes ensured survival, as illustrated by Raul Colombo (1956–65). Several *presidentes* have been members of Unión Cívica Radical including Tiburcio Padilla (1934–35), Pedro Canaveri (1946–47) and the present incumbent, Julio Grondona.

Never have the state and the AFA been more closely tied than in the 1940s when the AFA *presidente*, Ramón Castillo, was the son of the President of the Republic. Oscar Nicolini, Cayetano Giardulli, Valentin Suàrez, Domingo Peluffo and Cecilio Conditti were all government officials who ran the AFA during the dictatorship of Juan Domingo Perón (1946–55). No government has failed to get involved in AFA business and no AFA presidency has failed to seek Government support.[13] In 1926 the President of the Republic intervened to resolve yet another rift between two rival football associations.

Football clubs were not slow to exploit the government's desire to enhance the profile of *fútbol*. In 1936 state subsidies were made available in the form of special grants which enabled clubs to rebuild or upgrade their stadium or even to build a brand new one. The most famous examples of new stadia at this time are River Plate's El Monumental (see Figure 1) in 1938 and Boca Juniors' La Bombonera in 1940. Furthermore, it has not been uncommon in the history of Argentine *fútbol* for the state to bail clubs out of financial straits and save them from bankruptcy.

FIGURE 4.1

River Plate fans celebrate at *El Monumental.*

It was during the Perónist period from 1946 to 1955 that state intervention in *fútbol* reached its peak. Policies were adopted which were directed at expanding the appeal and strengthening the infrastructure of the sport. Perón undertook responsibility for sport as a mechanism of national integration via the socialization of the youth and as political propaganda. It was important to export a positive image of the country and *fútbol* was promoted in order to do this.

Sporting success was equated with Perónist success to such an extent that medals achieved under Perón were named *medallas peronistas* (Perónist medals). In return for state backing, the AFA supported Perón as a presidential candidate. Perón himself was reputedly enthusiastic about *fútbol* and frequently attended matches. His wife, Evita, patronized the Evita Youth Championships in the 1950s during which *fútbol* was used as part of the country's child health programme. It was compulsory for all participants to pass a health check before entering the competition. Undoubtedly, these championships served to win over many youths to Perónism.

Links between the state and football were strengthened during the Perónist period. Clubs used their connections with power in order to develop. Most of the club *presidentes* were, and still are, either rich businessmen or politicians or both. It became normal practice during the Perónist period for football clubs to have a *padrino* (literally: a godfather, or patron) within government, who often also doubled as directors at the club. The *padrinos* were occupants of high positions of power who looked after the interests of a particular club. They had no official status as such but many clubs looked to their support when they were in difficulties. At this time *fútbol* was still enjoying a steady rise in popularity, such that clubs continued to outgrow their stadia. The state policy of aid for redevelop-ment was extended. Huracán, Racing Club and Vélez Sarsfield opened new stadia in 1947, 1950 and 1951 respectively. Racing accomplished a particularly favourable negotiation via their *padrino*, Ramón Cereijo, who was no less than the government treasurer at the time.

In Argentina the fans also came to play an important role since they constituted the masses, the voters and the consumers. Their existence explains why everyone wants to become involved in the sport. One of the prime reasons why the state originally became interested in *fútbol* was to control the masses by structuring and defining social identities and reinforcing national sentiments as international football became more important. The state targeted *fútbol* as being a location where the masses could gather and channel their frustrations. For businesses, involvement in *fútbol* was premised on the fans' role as consumers.

However, above all it is the political role of the fans which has been distinctive in Argentine *fútbol*. The fans have been voters not only in elections for club officials, which as we have seen have been themselves party political, but also in local, regional and national elections. Therefore, ambitious politicians needed to cultivate a solid fan base of support. The more militant fans (*militantes*) participated in more than committed support for the team and the club; they also undertook political work on behalf of a politician who might be the club *presidente*, a candidate for club *presidente* or one of the club *dirigentes*. This direct relationship between politicians and fan groups was to reach its apotheosis during the mature stage of the game's development in the form of the *barras bravas*.

Mention of the *barras bravas* (which translates roughly as the fierce opponents) raises the issue of the extent of violence in Argentine *fútbol* during the adolescent period. It is difficult to specify exactly when such violence began. Certainly we know that Estudiantes de La Plata had their ground closed in May 1912 following an attack on a match referee. There is evidence that the term *barras de hinchas* was used already in 1929 to describe gangs of ruffians who defended the honour of their club against others. O. Bayer has suggested that such incidents between fans began in 1932.[14] The aim of the fighting was to capture emblems and banners as trophies of war from the opposing fans. We have presented a more detailed argument regarding the separate evolution of football hooliganism in Argentina in an earlier published article.[15]

In the 1930s and 1940s the violence was mostly apolitical in nature, largely related to events that took place on the pitch and directed towards players and match officials. However, there is also evidence of fighting between rival groups of fans. A complex system of enmities and alliances developed to the extent that a meeting of certain clubs would guarantee a fight. These traditional rivalries often involved clubs from the same neighbourhood in Buenos Aires (e.g. Huracán and San Lorenzo in Almagro; Racing Club and Independiente in Avellaneda), or from adjacent neighbourhoods (e.g. Atlanta and Chacarita Juniors), or from the same provincial city (e.g. Newells Old Boys and Rosario Central in Rosario). The Rosario case highlights another kind of rivalry between the workers' club (Central) and a club associated with wealth and the middle classes (Newells). This situation is mirrored in La Plata (Gimnasia y Esgrima and Estudiantes) and Santa Fe (Colón and Unión). With the rise of the *barras bravas* what is different in the stage of maturity is that the violence became more organized, more political and more lethal in its consequences.

The network of links between *fútbol* and politics was established during the adolescent period. Motivation for ties between the state, the AFA and football clubs was high. The state did what it could for *fútbol* via the AFA. As the AFA was usually run by government officials or supporters, they toed the party line. The state tried to benefit by exploiting *fútbol* as a social drug and/or as a vote-winner in times of democracy. Individual politicians, the *padrinos*, did what they could for individual clubs. It enhanced their profile and status in society. Clubs benefited by having someone in power to represent them so it was in their interests to offer support in return. The fans were not just spectators providing gate money for the clubs because they were also the voters in both club and national elections. As such, politicians and football clubs could not afford to ignore them.

MATURITY AND CONSOLIDATION OF THE LINKS BETWEEN
FÚTBOL AND POLITICS

By this stage of maturity, the complex structure of links between *fútbol* and politics in Argentina was already in place and all that remained was the consolidation of the various networks involving the four main elements. In other words, the relationships were institutionalized. These relationships have been described in detail in the previous section. Two additional features of maturity are worth mentioning. First, the relationship between the state and *fútbol* reached new heights in 1978 when Argentina hosted the World Cup Finals for the first time. Second, the rise of the *barras bravas* inaugurated a period of increased violence associated with *fútbol*, violence which was more organized, more political and resulted in more fatalities. Both of these features will be considered in detail below, following a more general consideration.

At the beginning of the mature period, social and economic changes were impinging on *fútbol*. In the late 1950s and early 1960s, *fútbol* began to be run more as a business venture and there was increased pressure on clubs to be successful. Average attendance at matches was declining, partly as a result of Argentina's humiliation at the 1958 World Cup Finals in Sweden. *La selección*, as the national team is known, reached its nadir in a 6–1 defeat against Czechoslovakia. This disillusion with *fútbol* coincided with the emergence of alternative ways of occupying leisure time, such as watching the television that was increasingly widely available.

Although most clubs traditionally enjoyed the financial backing of a figure in the local business community, they were still aware of the importance of match results – success guaranteed fans and publicity and it is the fans who constitute the customers that businesses hoped to attract via their advertising and sponsorship. Thus the phenomenon of *fútbol-espectáculo* (football spectacular) was born. The two main protagonists in *fútbol-espectáculo* were the *presidentes* of the two largest clubs – River Plate and Boca Juniors. They invested huge amounts of money in their clubs, made big-name signings to attract the crowds and expected success. It is this increased pressure for success which some argue has led to the corruption and violence that frequently controls *fútbol* match results.[16]

While results have become ever more important, football clubs in Argentina have maintained their social function in the *barrios*. This goes way beyond the running of a football team. Clubs encourage support and reward loyalty by providing other facilities for the local community.

Even at the smallest clubs, other sports teams and not just *fútbol* are run for members of the local community of all ages and both sexes. Special social events are often held for women and their involvement is encouraged. At large clubs, the responsibilities of the club extend far beyond the professional football team. Promising young footballers might be invited to pursue their education at the club schools which opened in the 1970s – at Boca Juniors there is a library situated within the stadium. Although progressive in these respects, facilities for spectators at many of the major grounds lag behind clubs of equivalent status in Europe. For instance, the majority of grounds retain large terraces for standing spectators (see Figure 2). The AFA had promised all-seater stadia by 1995 but a combination of opposition from fans, lack of finance and simple inertia have preserved the status quo.

It is early in the period of maturity that the phenomenon of the *barras bravas* appeared on the scene. The existence of the structures linking *fútbol* and politics, coupled with the increased importance of results in the 1960s, meant that there was a temptation to manipulate violence. A. Romero has claimed that the style of violence by interested parties in Argentine *fútbol* is as distinctive as their style of play.[17] Much of this

FIGURE 4.2
A packed terrace of River fans at Vélez Sarsfield as they clinch the championship in July 2000.

violence is organized and politically motivated. The term *barras fuertes* was used in 1958 to refer to groups of violent fans who appeared to be organized in a formal manner. Immediately after the military coup of 1966, this kind of behaviour was reinterpreted in the context of the new terminology of football hooliganism from Europe. According to Scher and Palomino, the murder of Hector Souto, a Huracán fan, in November 1967 marked the beginning of the era of the *barras bravas* and the institutionalization of violence.[18] However, what was different from the late 1960s onwards, was not fighting between rival groups as such but an escalation in the killing of rival supporters.

In terms of organization, the emergence of the *barras bravas* represented the militarization of *fútbol* support. They have a strict hierarchical structure with a leader at the helm. Most of the group members are aged between 20 and 25 although the leaders are frequently over 30. Members are recruited and set a series of trials to test their commitment and strategies. It is common for core members to be full-time professional militants and not, therefore, in conventional employment. Attacks are only carried out on match-days, despite the fact that rival *barras bravas* know where each other meet during the week.

Most of the activity of the *barras bravas* can be explained in terms of political motivation. They have connections with those involved in the running of their club, for instance a particular candidate for club *presidente* who needs their support. They might also take part in political demonstrations on behalf of the club *padrino*. Occasionally political action takes precedence over *fútbol*. It is not unknown for gaps to appear on the terraces where the *barras bravas* usually stand. This means they are otherwise engaged on political business.

The *barras bravas* engage in political activity in return for some kind of payment, either in cash or in kind. Common forms of payment in kind are the funding of their transportation to away matches (sometimes including refreshments), or the gift of match tickets to sell on the black market. Particularly prized are tickets for the *clásicos* (derby matches or games between leading clubs) which are in big demand and command a high price. This understanding goes beyond *fútbol* at club level and penetrates the AFA. By way of example, leading *barras bravas* were provided with both match tickets and air fares in 1986 in order to maintain the backing and co-operation of the *barras bravas*, while at the same time ensuring vocal support for Argentina at the World Cup Finals in Mexico. During the USA World Cup Finals in 1994, it has been estimated that $150,000 was spent on tickets for *barras bravas*, many of which were sold on the black market at three times their face value.[19]

It is not only rival supporters who are targets for the activities of the *barras bravas*. Sometimes the violence is directed towards the club's players, manager or directors. Victims are rarely chosen at random, the attacks are usually carefully planned and with clear motivation. In 1988, a San Lorenzo player was seriously injured as the result of an attack by *barras bravas* in the changing room at Córdoba. In February 1993 the River Plate manager, Daniel Passarella, was beaten up by a faction of the River *barras*. One of the authors saw River Plate clinch the championship in July 2000 against Ferrocarril Oeste at Vélez Sarsfield (see Figure 2). After the final whistle, the River *barras* stormed up and over the high wire fencing onto the pitch; wise players voluntarily donated their match shirts to the fans as valuable trophies, whilst the others were attacked by their own supporters and their shirts were ripped off their backs.

Another angle to the politicization of violence in Argentine *fútbol* centres around the relationship between the police and fans. The police were blamed for the death of Adrián Scassera at a match between Independiente and Boca Juniors on 7 April 1985 and 35 Vélez fans were injured when fighting broke out between police and fans in 1992. According to Romero, the police are responsible for 68 per cent of *fútbol*-related fatalities.[20] The role of the police in Argentine society is extremely significant. They have a long history of violence against the people, often on behalf of a repressive state. They are seen as agents of the state. Figure 3 shows the riot police preparing for a match at Platense and standing in a line by the entrance for *socios*.

It is not unknown for *barras bravas* from different clubs to unite when faced with police hostility and to become temporary allies. One famous example occurred when rival fans from River Plate and Argentinos Juniors joined forces in protest, chanted obscenities and gestured aggressively as police attempted to arrest two youths in *El Monumental* in May 1983. On occasion the police have also been criticized for their lack of action, or apparent indifference. Their passivity in certain situations has been considered by some to indicate complicity.

Covert activities carried out by the *barras bravas* are crucial to the internal structures of *fútbol*. These operations involve blackmail and are carried out on behalf of the *dirigentes* or *presidente*. The victims are usually the players. It is not uncommon for clubs to sort out their problems on the pitch via the *barras bravas*. If they want to get rid of a

FIGURE 4.3

The riot police get ready at Platense by standing in line
at the entrance for *socios*.

FIGURE 4.4

The players emerge at Independiente
(Colón Santa Fe match, June 2000).

player or sometimes a manager, it is easy for them to pay for the *barras* to gain information on his private life and then use that information to blackmail him. So the *barras bravas* make sure it is their responsibility to know which players are taking which drugs (they might even be involved in supplying them) and all about their sex lives.

Abusive chanting in the stadium is another *barras* activity to destroy an unwanted player on the pitch. Chants at *fútbol* matches have little or nothing to do with events on the pitch. If the *barras bravas* chant abuse at a player when his contract is due to be renewed, it makes it much easier for the *presidente* to lower the conditions of his contract or can even provide the club with an excuse to get rid of him. *Barras* are prepared to do this if they are offered the right price. Concern for the safety of players and officials in Argentine *fútbol* is evident in Figure 4. At all professional matches the players and officials emerge on to the pitch through long inflatable tunnels, which have the appearance of giant condoms.

Understandably it is in the players' interest to try and keep the *barras* sweet. This provides another source of income for the fans, often in the form of match tickets. If the players are not intimidated by threats and do not respond to the *barras bravas*, they can expect punishment. The threat of punishment is usually enough to see that the *barras bravas* achieve their objective. Some who have not heeded warnings have been physically attacked or shot. So long as players, directors and chairmen are aware that the threats are not empty, intimidation is indeed effective. There have been many examples of intimidated players and managers during the 1980s and 1990s.[21]

The mutually beneficial relationship between the *barras bravas* and the club officials has been possible because of the historical links between *fútbol* and politics. Moreover, it is perpetuated by the internal structure of football clubs in which the *socios* elect the *presidente*. Electoral politics continue to play a leading role and it is through this function that the *barras bravas* have been implicated in covert activities and have become an essential cog in the workings of a club. It is in the interests of the club to keep them sweet and it therefore unsurprising that the media frequently accuse clubs of protecting the *barras bravas* and encouraging their violent activities. In the case of the Boca *barras*, they have often been known to stay at the same hotel as the official club delegation.

In wider political elections, which may be local, regional, national, or even trade union, typically a *barras bravas* from one club supports a candidate in opposition to another candidate backed by a different *barras bravas* from another club. Connections with trade unions also date back a long way. On one occasion in 1973, Quilmes received reinforcements from their allies, Nueva Chicago, in a match against Banfield. Members of one of the most powerful trade unions in Argentina were present among the *barras bravas*.

The *jefes* (leaders) of the main *barras bravas* have become celebrities and well-known figures, appearing frequently in the media and also in the company of the club *dirigentes*. One of the most celebrated and feared leaders was José Barrita, the *jefe* of the Boca *barras* in the 1980s and 1990s. He was more popularly known as *El Abuelo* (the grandfather) because of his prematurely grey hair and was frequently seen alongside the club *presidente*. In April 1997 *El Abuelo* was finally convicted for organizing an extortion racket (along with eight other Boca *barras bravas*) and jailed for 13 years.

The period since the restoration of democratically elected government in Argentina in 1983, has coincided with some of the worst violence from the *barras bravas*. Pressure to at least be seen to take action led to new laws in May 1985 and March 1993 that were specifically intended to combat *fútbol* violence. However, the level of *fútbol* violence today is as high as ever. In a previous article, we presented data which indicated a marked escalation in *fútbol*-related deaths, from an annual average of 0.44 (1958–66), to 1.32 (1967–85), to 5.25 (1986–93).[22] Since 1993 the rate has remained around 5.00 per annum. Romero has argued that organized violence in Argentina has spread from *fútbol* to the rest of society, especially in relation to political activity.[23] It is important, however, not to paint a totally negative picture of the activities of the *barras bravas*. During the last military dictatorship (1976–83), democratic politics continued in the organization of the football clubs, at a time when it was banned at the national level.

As we have seen, the period of maturity produced a strengthening of the relationship between politicians, football clubs and fans, leading to the institutionalization of violence in the shape of the *barras bravas*. At the top of the *fútbol* hierarchy, little has changed. The current *presidente* of the AFA (since 1979), Julio Grondona, is a member of Unión Cívica Radical, an important businessman in the steel industry and a former *presidente* of Independiente.

Government involvement in *fútbol*, always extensive, reached new heights during the last military dictatorship. Following the military coup of 1976, involvement became more open and the links between *fútbol* and politics were at their most visible. In 1978 the World Cup Finals were to be held in Argentina for the first time and the state wanted to project a positive image to the rest of the world. The leaders of the *barras bravas* were called together by the military dictatorship and a truce was established so that they would instigate no violent incidents for the duration of the finals. It is significant that co-operation was achieved, reflecting the fact that the state would, and could, do business with the *barras bravas*.

Huge amounts of money were invested to promote the national image, most notably in the form of improvements to the country's infrastructure. Road networks and the public transport system were developed and stadia and a television centre built. Some complained that the money could have been better spent on much-needed hospitals, housing and schools. Moreover, strong rumours circulated regarding additional expenditure on football bribes (for instance, in order to achieve Argentina's 6–0 win over Peru).

In 1978 a state official was appointed to investigate allegations of financial corruption. These efforts were thwarted when a bomb exploded at his home. At the time, no exact figure was available regarding the full cost of staging the World Cup Finals. Steps were taken to silence the critical media for the duration of the event and also to remove from Buenos Aires anyone who was considered a potential threat to the regime. The Argentine press was specifically ordered not to print anything critical about the national team.

The opening ceremony was presided over by the President of the Republic, Videla, who gave a moving speech on peace, friendship, human relationships and living together in harmony. These values contrasted sharply with the country's flagrant violation of human rights, including the 'disappearance' of thousands of its subjects and the torture of opponents of the regime in buildings a few blocks from where the speech took place. Politicians equated Argentina's win in the final against Holland as a success for the dictatorship. The triumph of the Argentine team was viewed as belonging to all Argentines. It was a victory for the country. The Dutch refusal to attend the closing ceremony was interpreted by the Argentine media as a demonstration of sour grapes. In fact it represented a politically motivated gesture against repression in Argentina.

Such was the concern with the Argentine national image that an American company was employed to promote it in the build-up to the tournament. The main person responsible for the organization of the World Cup Finals was Carlos Alberto Lacoste, vice-president of the organizing body Ente Autuartico Mundial (EAM'78). The original president of EAM'78, General Omar Actis, was assassinated in August 1976. Strong rumours at the time suggested that Lacoste was responsible for the assassination, because of disagreements on some of the fundamental principles of World Cup organization.

After the tournament, Lacoste was rewarded for his success. Aided by relationships and family ties with *Presidentes* Videla and Galtieri, his political career took off and he became an important public figure. Others who benefited included those involved in the construction industry, tourism, the mass media and communications not least because the state helped to finance those areas of national interest. The military dictatorship ended in 1983 and Argentina returned to democratically elected government, a thorough re-analysis of Argentina's recent history ensued, with the voicing of previously censored views. Financial irregularities were exposed in EAM'78 and Lacoste was investigated for fraud. Lacoste was a notable example of the links between *fútbol*, politics, business and repression.

1979 witnessed a shameful illustration of the exploitation of *fútbol* to cover up deep social unrest. Argentina, captained by Diego Maradona, won the Youth World Cup. This victory coincided with the investigation into allegations of state breaches of human rights, which involved the presence of several prominent foreign political figures in Buenos Aires. The families of those who had disappeared at the hands of the state gathered in the Plaza de Mayo in Central Buenos Aires to demonstrate and demand an explanation of what had happened to their loved ones. Utilizing the compliant media, the regime's response was to invite people to go to the Plaza de Mayo to fete the victory of the youth team. Thus protest was conveniently masked by a celebration of national pride. The state found in *fútbol* a good friend yet again.

CONCLUSION

In the twentieth century, *fútbol* has been exploited in Argentina by regimes of varying kinds. We have demonstrated that during the adolescent period, the Argentine take-over of the game established the key structures linking politics and *fútbol*. In maturity, the network of links between the AFA, football clubs, politicians and fans was consolidated. The relationship between the state and *fútbol* reached new heights for the 1978 World Cup Finals and *fútbol* violence became institutionalized in the form of the *barras bravas*.

Fútbol at the end of the twentieth century is as large a business as it has ever been and the mechanisms that link it with politics are as strong as ever. Interestingly, the new laws mentioned earlier, which were reluctantly introduced with the aim of reducing violence, took into consideration the role of *fútbol* as an industry. A sentence is increased by one-third if any crime leads to a match being cancelled or suspended. What politics is protecting is *fútbol* as an industry.

The sport's combined political and commercial roles mean that those involved in *fútbol* whether as politicians, chairmen, directors or fans, will continue to enjoy a certain degree of protection. Football clubs are still looked after by their *padrinos*. In 2000 a new law was introduced exempting football clubs from the normal rules of bankruptcy, basically in order to keep Racing Club going. Significantly, both the vice-president of the republic and the mayor of Buenos Aires are Racing fans. Moreover, no one accepts responsibility for *fútbol*-related violence. As a consequence of these facts, many observers criticize the way that politicians, club directors and the judicial system are seen to protect the *barras bravas*.[24]

Towards the end of the twentieth century, television exerted a growing influence on sport around the world. In Argentina, possibilities of making money through the televising and merchandising of *fútbol* has led to new business initiatives, and the first clear threat to the established structure linking politics and *fútbol*. Attempts have been made to change the status of Argentine football clubs from private member associations (where the *socios* elect the club officials) to private limited companies but the clubs voted overwhelmingly against this. Not surprisingly, most *socios*, *dirigentes* and *presidentes* were against reform. There have been calls to reduce the concentration of professional clubs in Buenos Aires with their traditional rivalries. The moving of clubs to other cities has been proposed (Argentinos Juniors did briefly move to Mendoza in 1994) and club mergers/ground sharing have been suggested. All of these ideas are anathema to the traditions of Argentine *fútbol*.

It is ironic that the democratic organization of *fútbol* in Argentina is helping to perpetuate violence. As long as the links between *fútbol* and politics continue, the system will be maintained. At present, there is little attempt to keep *fútbol* and politics apart. The desire for power and money provides the motivation for the continuation of the relationships between the key 'players'. It is in their interests to preserve the system. So long as the structures in Argentine *fútbol* stay the same, the relationship between *fútbol* and politics will also remain unchanged.

116 *Sport in Latin American Society*

NOTES

1. Examples of very different football cultures are featured in our previous book; see Vic Duke and Liz Crolley, *Football, Nationality and the State* (Harlow: Longman, 1996). Also recommended is Richard Giulianotti, *Football: A Sociology of the Global Game* (Cambridge: Polity Press, 1999).
2. Amílcar Romero, *Las Barras Bravas y la Contrasociedad Deportiva* (Buenos Aires: Nueva América, 1994), p.18.
3. Between them the authors have visited Buenos Aires three times in the last decade. In 1994, Vic Duke was supported by a grant from the Nuffield Foundation. Access to the archives at *El Gráfico* was invaluable on all three occasions. We are grateful to the following for their assistance: Pablo Alabarces, Eduardo Archetti, Andres Cruzalegui, Miguel Cruzalegui, Pablo de Biase, Natalio Gorín, Ariel Scher and Eric Weil.
4. A brief English language summary may be found in Tony Mason, *Passion of the People?* (London: Verso, 1995), Chs.1 and 2.
5. Osvaldo Bayer, *Fútbol Argentino* (Buenos Aires: Editorial Sudamericana, 1990), p.18.
6. Many of the English-language schools in Argentina formed football clubs, see Andrew Graham-Yooll, *The Forgotten Colony* (London: Hutchinson, 1981), pp.194–5.
7. Ibid., p.130.
8. Ariel Scher and Héctor Palomino, *Fútbol: Pasión de Multitudes y de Elites* (Buenos Aires: CISEA, 1988), p.231.
9. Mason, *Passion of the People*, p.6.
10. Creolization refers to the take-over of Argentine football by clubs whose players were mostly Italian and Spanish immigrants, by officials from the same ethnic background and by their *criollo* style of play (rather than the English style).
11. Pioneering work on the early football clubs and football organizations in Buenos Aires has been undertaken by Julio Frydenberg; see 'Prácticas y valores en el proceso de popularización del fútbol: Buenos Aires 1900–1910', *Entrepasados Revista de Historia*, 6, 12 (1997), 7–31; and 'Redefinición del fútbol aficionado y del fútbol oficial: Buenos Aires 1912' in Pablo Alabarces, R. Di Giano and Julio Frydenberg (eds.), *Deporte Y Sociedad* (Buenos Aires: Eudeba, 1998).
12. Example provided by Pablo de Biase from his thesis at the School of Social Sciences, University of Buenos Aires, 1999.
13. Scher and Palomino, *Fútbol*, p.196.
14. Bayer, *Fútbol Argentino*, p.46.
15. See Vic Duke and Liz Crolley, 'Football Spectator Behaviour in Argentina: A Case of Separate Evolution', *Sociological Review*, 44, 2 (May 1996), 272–93.
16. Romero, *Las Barras Bravas*, p.159.
17. Ibid., pp.14–15.
18. Scher and Palomino, *Fútbol*, p.118.
19. Romero, *Las Barras Bravas*, p.44.
20. Amílcar Romero, *Muerte en la Cancha* (Buenos Aires: Editorial Nueva América, 1986), p.11.
21. See Juan Sebreli, *La Era del Fútbol* (Buenos Aires: Editorial Sudamericana, 1998), pp.59–70.
22. Duke and Crolley, 'Football Spectator Behaviour in Argentina', 278–9.
23. Romero, *Muerte en la Cancha*, p.40.
24. For evidence of external protection by the judiciary see 'La violencia en el fútbol', *Clarín* (19 Dec. 1990); similarly, examples may be cited for directors, see 'Las Barras Bravas' (informe especial), *El Gráfico* (7 June 1983); and politicians, see 'La ley del más fuerte', *El Cronista* (18 May 1992).

Baseball Arguments:
Aficionismo and Masculinity at the
Core of *Cubanidad*

THOMAS CARTER

Every morning, Manolo begins his day by dressing in slacks and *guayabera*, the tropical version of a dress shirt, and downs his coffee, a concoction closer to espresso than anything else, as the sounds of Havana rise to his third-story apartment. He leaves his apartment between ten and noon, descends the decaying marble staircase of his building and walks the three blocks to Parque Central where he argues baseball with other men gathered there. Manolo is a white-haired, spry, bespectacled man in his late seventies.[1] He is a proud man who supported the Revolution when it came 40 years ago and continues to be proud to be Cuban. As long as it is not raining, he meets other men, some have been friends for decades while others are younger men unknown to him, who come to the central square of Parque Central in Havana. Within direct sight of a statue honouring José Martí, the father of Cuban independence, and of the multitudes of tourists streaming in search of Cuban treasures, Manolo meets these other men to discuss the state of baseball, sport and current events. He spends the entire afternoon there if the conversation or people interest him, or as little as an hour if nothing piques his imagination. While almost any topic can be the focal point of discussion on a given day, the consensus among Manolo and his companions is that they meet to 'argue baseball'.

Cuban baseball fans do not 'talk baseball' ('*hablar pelota*'), instead they 'argue baseball' ('*discutir pelota*'). This is no minor linguistic distinction. To argue baseball rather than talk baseball connotes two contextually different activities with specific implicit cultural values and mores. To argue suggests confrontation with the additional implication of opposition or an opponent. To talk suggests discussion without any implicit opposition involved. It is this particular practice of arguing baseball and its implicit value of confrontation that marks baseball fans in Havana specifically Cuban and masculine.

The value of confrontation is a core aspect of Cuban masculinity. Baseball fans who come to Parque Central to argue baseball display their masculinity through their arguments by embodying and displaying valued characteristics considered by Cubans to be emblematically part of being Cuban (*cubanidad*). The values these men embody and display include discipline (*disciplina*), struggle (*lucha*) and lucidity.[2] Fans' assertive disagreements emphasize their masculinity as evidenced by their willingness to argue and their ability to maintain self-control in the face of obvious antagonism. Only in extreme cases do arguments degenerate into violence. The fans who gather in Parque Central have a public venue for displaying their own sense of masculinity as well as affirming publicly displaying their sense of being Cuban. While men's passions are potential connections to more encompassing group identities, these intense feelings are not limited solely to sports fans or to masculinist or nationalist constructs. Since sport remains a male-dominated practice, how sports fans relate to each other as men remains an essential consideration in the construction of *cubanidad*.

This is just one consideration that makes Cubans' passion for baseball a distinctly Cuban experience. There are numerous ways to assert an identity, particularly a gender identity. Neither masculine nor feminine identities are essentialized within any given society; instead there are many different forms and expressions of either gendered identity. That various masculine constructs can be, and are, contradictory does not lessen either construct in terms of an individual having greater or lesser degrees of masculinity. Since the scope of Cuban masculinity and the entirety of Cuban baseball fans is too broad a topic to cover in a single essay, I will focus on one particular group of fans in Havana's Parque Central. In so doing, I will discuss the historical connections between baseball and Cuban nationalism and provide an analysis of one form of men's social groups in Cuba, known as *peñas*. I will then briefly discuss the historical significance of Parque Central since the historical setting of the group helps to define the context of *peña* members' activities. The historical connections of Cuban nationalism and baseball, the social importance of Parque Central and the background of *peñas* all provide the grounding for the ethnographic portrayal of arguing baseball in Parque Central. This essay, then, will illustrate how these sociohistoric factors inform *peña* members' constructions and displays of their own masculinity.

HISTORICAL SITUATION:
BASEBALL AND BASEBALL FANS IN CUBA

Baseball is a cultural practice dominated and almost universally practised by Cuban men. Men's discussions about baseball form an important aspect of their constructions of themselves as Cuban. Their constructions touch on values originating over 100 years ago, when Cuban identities were nascent. Embedded in the Victorian notions of the sporting male, attached to the ideas of physical invigoration, moral character and manly struggle was the idea that baseball prepared one for armed struggle, violence and rebellion. All of this came to embody *cubanidad*, the modern Cuban nation and modern Cuban man who were ready to fight for their own and their nation's independence – baseball symbolism that Revolutionary Leaders resurrected.[3]

Baseball arrived in Cuba sometime in the 1860s. University students returning from the United States brought baseball knowledge and equipment to Havana where the game quickly became a Sunday afternoon excursion for the Cuban elite. The sport rapidly gained popularity. Proponents and fans of baseball appeared as quickly as the sport itself. By the late 1870s a Cuban league appeared that produced the passions of *aficionismo* among Havana's residents. These early teams were composed of young gentlemen who belonged to specific elite social clubs. While these young baseball players were part of the Cuban elite, baseball fans did not necessarily have to be from the same class. By virtue of publicly expressed partisanship, anyone could, and many did, create an imagined link that many Cubans may not have otherwise possessed to Havana's elite. Wenceslao Galvéz y Delmonte, an historian, shortstop and member of the wealthy *criollo* class,[4] described his and his Almendares teammates' passage through the streets of Havana to a Sunday game against their major rivals, Habana:[5]

> One by one we, the Almendares players, arrive at Aurelios Gymnastic Club. We put on our uniforms and swing from the trapeze while the ten was completed.[6] The most enthusiastic or most presumptuous [fans] come in to see us get dressed, witnessing it all, somewhat indecorous at certain points. And in their delirium for the team they might praise the beauty mark on so and so's right thigh. They would help us with our toilette, tying the string on our undershirts and the brand new blue silken scarf, which was purchased at the Chinese boutique.

'How about dedicating a hit to me today? I have already seen the *habanistas* [team members of Habana] at the gym on Consulado Street. Don't strike out. Have you had much wine?' They continued in their impertinent and foolish manner until it was time to leave.

'I'll go with you. Can I carry your bat?'

'No, man, I'll carry my own bat.'

No sooner do we appear outside the gym door than the curious began to stop in their tracks and stand in front of us and, those who recognised us point us out to their friends as if we were some sort of monument.

'There's Carlito Macía', pointing his finger at my teammate.

'Look, that's Alfredo Arango.'

'So fat? I thought he was much thinner.'

'Well, I'll prove it to you. Psst, psst, hey aren't you Alfredo Arango? ... Yeah, man, that's him. He just doesn't want to answer.'

Finally, we arrived at the park by threes in cabs with their tops down (the cabs' not the cabbies') passing along the Prado, the Campo de Marte, Reina Street, and Carlos II Boulevard.

We were first seen by those atop the laurel trees and they shouted the news of our arrival.

From the stands there came twenty thousand cheers, greetings, a fluttering blue flag that could make one dizzy, applause, whistles, and boos. Onward![7]

Galvéz y Delmonte's description of fan behaviour indicates that it has not changed much in the last hundred years. However, nineteenth-century baseball games were only one part of a full Sunday's extravaganza. Occurring about once a month, afternoon games preceded dinners and dances. A social club might challenge another club's team and then host a dinner and dance in which the athletes from both teams mingled with other club members. Members of Havana's elite may have attended the game for the enjoyment of the spectacle but they also attended to be seen by others.

Not all baseball fans were members of the elite. In Galvéz y Delmonte's account, 20,000 fans awaited his team's arrival to the park. Obviously, it is safe to conclude that not all of those fans were members of either social club. Being a fan indicated social aspirations as well as social status. Members of the two clubs and their guests sat in the shaded comfort of the *glorieta*, a building erected in a garden usually as a place for dining. The *glorieta*'s walls were trellises which allowed tropical breezes to carry the flowers' scents into the interior of the structure while its roof protected its inhabitants from the punishing tropical sun and rains. It was here that the elite watched the game, socialized and, once the game ended, dined and danced. The rest of the crowd sat in the *gradería* (stands), which were not protected from the elements.[8] Social distinctions were clearly marked, based upon where one sat and was seen by the rest of the crowd. Thus, cheering and supporting a given club publicly demonstrated one's position in society.

That social relationships and aspirations can be expressed by one's *aficionismo* challenges many assumptions about fans. Such a challenge further suggests that one's very social identity can revolve around one's loyalty to a sports team. Such constructions are as equally legitimate as constructs based on race, gender, or religion, yet the mass media frequently denigrate fans' identities on the basis of team loyalty.

A more recent trend in masculinity studies focuses on sporting events and the immediate ephemeral attachments fans' make with specific athletes. Other studies focus on issues of mass representation, particularly the relationship between mass media and sport, often in terms of 'popular culture'.[9] Still others focus on issues of masculinity and nationalism within sport. However, most anthropological studies have historically ignored the role of sport in defining gender and studies of Cuban masculinity have focused primarily on issues of sexuality rather than the social relationships of men in a non-sexual context.[10] The more recent studies that do address the relationship between nationalism, sport and masculinity do so by examining the cultural ideals of masculinity or 'hypermasculinity' found in modern sport. All of these studies recognize and/or reveal sport's power to move people emotionally, to mobilize people and to make them feel part of something larger than themselves.[11]

Clearly, fans engage in feelings of belonging to an 'imagined community'.[12] Team sports are particularly suited for community adoption as 'any imagined community seems more real as a team of eleven named people'.[13] Teams bearing a nation's name become a kind of collective representation and objectification of that nation, with the triumphs and trials of the team perceived to be a direct reflection of national fortunes. Not only do a nation's fortunes rise or fall with the team but contact with the individual athletes of the team becomes socially important. As B. Buford demonstrates in relation to twentieth-century English football hooligans and as Galvéz y Delmonte shows for nineteenth-century Cuban baseball fans, *aficionismo* is used to forge or reinforce social connections considered either in danger or in question.[14] In each case, the forged social relationships of nationalist sentiment exist on a personal level for the fan.

Buford's description of rioting English football fans clearly illustrates working-class youths' xenophobic nationalist sentiments. These disaffected, underemployed white men act out their fears and frustrations with violence. They feel that the state has sold them out to minority populations who recently immigrated to England. For international matches, they perceive themselves as an extension of the national team of England, defending the nation's honour against foreigners. Consequently, they perceive themselves as defending the nation, as they imagine it, from both internal and external non-English influences.

Galvéz y Delmonte's history also demonstrates players and fans' attachment of nationalistic sentiments to the playing of baseball. He considered baseball as a vehicle for the creation of the good Victorian man with the added benefit of preparing Cuban youth for armed struggle. Aurelio Miranda, one of the founders of the Havana Base Ball Club, believed that baseball 'promised to promote the physical development of our youth … Exercise invigorated the body, promoted valour, the will to win, and tempered the spirit' as well as teaching discipline and patience. Miranda insisted that 'the baseball player must learn to wait for his pitch, his play, his moment. An untimely move, a base taken prematurely, a ground ball fielded hastily leads to a game lost. The same impatience, the absence of the virtue of knowing how to wait, leads to a loss and often leads to the loss of the nation.'[15]

Baseball was more than a political symbol; it became a political act after the Spanish banned the sport for its 'revolutionary potential'. *Criollos* explicitly contrasted baseball with the public spectacles of Spanish *corridas* (bullfights), characterizing baseball as a modern, civilized game that made men out of upper- and middle-class boys, yet, unlike the bloody, barbaric killing of animals, was genteel enough for women to watch.[16] Thus, to be a baseball fan in nineteenth-century Havana was to adopt a specific political position that asserted the modernity and independence of Cuba as a contrast to its colonial relationship with Spain.

While nineteenth-century baseball was promoted in nationalist terms by the *criollos*, the class most interested in Cuban independence, rivalries also emerged between these social clubs. In Havana, teams represented specific neighbourhoods and the associated rivalries continued in the emergent professional leagues until the 1959 Revolution. During the 'Golden Era' of Cuban professional baseball (the 1930s–50s), fans' passions were not so much nationalistic as they were localized.[17] The main rivalry between Habana and Almendares played itself out weekly in Havana throughout the Golden Era. The undercurrents of this rivalry occasionally took on nationalistic overtones. Habana's colour was red and Almendares was blue: the two colours of the Cuban flag. With the arrival of radio, rivalry spread across the island. This rivalry, however, was not so much Cubans struggling symbolically against outsiders, as it had been in the nineteenth century, but Cubans struggling over different ideas of Cuba. However, these passions and sentiments were not at the forefront of most fans' minds. Loyalty to one's team took prominence and potentially overrode other loyalties, including those of kinship. A middle-aged Cuban writer I interviewed in 1997 described his and his brother's passions for Habana and Almendares, passions so strong they divided the brothers:

> When I was a boy I was *habanista* [a fan of Habana]. My room was covered in red. I had all the, what do you call it, memorabilia. Pictures, pennants, everything. My whole room was red. My brother was blue [a fan of Almendares]. Lord, how we would fight! We wouldn't agree on anything. We drove our mother crazy. Our arguments meant we couldn't agree on anything else. If he liked something, I simply couldn't like it. This was at all levels. From our food, to our taste in music, clothes, girls, everything. If mama made *arroz morro* (rice with black beans) for him, I wouldn't touch it. She had to make something different for me. Everything.

While the basis of the brothers' relationship was constant rivalry, it nonetheless forged strong ties between the two men. Competing loyalties to teams can both divide individuals and forge a basis for a social relationship that might not otherwise exist. The men that gather in Parque Central to argue baseball do not agree with each other very often. Instead, their relationships are based on ideas of masculine respect centred on articulateness and knowledge. Rivalries based on the testing of each other's knowledge and ability to think quickly and speak clearly in heated debates create the environment for the relationship between these men. Indeed, one elderly man who frequented Parque Central commented that he no longer enjoyed coming to the park anymore since his rival had died the year before.

OF *PEÑAS, PIÑAS* AND LA PEÑA

These friendly rivalries exist within a loosely based, socially recognized institution known as a *peña*. Most are small, anonymous groups organized within a neighbourhood or workplace and their degree of organization varies widely. Cubans variously describe a *peña* as a group of friends who meet to pass time, as a large organization that supports a specific activity such as playing softball in an open field, as a smaller group such as musicians who meet at someone's house to play music, or as another kind of organized associations such as a fan club. In general, a *peña* is a loose association of people, usually men, who regularly meet for a specific reason. *Peñas* can be organized around one's work, one's craft, or one's passion. Many peñas meet on street corners or in parks to argue baseball. Some *peñas* are extremely well organized, well financed and well known. For example, many people in Havana know that there is a *peña* that meets in Plaza Martí in Santiago de Cuba, the capital of the *Oriente* or eastern half of Cuba, to argue baseball. This particular *peña* is renowned for setting up a television and loudspeakers so its many members can watch the Santiago baseball team when it is playing teams in the Occidente or west, such as Habana or Pinar del Rio.

Peñas are not government-organized groups. Nor, insist *peña* members and other fans, are they in any sense political – every Cuban I spoke to insisted on that point. As one of the men of Parque Central explained, 'The government would not allow them if they were, which means they can't be political or the government would break them up or co-opt them'. Yet, *peña* members are acutely aware that others may interpret their actions as being political. Indeed, they described their anger towards a group of journalists who filmed them arguing baseball during the 1997 World Series. Interest in Cuban baseball was enormous at that time because a young Cuban defector, Liván Hernández, was playing for the Florida team in the World Series. Friends in London sent *peña* members a copy of this documentary. *Peña* members were upset because they felt that the documentary portrayed them as anti-Castro. These *peña* members vehemently denied they were anti-Castro and insisted they had been misrepresented. They were right to be concerned since if government officials had interpreted their actions portrayed in the documentary in this same manner, they could have serious trouble with state authorities.[18]

One of the most famous baseball-oriented *peñas* is La Peña de Parque Central. Known by Havana's residents as simply 'La Peña', it comprises men who meet in the middle of Parque Central to talk sports, especially baseball, and most especially Major League baseball (professional baseball in the US). The *peña* in Parque Central fits the more rigid definition of a *peña* as used by *aficionados*, rather than the more general cultural usage. La Peña is a formal organization that has officers and dues, but although *peña* officers do meet monthly to reassess the group's resources and strategies for surviving in the volatile economic situation that is Havana, its members usually meet informally. They also hold formal meetings on special occasions, such as when a foreign guest volunteers to give a brief talk on US baseball. Other than that, as Manolo, a founding member and former treasurer, told me, 'There is no organisation. We just come because there is nothing else for us to do'. Members and non-members come every day to Parque Central for varying periods of time to talk baseball. One does not have to be a member of the *peña* to be included in the discussions at Parque Central. Most who come are *aficionados* but few are actual dues-paying members.

Cuban baseball *peñas* are segregated men's spaces, similar to other masculine Latin American social associations described in anthropological literature.[19] Such associations revolve around members' creations of individual masculine identities based on reputation. A man on the corner, in the bar, or in a *peña* must learn how to argue, tell stories, drink and demonstrate spiritual, social and physical strength. Furthermore, knowledge, frequently based on life experiences, also enhances one's reputation.

A good ethnographic example of a Latin American masculine association is the *winkel* of Suriname.[20] *Winkels* are associations of underemployed working-class men who have a singular kind of relationship with women, in that they are marginal players in their own households. As a result of their economic marginalization outside the household and their domestic marginalization within the household, these men interact regularly with other men who share their marginal social context. Members of a *winkel* pass their time drinking and talking with each other, discussing incidents, personal problems and news of their neighbourhood. Women pass, talk and flirt with the men of the *winkel* but do not linger amongst them.

Like *winkels*, *peñas deportivas* (sports groups) are a form of masculine association that serve as social gathering spots for men. However, *peñas* differ in a number of ways from G. Brana-Shute's description of *winkels*.

The men of La Peña are primarily urban middle class. Furthermore, the basis of a man's reputation rests not on his ability to imbibe alcohol or on his life experiences but on his ability to memorize baseball knowledge, especially statistics, and the speed and accuracy with which he can articulate that knowledge. The very tightness of the circles of men arguing baseball also discourages any sort of outside interference, such as flirtation with passing women. In over nine months of fieldwork, I never once observed a woman approach a man involved in *discutiendo pelota* in the *peña*. Tony, a large, barrel-chested, young, well-dressed Afrocuban who frequents the *peña*, explained that it is a combination of women's lack of baseball knowledge and the rough language of the *peña* that keeps them away:

> Women simply do not know anything about baseball. They don't go to the stadiums. They might if they know someone there personally; an athlete, security guard, or journalist who is a family member or boyfriend, for example. They might have *antes* ['before' indicating 'before the Revolution']. But even then, they do not grow with it. Their fathers, uncles or brothers do not teach them. Besides, the language in a *peña* is rough, and it is not meant for a woman. It is not sincere [the insults] but it offends them [women]. So, yes, the sports *peña* has only men, always.

It is this aspect of specific knowledge that is the defining factor of belonging in the *peña* and acts as a factor in confirming one's claims of masculinity. Even if a woman was not offended by the *peña's* rough language, she would still have to somehow obtain the cultural knowledge of baseball that is most often passed from father to son.

Tony's comments point to the centrality of the discussions in the *peña*. *Peña* gatherings are inwardly focused, its members' concerns revolve around their arguments and themselves. This contrasts with Brana-Shute's analysis of *winkels*, which are outwardly focused. *Winkel* members' concerns centre on their neighbourhood's goings-on. As I attempted to gain entry to the *peña*, men on the edge of a circle asked me '¿te gusta piña, no?' ('You like pineapple, don't you?') They proceeded to explain the metaphor once it was evident to them that I did not quite understand: 'We are like pineapples. We cluster around each other; even if you pluck one [leaf or man] out, we get in closer together. Also, we don't like outsiders bothering us. Foreigners don't do anything for us. We want nothing to do with them. So we are prickly towards others. Get it?'

La Peña differs from most of the masculine associations described in anthropological literature and even from some other non-sport oriented *peñas*, in that alcohol is not consumed during meetings of the *peña*. To be sure, many of the men of La Peña drink, but they do not drink in Parque Central. Here, to be publicly drunk is considered a failing of one's masculinity and the social stigma, along with the added legal reinforcement by Cuban police, acts as a strong deterrent to drinking in the park. The men of La Peña certainly have their networks of friends with whom they share rum or beer but those are networks of *socios*, trusted friends who provide support, information and, at times, immediate economic assistance within understood reciprocal relations.[21] Many of the men who come to La Peña arrive to meet some of their *socios* and, after some time amongst the circles of arguing fans, move on to a nearby drinking establishment. *Socio* networks extend out much farther than the *peña* and are based on a variety of social factors. Men's relationships with each other in La Peña revolve solely around their passion for baseball. Other social necessities intrude but they are not the basis of their relationships.

Drinking is clearly an important masculine activity and the drinking establishment remains an important male gathering spot throughout Latin America (and elsewhere). A Mexican anthropologist took American anthropologist Matthew Gutmann to *cantinas* in Mexico City because of Gutmann's interest in masculine identities. He told Gutmann: 'You know nothing of the Mexican man if you don't know the cantina'.[22] In a similar vein, Cesar, a Cuban journalist, told me, as we sat with a bottle of rum between us, that to understand Cuban men you have to know baseball. Cesar was not referring to the written rules of the game, rather he meant that I must understand the masculine ideals embedded in how La Peña's members argue baseball.

SOCIAL HISTORY OF *PARQUE CENTRAL*

The men of La Peña have socially constructed the space of Parque Central; that is, they have reinforced a specific social meaning of the park. The social construction of space is the transformation of space – through people's memories, social exchanges, images and daily use of the material setting – into scenes and actions that carry social and symbolic meaning.[23] In so doing, the actions of La Peña reinforce the gendered meaning of the park as masculine space, through their daily occupation of the central portion. However, their appropriation of this space is not uncontested. The park serves as a public transportation hub for Havana's *camellos* (large trailers pulled by lorries), taxis waiting to serve tourists and as an entrance to the tourist sites of Old Havana – the original colonial part of the city.

During Cuba's colonial era, Parque Central was one end of the major axis through which Havana's traffic travelled. As such, it was a major turnaround point for the *volantes* – two-wheeled carriages elaborately decorated with leather hoods, brass buckles, imported fabrics and even small Persian rugs – that carried Havana's wealthy women.[24] The female elite of Havana would ride in these vehicles during the evening hours; the degree of décor provided a clear indication of the family's status. Such jaunts were frequently the only time that aristocratic women could get out of the house. Although these outings normally lasted, at most, two hours, they were of great social value among upper-class women. Men could observe their passing from the park's benches and many courtships began with stolen glances and nods. As 'their only means of escape', such excursions contributed to a distinctly gendered, spatially defined and class-specific use of Parque Central in the nineteenth century.

With the advent of the Republic in 1902, Parque Central remained a key spatial site for socializing. New, monumental buildings linking the state, private initiatives and elite residences together surrounded the park. The nation's main theatres (Nacional, Payret, Irijoa, Politeama, Alhambra) and the first tourist hotels (Inglaterra, Plaza, Telégrafo, Sevilla Biltmore) were located in this area. In this setting the first European-style shopping arcade in Cuba, the Manzana de Gómez, emerged.[25] Today, the Hotel Inglaterra, the reconstructed Sevilla Biltmore, the Teatro Nacional (now known as the Garcia Lorca National Theatre) and the Manzana de Gómez remain tourist attractions, serving as gateways into the narrow streets of Old Havana.

Parque Central still occupies a central point in Havana's social activities. Tourists pass through on their way to and from Old Havana. They frequently stop and take photos of the José Martí statue with the Hotel Inglaterra's ornate Victorian architecture in the background. Cubans use the benches in the shade for a variety of reasons. Some try to talk tourists into exchanging money or purchasing other illicit goods, such as cigars, rum, *ganja* (marijuana) and sex. Others wait for the *guaguas* (coaches) and *camellos* as they sit on benches near the edge of the park. A few meet lovers or friends during lunch hours or the early evening hours. Policemen occasionally drift through the park, checking for illicit/illegal activities by examining identity papers.[26]

The park itself is divided into three rectangular sections. The two outer sections are shaded areas with benches, paths and trees which provide a cool place to stroll or rest, as well as some concealment for more illicit meetings. The central third of the park is an open plaza which faces Calle Obispo, one of the main shopping streets at the end of Old Havana. The bar/café, La Floridita, the birthplace of the daiquiri, sits right across from the park, on the corner of Obispo and Avenida Monserrate. The Hotel Inglaterra and the Garcia Lorca National Theatre are on the other side of the park. Lining the pedestrian plaza on both sides are marble benches. Along the benches on the south side of the plaza, where trees provide a little shade, continuously shifting circles of men meet and argue baseball. Because *peña* members ignore the foreigners passing through the park, as well as the curious foreigners who hang about for short periods of time, it is abundantly clear that they are not engaged in the *bolsa negra*, the illegal tourist-driven economy. Since the reason why these men gather in the park and what they are doing is public knowledge, their 'loitering' is tolerated by the police. Thus, state officials, in the form of the police, assign a different significance to Parque Central than do other residents of Havana, who know the park as La Esquina Caliente or the Hot Corner.[27]

EN LA ESQUINA CALIENTE/ON THE HOT CORNER

The Hot Corner is a baseball metaphor referring to third base. It is so named because of the speed with which batted balls arrive at the fielder. La Peña's discussions are so named because of the rapidity of questions and answers tossed around by discussants. Debates in Parque Central are loud, heated, multi-vocal and simultaneous, making it very difficult to present any coherent record of the conversations that occur. At first glance, the noise, gestures and number of men make *peña* gatherings seem intimidating, chaotic and potentially violent. Pedestrians passing through the park move around the solid circles of arguing men. Anyone standing in a circle can inject a comment at any time, leading to several people attempting to speak at once and shouting down other speakers to be heard. Debates coalesce into one discussion, break apart into a variety of side arguments and then rejoin once again in a continuous cycle. Two or three debates often occur simultaneously as men participating in one discussion pick up and follow a different thread of an argument and form another group.

A variety of strategies are used in debating. Speakers turn and ask for support from bystanders. They ask other listeners, often with mocking incredulity, if they heard their antagonist correctly or whether the encircling men can believe what the antagonist is saying. Often an argument is dismissed with a simple 'No se sabe' ('He does not know [baseball])' or 'You don't *really* know [baseball]'), accompanied with a wagging finger in the antagonist's face. As arguments heat up, insults get nastier and more personal until, finally, one of two outcomes occurs. On rare occasions, one man gets so frustrated or angry that he stalks away as the other man continues shouting at him until he is out of earshot: 'Amarillo! Mentirosa! No sabe pelota! ¿Qué es su problema? No sabe que … ' (Amarillo![28] Liar! You don't know baseball! What is your problem? You don't know that … !'). Even once the man's antagonist is out of earshot, his challenger will continue to reinforce his point to those who are listening to their debate 'El no se sabe. ¿Por qué hablo con él? No se sabe nada' ('He doesn't know anything. Why do I talk with him? He knows nothing'). However, the disgusted, disgruntled individual invariably returns. Eventually, after several days, the original two antagonists renew their debate.

The other eventual outcome occurs if one of the few regulars with statistics is there to resolve the dispute. Disputes do not get resolved unless the points of issue can be quantified. Statistics are essential to baseball discourse. In the *aficionados*' eyes, they provide a means of settling disagreements fairly. Many fans prefer statistics to baseball lore.[29] Frederico, another founding member and former president of the *peña*, explained that statistics are the best way to resolve an argument:

> Numbers are non-negotiable. You can't argue about the numbers. You can argue over who is the better player. You look to see who hit more home runs, better average. End of debate. There is no question about the numbers. You look and see Marquetti hit so many homeruns and Mesa hit a few less in more years. The numbers decided it. You can't argue with numbers. You can argue with a man, with his opinions, but you can't argue against the numbers. They just are.

Statistics provide men with a safe means of resolving challenges to their masculinity without resorting to violence. The establishment of each man's reputation, in comparison to others' reputations, lies in his ability to establish his position and to answer questions of esoteric knowledge posed by his challenger (which may or may not be relevant to the initial debate). Then, if it comes to an ultimate showdown, he must justify his position by accurately quoting the relevant statistics. The accuracy and speed of mental ability, along with ability to articulate clearly and quickly, are the determining factors. Two antagonists argue with one another, each challenging the other's assertions and supporting his own until, finally, an 'expert' is called on to confirm or destroy a point supporting a position. These 'experts' are men who, like Frederico, have memorized specific sets of statistics that interest them – there does not appear to be any system determining who memorizes what – and have proven their memories against printed materials time and again. Even when the 'expert' is called on, this does not necessarily end the debate; usually the parameters of the debate shift and the argument continues.

No one is immune to this sort of questioning or testing. Any man who stays long enough will be challenged, merely to see if he 'belongs', or has legitimate 'business' there. My own claims of *aficionismo* were challenged through several sets of esoteric questions, some that did and some that did not have ready, clear-cut answers. Such questions serve two purposes. They confirm that this unknown individual is, socially speaking, a man and determine his degree of masculinity in relation to the other men in the park through his willingness to engage in argumentative confrontation. In confirming an individual's masculinity through *discutir pelota*, such questions and ensuing debates also suggest that the masculinity being displayed is specifically Cuban. Initial questions ask for baseball knowledge that has definitive answers, such as 'How many Latinos are in the [US Baseball] Hall of Fame? Who are they and what country is each from?'[30] As an individual proves his knowledge, he demonstrates his masculinity through his willingness to *discutir pelota* as he becomes involved in broader questions. Such questions are topics of conversations that can go on interminably, such as 'Who is the best pitcher in Cuba?' An argument revolving around this question can continue for days, as fans negotiate the temporal boundaries of the question; different positions can include whether the point of contention will be encompassed by a decade, a generation, or some other demarcation. Where these lines are drawn is continually negotiated since many players cross any agreed boundary and since the constant flow of arriving and departing men ensures that some are unaware of the initial boundaries.

Debates like this ensue on almost any given day. The argument topics and parameters vary. One constantly raging argument centres on which has been the best Cuban team. This particular topic is a *peña* favourite.

One parameter that has to be immediately established is whether the argument will be about pre-Revolutionary baseball or the current era of baseball that began in 1962. When arguing about more recent generations of players and teams, the *peña* members are discussing the Serie Nacional, the Cuban professional league that currently consists of 16 teams and plays anything between 75 and 95 games in a season.

On one sunny afternoon, the negotiated parameters of one debate centred on the quality of competition and the number of times a team has been a champion included: the number of championships won in the Serie Nacional; which team has historically developed the best talent (indicated by the number of players it has sent to the national team); the number of wins each championship team had earned (significant because the number of games per season has increased steadily since 1962); and the quality of the team's competition in winning championships. Several men, one of whom came from the Oriente region, sat on one of the marble benches lining Parque Central's plaza surrounded by a semicircle of men and debated the Oriente's claim that Santiago was the best Cuban team in Serie Nacional history:

> 'Santiago is the best team. There is no doubt. Santiago has been champions more often than any other club.'
> 'Nah. Santiago doesn't have any competition in its region.'
> [The speaker's implication is that the team does not need to play good baseball until the national championship series against the Western champion.]
> 'You can't say that. Santiago has Villa Clara as a rival.'
> [Villa Clara is geographically in the centre of the east–west axis of the island, as well as being conceptually part of the Oriente from Habaneros' (people from Havana) viewpoints. Anything east of Matanzas, approximately an hour's drive east of Havana is Oriente from a Habanero's point of view.]
> [A man standing in the semicircle around the bench asked the man from the Oriente:]
> 'How many championships has Santiago won?'
> [Before he could respond, another man interjected:]
> 'Industriales has won the most [titles] since '62.'
> [1962 was the inaugural year of the Serie Nacional. Industriales is one of two teams representing the capital, the older and more successful of the two that represents Havana.]

[The Santiago supporter from the Oriente countered:]
'But in the 90s, Santiago has won the most.'
[Another Industriales supporter reacted by comparing Industriales and Santiago in head to head competition in national championship series throughout the history of the Serie Nacional:]
'Industriales has been to the championship versus Santiago and won seven times and only lost twice.'
[The Santiago supporter ignored that comment, continuing to focus his argument on Santiago's success in recent years:]
'Santiago won in '90, '92, and '93.'

The debate continued in this manner for approximately an hour with various men coming and going, adding comments and meeting other men. Debates in this context are more than verbal duels between two men in a fishbowl of spectators; they are a free flow conversation of information, ideas, opinions and positions among all members of the group. At one point, one of the men sitting near the Santiago supporter said that Camagüey was the best Cuban team, eliciting cries of disbelief and howls of laughter:

'What? *Coño*! How can you say that?'
[Several participants shouted in an aside to men in engaged in other arguments:]
'Hey! Camagüey is the best Cuban team according to this cretin',
[Arms were raised above the circle's heads and pointed at the supposed cretin who could make such a statement. The Camagüey supporter defended his assertion:]
'Look at their pitchers! They produce more pitchers for the national team and they consistently have the best pitchers of any team in the Serie Nacional.'
[One man who had been quietly listening until this point yelled:]
'What are you talking about? Villa Clara has a better team than Camagüey. Camagüey can't hit at all. You don't know anything.'
[A Santiago supporter and the Industriales fans also lent their critiques of the Camagüey fan's position. The Santiago supporter attacked the Camagüey fan by retorting:]
'What? Santiago has beaten Camagüey in every playoff series. They have never won a championship.'
[Industriales' supporters shouted at all three men, saying that none of them knew what they were talking about:]

'The Occidente has better teams, Industriales and Pinar.'

'Pinar won the last championship and they'll win this year's too.'

'Pinar or Industriales have won more championships than all the teams in the Oriente. None of you know what you are saying.'

Industriales' fans argued with all three men who were supporting other teams and the main conversation broke into three separate debates for several minutes. Then, some of the men got up and left and the group reformed and continued its original debate with the *Santiago* supporter's assertion.

The above is representative of any given argument amongst the fans of Parque Central. However, these arguments are not so much about actual confrontation as they are about demonstrating manliness. Although there are a few instances in my notes of an argument growing so heated it clearly becomes a confrontation, the park, in general, is a place for men to gather, socialize and display their masculinity in a relatively secure context. Cuban men assert claims of their own masculinity while simultaneously implicitly recognizing another's claim through the engagement of argument within the *peña*.

CONCLUSION

On the surface, the arguments of La Peña appear to conform to earlier claims that men cannot openly disagree with one another without, at least, a latent threat of violence.[31] However, if one digs a little deeper, it becomes increasingly evident that it is the very act of disagreement that is vital to asserting and displaying one's masculinity. These public disagreements are structured with the implicit understanding that violence is not an acceptable option. To react with physical violence is to refute one's claim of masculinity because one is clearly displaying a lack of self-control (*disciplina*). To willingly involve oneself in these arguments displays willingness and ability to engage in struggle (*lucha*). Both *disciplina* and *lucha*, or the lack of them, are clearly evident in one's lucidity within *discutir pelota*. Thus, the very act of publicly disagreeing with another man by confronting him with baseball knowledge demonstrates masculinity and *cubanidad*.

It is not whether one is masculine or not that is implicitly questioned in *discutir pelota* but rather the kind and degree of masculinity. How one participates, and to what degree, are the important characteristics that are based on how well and how quickly one articulates baseball knowledge. The confrontations within La Peña are not 'real' confrontations, in that the results and commentary are not direct attacks on an individual's claim to manhood. What is revealed in La Peña is what sort of man the individual in question is. Most arguments never reach a conclusion and in so doing affirm the participants' claims of masculinity. Arguments are not supposed to reach a conclusion; they wind down at day's end only to be picked up again the following day. Consequently, *discutir pelota* is supposed to remain open-ended because it is the public display of disagreeing with one another that demonstrates each participant's masculine qualities of *disciplina*, *lucha* and articulateness to the other participants and to the rest of the world passing through Parque Central.

That these arguments take place as men-only affairs in the centre of a public space further reinforces participants' claims and displays of masculinity. Their gathering also demonstrates the very spatial centrality of masculinity in *cubanidad*. La Peña dominates the park both in terms of physical and cultural space. Physically, the clusters of men arguing baseball occupy the central part of the park, at times, encircling the statue of José Martí. Thus, not only are these men occupying the park's central space but they are symbolically encircling the father of the Cuban nation. Furthermore, La Peña's occupation of the central plaza forces pedestrians to walk around the circles of arguing men. Passers-by cannot help but notice this occupation; they are forced to take a more indirect route through the park.

La Peña also dominates the park culturally. Parque Central is known throughout Havana as the place that one goes to argue baseball. La Peña of Parque Central is not the only *Esquina Caliente* in Havana but La Peña is the Esquina Caliente of Havana. That the park is known city-wide as the place for *discutir pelota* also implicates the park as a gendered space.

By Cubans' cultural logic, it makes sense for a man to spend time in Parque Central but not for a woman – there is no socially defined reason for women to be there. Of course such cultural logic is contestable. Other activities occur within the park's confines, sometimes simultaneously with *La Peña*'s arguments. Like all parks, Parque Central is a socially contested space. That a park acquires a certain 'reputation' for a specific kind of activity, however, socially constrains that space. Public spaces become symbolically embedded in the constructions of social identities. Such locales become known as places one goes for a specific kind of experience. In the case of Parque Central's, baseball dominates this conceptualized space even though baseball is never played there. The park itself is associated with *discutir pelota* and, consequently, marked as a masculine space.

That the men of La Peña socially dominate the space of Parque Central is not a new phenomenon in terms of gendered public space. As was discussed earlier, parks, streets and other venues have always been the province of men, especially upper-class men with leisure time. The movements of upper-class women were restricted to select hours and methods as the case of the *volantes* illustrates. The men of La Peña are merely the newest configuration of the socially defined masculine space of Parque Central.

In this chapter, I have attempted to show that sports fans create and maintain legitimate social identities linked to what is usually considered the more 'serious' forms of social identity, in this instance, gender and nation. To be a baseball fan in Parque Central is to both declare and display one's manliness. Furthermore, such declaration and display of masculinity is a historically specific gendered construct. The men of La Peña embody the continued century-old associations between baseball, masculinity and *cubanidad* that have permeated the island since Wenceslao Galvéz y Delmonte played and wrote about the sport. They do not simply declare their masculinity, they demonstrate, through their passion for baseball, that their masculinity is specifically Cuban.

ACKNOWLEDGEMENTS

Funding for this research was provided by the Latin American Institute of the University of New Mexico as well as several other university institutions. The chapter was much improved through conversations with Nelson Valdés, Karl Schwerin, Carole Nagengast, Les Field, Milton Jamail, Peter Bjarkman, Robert Lavenda and Paul Ryer. Comments on earlier drafts made by Karl Schwerin, Paul Ryer, Andrew Sussman, Elaine Fuller Carter and Georgeanne Gabrielli greatly improved the final version. As in baseball, all errors that may have occurred are my own and none of the above individuals can be held responsible for this chapter's assertions, interpretations, or content.

NOTES

1. As is standard ethnographic practice, all names have been changed. This is particularly important when conducting ethnography in Cuba because of the potential for state authorities to disapprove and punish citizens who participated in my research.
2. For a more detailed and in-depth examination of each of these values of Cuban masculinity as the embodiment of *cubanidad* amongst Cuban baseball fans, see T. Carter, *Playing Hardball: Constructions of Cuban Identity*, Ph.D. dissertation (Albuquerque: University of New Mexico 2000).

3. Ibid., pp.235–78.
4. The *criollo* class were members of the Cuban elite who distinguished themselves from other Cuban members of the Cuban elite on the basis of where they were born. *Criollos* were born in Cuba and contrasted themselves with those who were born in Spain.
5. Many current teams are named after provinces. To facilitate discernment of the difference between province and team names, the teams are italicized while the provinces are not.
6. Nineteenth-century Cuban baseball was played with ten members to a team. The tenth player's position was a short outfielder much like the tenth member of a modern-day softball team.
7. W. Galvéz y Delmonte, *El Base-Ball en Cuba* (La Habana: Imprenta Mercantil de los Herederos de Santiago S. Speneer, 1889), pp.98–9. Unless otherwise noted, all translations are my own.
8. R. González Echevarría, *The Pride of Havana: A History of Cuban Baseball* (New York: Oxford University Press, 1999), pp.95–6.
9. On the role of fans, see J. Lever, *Soccer Madness. Brazil's Passion for the World's Most Popular Sport* (Prospect Heights, IL: Waveland Press 1995) and N. Trujillo and B. Krizek, 'Emotionality in the Stands and in the Field: Expressing Self Through Baseball', *Journal of Sport and Social Issues*, 18, 4 (1994), 303–25. For discussions on the relationship between sport and popular culture, see A. Baker and T. Boyd (eds.), *Out of Bounds: Sports, Media, and the Politics of Identity* (Bloomington: Indiana University Press, 1997); G. Lipsitz, *Time Passages: Collective Memory and American Popular Culture* (Minneapolis: University of Minnesota Press 1990); D. Rowe, *Popular Cultures: Rock Music, Sport and the Politics of Pleasure* (London: Sage, 1995).
10. See M. Leiner, *Sexual Politics in Cuba: Machismo, Homosexuality, and AIDS* (Boulder, CO: Westview Press 1994); I. Lumsden, *Machos, Maricones, and Gays: Cuba and Homosexuality* (Philadelphia: Temple University Press, 1996).
11. For a cogent examination of 'hypermasculinity' and politics in sport, see V. Burstyn, *The Rites of Men: Manhood, Politics, and the Culture of Sport* (Toronto: University of Toronto Press, 1999) as well as M. Messner and D. Sabo, *Sport, Men, and the Gender Order: Critical Feminist Perspectives* (Champaign: Human Kinetics, 1990). Finally, for important studies on the relationship between masculinity, nation and sport, read E. Archetti, *Masculinities: An Anthropology of Football, Polo, and Tango* (Oxford: Berg, 1999); S. Brownell, *Training the Body for China: Sports in the Moral Order of the People's Republic of China* (Chicago: University of Chicago Press, 1995), A. Klein, *Sugarball: The American Game, the Dominican Dream* (New Haven: Yale University Press, 1991) and A. Klein, *Baseball on the Border: A Tale of Two Laredos* (Princeton: Princeton University Press, 1997).
12. B. Anderson, *Imagined Communities: Reflections on the Origin and Spread of Nationalism* (London: Verso, 1991).
13. E. Hobsbawm, *Nations and Nationalism Since 1780: Programme, Myth, Reality* (New York: Cambridge University Press, 1992), p.143.
14. B. Buford, *Among the Thugs* (New York: Vintage, 1991) and W. Galvéz y Delmonte, *El Base-Ball en Cuba*.
15. A. Miranda, 'Mi recuerdos y mi opinion' in R. Mendoza, J. Herrera, and M. Calcines (eds.), *El Base Ball en Cuba y América* (La Habana: 1908), pp.27–9.
16. L. Pérez, 'Between Baseball and Bullfighting: The Quest for Nationality in Cuba, 1868–1898', *Journal of American History*, 81, 2 (1994), 493–517.
17. Instead, nationalistic overtones of competing against outsiders were evident in Cuban sentiments towards the Havana Sugar Kings of the International League. Despite being owned by Americans, the Sugar Kings were 'Cuba's team' and were a symbolic means of competing with and beating 'Los Yanquis' even if the majority of the Sugar Kings players were not Cuban. The Sugar Kings won the International League championship against the Minneapolis Millers in 1960 and then were moved to New Jersey because of heightening tensions between the new Cuban government and the US government. The apparent contradiction of Cubans' attitudes towards Habana and Almendares compared to the Sugar Kings goes beyond the scope of this essay.
18. This particular *peña* is used to foreign journalists 'bothering' them whenever a Cuban player is playing in the US Major Leagues' Championship Series (The World Series). Most *peñas* do not receive any foreign attention and thus, such potential 'misinterpretations' are highly unlikely.

While *peña* members do discuss how Cubans fare in the Major Leagues, they insist players' decisions to defect are individual economic decisions and not political challenges to the state. In general, fans are proud of Cubans' accomplishments in the Major Leagues because they are proof of the skill and calibre of Cuban athletes. Fans consider Cuban players overseas in the context of *cubanidad* (Cuban cultural national identity) without explicitly critiquing the State's socialist nationalist construct (*cubanía*) or the politics involved in the 40-year struggle over the Cuban nation-state.

19. For ethnographic examples of Latin American masculine social groups, see G. Brana-Shute, *On the Corner: Male Social Life in a Paramaribo Creole Neighborhood* (Prospect Heights: Waveland Press, 1979); M. Gutmann, *The Meanings of Macho: Being a Man in Mexico City* (Berkeley: University of California Press, 1996); J. Limón, *Dancing With the Devil: Society and Cultural Poetics in Mexican-American South Texas* (Madison: University of Wisconsin Press, 1994).

20. Many would consider the label 'Latin American' dubious in reference to Suriname. However, I argue that Suriname, despite its differences in colonial overlords and language, is part of Latin America precisely because of historical and colonial trajectories Suriname has had in comparison to other Spanish and Portuguese speaking countries. Furthermore, when one compares the construction of gender as I do here, one finds similar structures in each society's construction of a dominant form of masculinity.

21. *Socios* are not *compadres* but form another set of relationships altogether. Cubans have at least three sets of reciprocal relations: family, *compays (compadres)*, and *socios*. There is not sufficient space to fully discuss the intricacies and differences between *socios* and *compays* in this chapter. Thanks to P. Ryer for this reminder.

22. Gutmann *The Meaning of Macho,* p.176.

23. S. Low, 'Spatializing Culture: The Social Production and Social Construction of Public Space in Costa Rica', *American Ethnologist*, 23, 4 (1996), 861–79.

24. R. Segre and M. Coyula, *Havana: Two Faces of an Antillean Metropolis* (London: John Wiley & Sons, 1997), p.31.

25. Ibid., p.58.

26. The police do not generally bother foreigners unless they are blatantly engaged in illegal or dangerous activity. The Cuban government has spent several years encouraging tourism, unnecessary police attention would attract world-wide negative publicity and directly impact on these efforts.

27. Some individuals do use the *peña* as a place to conceal what they are doing. They cling to the edges of the discussion groups in order to watch the passing tourists, looking for prospective customers. However, these individuals are marginalized by La Peña and are occasionally pulled out by police who do not recognize them as frequenters of La Peña.

28. An 'Amarillo' is not a coward. To question a man's courage by calling him a coward is an invitation to fight because you are saying that he does not have the courage to try or to struggle. Therefore, while *amarillo* literally translates as 'yellow', it does not carry the same connotations of cowardice as calling someone yellow has in the United States. It appears that 'Amarillo' is a Havana taunt directed at men from the Oriente that implies they do not have the heart, the strength, or the skills to complete what they have started. Fans in the Estadio Latinoamericano chant 'Amarillo' at starting pitchers who have been knocked out of the game but only when the opposing player is from the Oriente.

29. Baseball lore consists of tall tales, eyewitness accounts and other narratives that fill the oral history of the sport and do not rely on physical documentation, such as box scores, line up cards and so forth.

30. This was one of the first questions the men of La Peña asked me. At the time of this fieldwork in 1997, the answer was five: Martín Dihígo of Cuba, Juan Marichal of the Dominican Republic, Luis Aparicio of Venezuela, Roberto Clemente of Puerto Rico and Rod Carew of Panama. Since then, Tany Perez of Cuba has been inducted into the US Baseball Hall of Fame. In English speaking areas, Tany Perez is often (incorrectly) called Tony Perez; his actual name is Atanasio.

31. E. Stevens, 'Machismo and Marianismo', *Society*, 10 (1973), 57–63.

6

The Crisis of Brazilian Football: Perspectives for the Twenty-First Century

CESAR GORDON and RONALDO HELAL

The twentieth century was, for Brazil, the football century. Since it was first introduced, the ancient 'British sport' has undergone a true process of cultural incorporation. Football has now become what Brazilians refer to as 'the national passion', as if they hope to affirm that the game is now practically Brazilian property, that Brazilians were custom made for football, that not only is Brazilian football the best in the world but that nowhere else is football as loved as it is in Brazil. This depth of feeling is synthesised in the epithet 'Brazil, the football country', an expression consolidated not only in the national imagery but also abroad and especially in light of the country's supremacy in World Cups, epitomized by four titles (1958, 1962, 1970 and 1994).

Football is more than a mere passion; it has been a primordial element in the country's recent history, in its transition from a rural society to a modern, urban and industrial one. As various scholars have emphasized, football in Brazil has been a powerful mechanism for social integration and for the consolidation of a national identity, as well as being revealing of certain imagined characteristics of the 'Brazilian *geist*'.[1] It was through football that Brazilians managed to 'add up nation and society … and feel confidant in our capacity as a people … to succeed as a modern country, and to also sing with pride its anthem and lose itself in the green field of its national flag'.[2]

However, towards the end of the 1970s, Brazilian football began to announce a 'crisis'. This crisis manifests itself in the declining number of spectators at football stadiums, in the rise of violence – especially among the so-called *torcidas organizadas* (organized band of supporters),[3] in the sale of Brazilian players abroad and in the financial indebtedness of football clubs. Initially felt and dramatized by the sporting press, this crisis later became the object of academic studies which sought to detect the problems afflicting Brazilian football and to point the way towards solutions.[4] During the 1980s, club managers and sporting analysts began to look for solutions to the crisis.

In spite of a brief interlude due to victory in the 1994 World Cup these problems continued to be present themselves. In August 1996, the Confederação Brasileira de Futebol (CBF, the entity responsible Brazilian football) organized a seminar on the topic.[5] Thus, the crisis of Brazilian football became conspicuous by the end of the 1990s and appeared to have paradigmatically reached its most dramatic stage by 2000. Scandals involving football's administrative elite and accusations of corruption and fraud aimed at Wanderley Luxemburgo, the former manager of the Brazilian national team, reached their zenith in two Parliamentary Commission of Inquiry (CPIs),[6] one in the House of Deputies and one in the Federal Senate, aimed at investigating the nature of contracts between the CBF and the Nike multinational corporation. The CBF also asked the Fundação Getúlio Vargas (a non-governmental organization for socio-economic research) to provide a *Plano de Modernização do Futebol Brasileiro* (plan for the modernization of Brazilian football). The initial diagnosis of this plan has already been presented to the press and points to the following problems:

- lack of a professional ethic;
- lack of credibility;
- lack of proper qualifications for managers and referees;
- low salaries for the majority of players and inflated salaries for a few;
- lack of leadership from the CBF;
- confusing timetables.

In the midst of all this, the Brazilian League in 2000 – this time organized by the clubs themselves and not by the CBF[7] – was considered a failure. The competition featured more than 300 clubs (divided into three modules) and was plagued by poor turnouts (an average of less than 11,000 paying spectators per match). The final match ended in tragedy after the gate separating the spectators from the pitch in São Januário Stadium broke and caused injury to 168 people. The match was suspended; earlier this year the Superior Court of Sporting Justice

(STJD), the highest authority in sporting justice, determined that a new match should be played.

These events present a scenario which discredits the institutions which controlling football in Brazil, as reflected by the poor spectator turnout at stadiums. An apparent disinterest in football began to take hold. We have now reached a point where certain analysts have begun, informally, to question the very importance of football to Brazilians. Recently a reporter on the main newspaper in Rio de Janeiro asked an anthropologist about the impact of Brazilian football's defeats in the Olympic Games. The anthropologist replied directly: 'None. National pride no longer suffers from defeats. We have diversified our interests in other sports and recreational activities; football no longer carries so much weight'.[8] He concluded that Brazil 'even wears ever smaller boots'. He was alluding to the famous Brazilian image of the country in football boots (*a pátria de chuteiras*) penned by the Brazilian playwright and writer Nelson Rodrigues which summarizes the relationship we have always perceived between Brazilian national identity and the national football team.

Radicalism apart, the phrase may express a sentiment or 'mood' which began to surface at the end of the century. If we compare the current situation to the strong emotions felt by Brazilians after defeat in the 1950 World Cup Final, for example, or after the third World Cup victory in 1970, we might speculate that we are about to witness a decline in interest. Today, unlike in previous decades, it is not unreasonable to question whether Brazil is still the land of football.[9] The very possibility of asking such a question would have been absurd in 1970. Recognition of this change in attitude allows us to glimpse the other changes that Brazilian football is currently undergoing.

The principal agents of Brazilian football interpret these changes as a 'crisis'. The aim of this chapter is to reflect on this crisis and to evaluate its real dimensions. We seek to explain the crisis through the changes experienced by Brazilian society during the last decades, through so-called globalization and the cultural transformations that stem from the globalization process – what we might term post-modernity. We thus hope to discuss football's possible role in the next century, in light of the process of the transformation of Brazilian society on the road towards post-modernity.

Interpretation of this variety cannot avoid speculation since we are analysing a process which is as yet unfinished. However, we can offer an examination of the role of football in the passing of a traditional, rural society to a modern urban one (with all its contradictions and conflicts), as well as an outline of what its role might be when this same society moves into post-modernity. In short, at the end of this essay we intend to ask the following question: if football in the twentieth century occupied a preponderant role in the history and formation of Brazilian cultural identity, how will it fare in the twenty-first century?

But first we must step back a little, in order to put the current phase of Brazilian football into perspective. If the present situation is conceived of as a crisis, it must be so in relation to a past moment. We feel that it is possible to, somewhat arbitrarily, delimit a period to contrast with the present. We might call this period 'the golden age of Brazilian football'; it begins with the professionalization of the game in 1933 and ends with the third World Cup victory in 1970. We intend to analyse these two periods separately and to highlight the ways in which Brazilian football was, and is, constructed, while at the same time describing contemporaneous Brazilian society.

Finally, our analysis of football as a cultural construct which finds parallels in the recent history of Brazilian society is a result of our belief that, as R. Da Matta has stated, football is the vehicle for a series of dramatizations of our society. We have taken our concept of drama from anthropologists such as Victor Turner and Max Gluckman.[10] As such, football is seen to be an idiom through which society allows itself to be perceived. From this point of view we believe that the transformations evident in football and the ways in which it is represented correspond to changes in society. In order to understanding the role of football in the next century, we must also consider Brazilian society itself.

FOOTBALL, NATIONALISM AND IDENTITY IN BRAZIL

Football was brought to Brazil at a time when important changes were occurring in Brazilian society. The old monarchical regime, which relied on slave labour, had just ended and the country had entered a non slave-based period of Republican government.[11] Thus a basically rural and agrarian society began to slowly give way to an urban and industrial one. In the first decades of the twentieth century, the country experienced growing migration to cities which lead to the formation of an urban proletariat. Brought to Brazil by English immigrants, football was absorbed by sectors of the new urban elite, who disdained the participation of the popular classes, particularly of blacks and mestizos. The first few decades of the Brazilian game are characterized by a struggle between the two forces: one set on keeping football restricted to the educated European elite and the other favourable to the idea of opening and expanding the game to the rest of society. Subsequently the conflict between those who wanted to maintain the sport's amateur status and those who sought to make it professional grew. We should note that the logic of amateurism cannot be abstracted from its ideological environment and cultural context. The defence of amateurism – either explicit or implicit – was the defence of an all-white football, closed to the working classes and restricted to the urban elite.

The debate around professionalism began to emerge towards the end of the 1910 but it became a central question in 1923 when Vasco da Gama became Rio de Janeiro state champion. For the first time a team made up primarily of mulatto, black and working-class players won a championship. Some players had been receiving payment from rich club members since 1915 and, in 1917, some of the clubs in Rio de Janeiro and São Paulo began to charge spectators to watch games. It was these factors that caused this period to be known as one of 'brown professionalism' or 'false amateurism'. However, up until 1923 the tournament-winning teams were composed predominantly of amateurs so the problem of brown amateurism did not cause upheaval. A title won by a team made up of players receiving wages resulted in a strong reaction on the part of those who defended amateurism and brought about the creation of a separate league excluding Vasco. A unified league was later re-established, integrating Vasco, but the debate about professionalism continued for a further ten years. Professionalization in 1933 meant that the lower echelons of society could find a job that did not require long periods of study or years of formal education. Football became a means of social mobility.

In this way, the 'modernizing' forces in the game managed to break the final shackles preventing full popularization of football in the country. Yet we cannot be sure if the adoption of professionalism alone was enough to achieve this end. At the same time, both sportsmen and politicians made a conscious and concerted effort to popularize football throughout Brazil with the aim of using its popularity to involve the wider populace in nation building and promote a sense of national identity. In order to understand this process we must outline the social context and the changes occurring in Brazil at the time.

The 1930s marked the passing of the so-called Old Republic and the start of the New State headed by president Getúlio Vargas. Strong political centralization and a preoccupation with national development, with the idea of integration and with the strengthening of the role of the state as a promoter of these were characteristic of this period. Another aspect of Vargas' presidency was its concern with labour matters. The 1934 Constitution provided a series of guarantees for workers, such as a minimum wage, set working hours, the right to union representation, social security, the establishment of a judicial body aimed at arbitrating conflicts between workers and bosses, etc.[12] Three years later, Vargas ordered a new Constitution to be written which some believed was influenced by Mussolini's *corporatism*[13] and which expressed the preoccupations of the time: the promotion of the harmonic accommodation of the different social groups in Brazil, thereby achieving the desired 'national unity'.

Simultaneously, social scientists who sought to explain Brazilian society were developing new ways of conceptualizing Brazil. Curiously, in the same year in which football became professionalized, Gilberto Freyre published his *Casa Grande e Senzala* (*The Masters and the Slaves*), which had an enormous influence in the ways in which Brazilian society was represented, both at home and abroad. The concept of a 'racial democracy' which played a large role in models that sought to explain national identity emerged as a result of this and other similar studies.[14] According to this theory, observable racial miscegenation was the result of harmonious rather than confrontational relations between the different ethnic groups which made up Brazil's population.[15] Before Freyre, miscegenation was seen by scientists as a major Brazilian problem. In this new formulation it emerged as a positive and advantageous aspect of our society. It is possible to see how the new sociological theories about Brazil combined with the theme of nationalism during the Vargas period, having *mixture* and *integration* as their basic concepts.

It is precisely in this context that we need to understand the rise of football. The growing popularization of football during the 1930s–50s was due in part to professionalization but above all to the work of the press and of intellectuals who helped make football a mass event and an element of popular culture. Mário Rodrigues Filho occupied a pivotal role in this transformation. He was the inventor of sporting journalism as a genre in Brazil and a promoter of the rise of a mass audience for football through his participation in various important sporting newspapers in Rio de

Janeiro (*O Globo*, *O Mundo Esportivo*, *Jornal dos Esportes*).[16] Through his use of the media, Mário Filho continuously promoted public football events and actively participated in debates about the end of amateurism. His sporting chronicles described football matches in epic proportions, not merely as sporting contests but as events where noble human values were at stake. He was an ardent defender of professionalism; he believed that it was 'a means towards the emancipation of blacks, a necessary condition for the constitution of football as a national sport'. For Mário Filho, professionalization was not only a matter of economics; it was a way of establishing a relationship of identity between players and the public, united in the same project of social emancipation through sports.[17] Filho was also responsible for the construction of the Maracanã stadium which was built in Rio de Janeiro in order to host the 1950 World Cup. Constructed in gigantic proportions and the largest stadium in the world at the time, the Maracanã was built, according to Mário Filho, 'to glorify the love of Brazilians for football'.[18]

Mário Filho and an entire sector of Brazilian intellectual life, especially the journalists and chroniclers who followed in his wake, suceeded in transforming football into a sport which closely corresponded with the expectations and tastes of the public.[19] According to Leite Lopes, this new way of communicating with the working classes was soon seized upon by the corporativism of the New State. President Vargas' public addresses, aimed at workers, often attempted to capitalize on football's popularity by taking place at São Januário Stadium (owned by Vasco da Gama and, until 1950, the largest stadium in Rio de Janeiro).[20] It was at São Januário, for example, that the government announced the establishment of a minimum wage in 1940. At the same time, the State intensified its part as a regulator and promoter of sporting activity. In 1942, football clubs were subjected to the Federal Government as part of President Vargas' centralizing and nationalizing policies. Law 3,199, dating from 14 April 1941, created the Conselho Nacional de Desportos (CND) with the objective of 'orientating, fiscalising and incentivating the practice of sports in the country'. The creation of the CND suggests that football was seen to be an important matter in the eyes of the government. On the other hand the CND was a government entity not directly identified with the clubs (private institutions with non-profit goals) and its mission was to serve the government's political interests. Before the 1988 Constitution, which abolished the CND, the structural organization of football was as follows: clubs were organized into regional federations; these federations were subject to the rules of the Confederação Brasileira de Desportos (CBD) and, after 1979, the Confederação Brasileira de Futebol (CBF) – all of these were executive entities while the CND acted as the normative agency. In practice, however, the CND was also an executive agency since it held the power to intervene in federations and clubs as it deemed necessary.

At the same time, the actions of journalists and intellectuals led to the appearance and diffusion of the idea of a typically Brazilian 'style' of football. It was believed that this style expressed specific traces of the Brazilian 'character' or 'spirit', particularly the theory of harmony between European and African, white and black.[21] The idea that Brazilian football appeared, on the pitch, as a sort of 'dance', which expressed characteristics such as cunning, art, musicality, *ginga* (swing) and spontaneity followed from this belief.[22] Mário Filho wrote a book (*O negro no futebol brasileiro*) which described these characteristics as a black and mestizo contribution to our football. In this work, the journalist credits football with the role of integrating blacks and mestizos into society and argues that it functions as a mechanism for the democratization of social relations. According to writer José Lins do Rego – one of the admirers and motivators of sport at the time – the Brazilian national team was a 'portrait of our racial democracy' where players from privileged classes joined with blacks and mulattos in the search for a common victory.[23]

In this way Brazilian football and society began to be seen as the result of positive racial mixing. This characteristic was seen to be the main element of integration, a factor capable of making the country 'work'. It was equally a mechanism for integration and racial democratization, the expression of a 'style' that was represented as the product of the mixture of races (and, as such, a defining element of an *identity*), a microcosm of society and nation: football was all this throughout the 1930s–50s. The metaphor is indeed powerful; it transcended its academic/intellectual origins and became a widespread common sense ideology.

The clarity and efficiency of this metaphor and the amalgamation of 'identity, nation and football' can be seen clearly during World Cups (initially in the defeat of 1950, but later in the victories of 1958, 1962 and 1970). Transformed into a metaphor for the nation ('the country in football boots'), the task of football and, more than ever, of the national team, was to show the supposed grandeur of Brazil to the world: it was not only a matter of collecting titles but also of 'carving a place among nations'.[24]

When the Brazilian team finally succeeded in winning the World Cup, the country was undergoing a new phase of economic and industrial growth and experiencing a period of optimism and euphoria. This was a time of intense cultural revitalization. Nationalist and integrationist trends were apparent at various levels from the construction of a new federal capital by President Juscelino Kubitschek (Brasília, situated in the central plateau, at the time an area of low population density), to artistic manifestations such as the new cinema, the bossa nova and popular art. Brazil's two consecutive victories in the World Cup were essentially the product of black and mestizo players such as Pelé and Garrincha. Victory represented the resurrection and supremacy of artistic football (defeated in 1950) together with swing and samba; the victory of art over strength, of intuition and spontaneity over reason, of magic over technology, in short, the victory of a football and a nation which were harmonized by the mixing of their differences.

The transformation of football into the 'national sport' was the product of a historical process carried out by agents of the cultural, political and sporting worlds which had at its base the powerful presence of the state and of nationalism. At this point, the modernization of football was no longer about overcoming the elitism of amateur status was prevalent in the first two decades of the century but, above all, of making football ever-more inclusive and representative of the nation and the people.

THE 'CRISIS' OF BRAZILIAN FOOTBALL

Brazilian football was at its peak during the 1960s and 1970s. The national team won the World Cup in 1958, 1962 and 1970 and Pelé's team Santos won the Taça Libertadores da América and the World Club Championship consecutively in 1962 and 1963. The public rushed to the stadiums to witness great events; it was as if football and its supporters were on honeymoon. The final match of the Rio de Janeiro State tournament of 1963 brought 177,020 paying spectators to the Maracanã – still the official record for spectators at a club match. In November 1969, Pelé scored his thousandth goal and consolidated his position as the greatest player of all time. The supremacy of Brazilian football appeared both unquestionable and indestructible.

In 1967, a tournament was organized between clubs from five Brazilian states – Rio de Janeiro, São Paulo, Minas Gerais, Rio Grande do Sul and Paraná. This championship was a substitute for the traditional Rio/São Paulo tournament that had been played since 1950.

The Sports Lottery was created in 1969, cashing in on football's success, to raise funds for government programmes.[25] In 1971, as part of the government's project for national integration established in 1964, the CBD (CBF as of 1979) began to organize a tournament to include clubs from most Brazilian states – now known as the *Campeonato Brasileiro* (Brazilian League).

The early 1970s brought about the construction of a number of stadiums holding over 70,000 people. According to CBF records, some, such as the Morumbi in São Paulo, the Rei Pelé in Macéio, and the Castelão in Ceará, even held more than 100,000 people. Under military rule, Brazil experienced the period of economic optimism which came to be known as the 'Brazilian miracle'. Official government propaganda, which served to stimulate national conceit, bore slogans such as 'Brazil, the country of the future', 'Brazil, love it or leave it' and 'Grand Brazil'. Thanks to its immense popularity, football became an effective means by which the government could transmit its message, principally the idea of an 'integrated country'. A marching tune popularized by the media at the time of the World Cup proclaimed: 'ninety million in action,[26] forward Brazil, land of my heart ... All of a sudden there is a wave of positive energy, it is as if all of Brazil are holding hands. All join together in the same emotion. We are all one heart. All together, let's go, forward Brazil, save our national team.'[27]

However, after defeat in the 1974 World Cup, Brazilian football began to show signs of ill health.[28] From the point of view of the organizational structure, the seeds of the crisis to come had already been sown in the lack of autonomy for clubs, in the politics behind the alliances between federations and the small leagues and in a timetable unable to cope with both the Brazilian and regional tournaments. Meanwhile, a re-organization was taking place in Europe which would give football a more business-like structure.

The situation worsened in 1975 when National Congress approved Law 6,251 which, among other measures, institutionalized unitary voting in football federation and confederations. This voting system, apparently modern and democratic, became a powerful tool in political bargaining and allowed the leagues from the interior of Brazil to control the federations. Many local club presidents sought to safeguard their personal political interests at the expense of the rational organization of the tournaments.[29] The federations and the CBD were therefore forced to organize tournaments for the participation of various small clubs. The long and unappealing nature of these tournaments resulted in the financial failure of some of the larger clubs.[30] For example, in 1978 the CBD organized the Brazilian League to include 74 clubs from all states; in 1979 the League expanded to include 94 clubs. The average spectator turnout fell dramatically to the lowest average ever (10,615 in 1978 and 9,137 in 1979).

The newspaper *O Globo* published a series of articles and debates involving journalists, club presidents and football managers on the theme of 'The Decadence of Brazilian football'.[31] The headlines for these articles are suggestive: 'Spectators, disenchanted, abandon stadiums'; 'Bad games and hisses are the routine'; 'In search of gains, just like businesses'; 'Structural reform: the only solution'; 'Politics: the main problem, according to the specialists'. An analysis of these articles reveals the tension between two distinct discourses or ethics: the 'traditional', centred on the exchange of favours, personal relationships and administrative amateurism, and the 'modern', seeking professionalization of club bosses, universal legislation and a managerial approach.

A few years previously the press had already reflected upon this tension in articles with equally expressive titles: 'Football, Inc: the bankruptcy of a business';[32] 'Throughout the land, a bankrupt football';[33] 'A football which once won three world cups is now in crisis';[34] 'The crisis of football';[35] 'Beyond the field, a football which rules only in incompetence';[36] 'São Paulo: from the deal with Coca-Cola we may even get a super-team';[37] 'The structure of a football in decadence';[38] '[João] Havelange predicts the end of football without support from advertising'[39] and 'Brazilian football Inc'.[40] The call for administrative modernization can be discerned in these articles and the references to football as business is symptomatic of the occurrences in Europe.

However, some of these articles also expressed concern about growing violence in football stadiums. Increasing urbanization and the rapid population growth experienced by urban centres in previous decades contributed to changes in the sociability and geopolitics of cities. By the 1970s, most big cities already had a peripheral urban ring populated by the under privileged. The existence of this ring facilitated the emergence of clusters of marginality and criminality. At the same time the so-called *torcidas organizadas*, organizations of supporters from the same region or neighbourhood who seek to express a particular, common lifestyle and behaviour, began to make their appearance.[41] The rise of violence during football matches coincided with the appearance and diffusion of this type of organized support.[42]

The golden age of football appeared to have reached its close and sporting insiders were already describing the crisis as the result of a series of interrelated factors which, if left unchallenged, would result in the collapse of Brazilian football. Analysts identified a series of diverse, and often overlapping, problems that found their reflection in the disappearance of supporters at football matches. Economic problems such as the financial failure of clubs, non-lucrative tournaments, the general poverty of the population were all related to the end of the economic 'miracle', the deepening recession at the end of the 1970s and inflation. Economists have subsequently come to refer to this period as the lost decade of the Brazilian economy. Analysts expressed concern about social problems such as the increasing violence and lack of security at stadiums. There were also obvious political-administrative problems such as the interference of the state and its refusal to allow clubs and federations autonomy; conflict between the personal and political interests of the heads of federations, the CBF and clubs and the paradox of having amateur administrators in an evermore professional and commercial activity. Technical problems such as the lack of great players were linked to the exodus of the best players to Europe which resulted in diminished club revenue.

Complications mounted and solutions began to be suggested. 1977 saw the introduction of publicity billboards around the pitch as a means of generating income. The money from these advertisements was divided between the federations and stadiums. Football also entered the television era and games began to be taped and transmitted. In 1983 publicity on club strips was introduced. This radical solution to the financial deficit initially caused a negative reaction on the part of supporters who saw it as a violation of the 'sacred' nature of the game. However, as the low stadium attendance continued and clubs earned little gate money, officials turned to the sale of Brazilian players to Europe as a ready and immediate solution to their financial problems. After 1982, a veritable exodus of players to Europe began which further contributed to the discontent of supporters. Live television coverage began in 1987 and generated even more controversy about the appropriate financial remuneration for contracts between clubs and television.[43]

With the end of the military regime and the start of re-democratization in 1985, Brazil began to turn against some of the ideas that had been typical of the previous period, such as 'planning', 'centralization' and 'national will'.[44] The supporters seemed to be of the opinion that the failure of the nationalist and developmentalist programme was due more to its ends than its means. The country had just left a period of dictatorship; it had been traumatized by excessive state power and now longed for liberty. However, the lack of a unified project for the democratic movement meant that the only possible political strategy was one of discarding the entire previous project. Certain specialists argued that it was necessary to apply the same anti-state reasoning to sports, by re-framing the existing sports legislation that had originated during the Vargas era and developed under the military regime (1964–85). The structure of football had remained unaltered since the 1975 sports legislation and was considered by some to be the 'preserve of reactionaries'.[45] It should be stressed that until 1990 two laws aimed at regulating the organization of sports in the country had been passed: Decree 3,199 (1941) and Law 6,251 (1975), regulated by Decree 80,288 (1977). Both were advanced during periods of totalitarian, centralizing rule which explains the strong interference of the state in the organization of clubs, federations and the CBF, the impediments to the professionalization of administrators and the prohibition on clubs organizing tournaments.[46]

The move for the transformation of the existing sports legislation gained momentum both in the media and in society; general opinion seemed to proclaim it as the necessary step for the administrative success of Brazilian football. In 1990, the president asked the recently retired player Zico (Arthur Antunes de Coimbra) to accept the newly created role of National Secretary of Sports. Zico's best known work as secretary was a law which sought to give greater autonomy to clubs and federations. It permitted the professionalization of administrators and ended the *Lei do Passe* (Transfer Law).[47] After various modifications at the request of politicians and club administrators, 'Project Zico', as the law came to be known, was finally approved by the National Congress and normalized as Law 8,672. Sanctioned by the president of the Republic on 6 July 1993, the law significantly altered the way in which clubs were organized.[48] It hoped to solve football's problems by reducing the role of the state and facilitating the transformation of clubs, or at least of their football departments, into profitable firms. The aims of Project Zico are the opposite of those proposed in the period considered previously. Nowadays, some of those in the world of sport believe that football is a matter for the market rather than the state.

However, these changes have not brought about their desired result. On the contrary, the commercial relations between clubs, the CBF and the sponsoring firms, which were seen to be the solution, are now themselves part of the crisis since they are at the centre of Congress' investigations into corruption and bad administration in football. Even after the 1994 World Cup win and other important international results, the problems surrounding Brazilian football remain and the idea of a crisis is still prevalent throughout the sporting press. It is curious to note that one of the defining factors of this crisis, the decline in public participation, is a less constant (and more complex) phenomenon than sports chroniclers have led us to believe.[49] As illustrated in Figure 1, the fall in the number of spectators for the main tournament in the country, shows significant fluctuations rather than uniform trends. Such fluctuation suggests that we are dealing with a conjectural phenomenon. Furthermore, it appears questionable to measure the interest level of supporters through an evaluation of the average attendance at football matches, insofar as the number of supporters who attend stadiums is always smaller than the number of supporters who follow tournaments solely through means of communication. Data from television stations shows that football attracts more television spectators than the vast majority of other programmes exhibited. Thus, if the low turn-out at stadiums is neither as dramatic nor as constant as we had thought; if Brazilian football has won important international titles in the 1990s, including the *Libertadores da América*, World Club tournaments and the World Cup (Brazil has reached two consecutive finals for the first time since 1962); if Brazil keeps turning out internationally recognized players such as Romário, Ronaldo, Rivaldo and Ronaldinho Gaúcho; if clubs and the CBF have come to agree sponsorship contracts with national and international firms and yet we still speak of a crisis, than it would appear that this is a crisis of a more problematic nature than we had first envisaged, a crisis that eludes simple definitions. Perhaps we should reach the conclusion that the crisis is more a matter of social representation than an easily definably phenomenon.

GLOBALIZATION AND POST-MODERNITY: BRAZILIAN FOOTBALL IN THE TWENTY-FIRST CENTURY

We do not intend to claim that there are no problems afflicting Brazilian football, nor that the degree of discredit attained by institutions and their bosses is a mere illusion. What we want to stress is that these facts have always been, in one way or another, part of the history of Brazilian football without being considered as constituting a crisis. In reality, there

FIGURE 6.1

AVERAGE TURNOUT FOR THE BRAZILIAN LEAGUE (1967–2000)

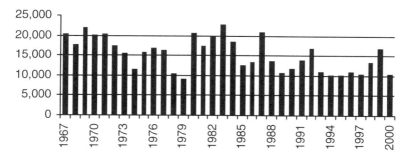

have been earlier crises which have emerged at certain specific moments as, for example, during the process of the construction or reconstruction of the Brazilian football within Brazilian culture. In short, the crisis manifests itself in key moments in the process of the social construction of football. At present, a reconstruction is taking place which accompanies changes in Brazilian society. This reconstruction carries the problematic label of 'modernization' and agents of the football world offer a solution to the crisis within this reconstruction in terms of 'modernization'. The adoption of a professional market ethic in the management of football is offered by them as the solution to the conflicts facing the organization of sport in the country. On the other hand, this ethic cannot put aside the more romantic, amateur aspect of this universe. The tension between the persistence of a traditional (romantic) vision and the tendency towards administrative modernization has become a key element for understanding football in Brazil. It is generally expected that a conciliation of these two aspects will once again lead Brazilian football into a golden age. However, we must question the very idea of 'modernization', since it has not always stood for the same thing.

At the beginning of the 1930s, those hoping for the 'modernization' of football saw the professionalization of players as the solution to a 'crisis'. Nowadays, the tendency is towards the professionalization of club and federation managers and administrators and in the adoption of a model known as the football-firm. These two movements are considered to be stages within a single process: the modernization of sport. However, we want to emphasize that these are essentially different processes which are, in some way, antagonistic in their purposes. Mário Filho's proposal of modernization through the professionalization of players could not dispense with the interference of the state as a promoter of sports. Filho sought to emphasize 'traditional' aspects by creating contexts for the 'sacralization' of teams and the icons related to them (strips, flags, almost mythical narratives of the game). The current idea of modernization that is contained within the notion of the profesionalization of administrators is distinct. It is to do with the removal of the state from decisions concerning football and the handing over of this duty to private investment: the *futebol-empresa* (football-firm). At the same time, various elements of the game are de-sacralized (the stadium, the shirt, even the clubs whose names become merged with those of private firms, such as the case of Palmeiras-Parmalat, where the club is transformed into merchandise for the sponsors), and subjected to the logic of the market and of gain, as if football were a commodity. Modernity during the 1930s–50s meant expanding the state over the field of football. Modernity in the 1980s–90s meant a retraction of the role of the state and an expansion of the market over football.

Still, the question is somewhat wider than this. We have seen how to solve the crisis of the 1930s and to pave the road towards football's golden period, it was not enough to make the game professional. A whole process was required to turn football into the national sport; a process brought about by conscious actions to this effect and by the adoption of a specific idea of the role of football in our society. This process can be characterized as an attempt at an association between football and the more inclusive and unifying elements of social reality: the country, the nation, the people. Football's agents no longer speak of this link although they simultaneously lament the loss of this relationship – perhaps the great paradox of the so-called crisis. One has the impression that the agents of the football world often fail to see that the 'football country' is not a natural reality but rather a social construction which depended on an *ad hoc* connection between football and more unifying influences of social life. If football is offered as a product to be consumed in an evermore diverse and plural entertainment market, without also being guided by a project which links it to these more inclusive instances, we ultimately strain the relationship which had been established previously. The metaphor loses its force and we end up feeling that something is lacking. Perhaps it is here that the real crisis lies.

It is clear that these facts reflect the changes of the so-called globalization era.[50] The difficulty in maintaining the nexus of football with national identity is not only due to the lack of a historical perspective on the part of the agents. In truth, it is the very idea of these unifying influences which post-modern globalization weakens. It is curious that at the same time as we detect the beginnings of the crisis, we also witness the gradual exhaustion of the idea of the state and the nation as the principle defining factors of collective identities. Many social scientists, as well as president Fernando Henrique Cardoso, have announced that the country 'has reached the end of the Vargas era'. What do they mean by this? That we have arrived at a moment in the reduction of the power of the state, of the emptying of the idea of nation and of the nationalist and corporativist project. The idea of globalization brings with it the negation of nation states and the fragmentation of identities. We no longer emphasize the relevance of people to a nation but rather to ethnic groups, to gender and, above all, to groups which define themselves by what they consume. At the same that time we witness the fragmentation of products, services and consumer goods which accompany and seek to achieve the destruction of identities within consumer sectors.

Therefore, the transformation of football into a product, into business, confirms its dissociation from more totalizing domains and places it within a myriad of entertainment (and consumption) products alongside so many others (such as the diffusion of television networks and the rise in media production) available in the market. Nonetheless, a large number of the agents in the footballing world believe that this transformation will succeed in bringing football back to its place as the national sport. That is precisely the paradox of the crisis.

In conclusion, if we have tried to make these points scrupulously clear it is because we believe that it is necessary to reflect on the crisis along these new lines. If football has been associated with integration and nationalism (indeed, with Brazilian identity) for such a long time, what happens when post-modernity no longer emphasizes this but instead stresses difference and fragmentation? If football was basically a mechanism for integration, what happens when we no longer have anything to integrate? How is football to be represented in Brazilian society if it is no longer important to join together (blacks with whites, the interior with the capital, the modern with the archaic) but instead to separate (ethnic groups, religious groups, specific regional identities, neighbourhoods, condominiums)? What will be the future of Brazilian football? Will it succumb to post-modernity, thereby revealing that it belonged, in fact, to modernity and, to some extent, helped to construct this modernity in Brazil? Or will it survive, announcing that this post-modernity can never be complete because we need to live under the sign of nationality, of cultural identity, of the integration of the country as one people, one nation 'as if all of Brazil held hands in one heart'? Understanding what football will become in the twenty-first century means looking at what is, and what will be, Brazilian society in the context of a world which claims to be globalized.

NOTES

1. For example, see J. Lever, *Soccer Madness* (Chicago: University of Chicago Press, 1983); R. Da Matta (ed), *Universo do futebol: esporte e sociedade brasileira* (Rio de Janeiro: Pinakothelke, 1982); R. Helal, 'Estádios vazios, ausência de ídolos: notas sobre uma reflexão sobre a crise do futebol brasileiro', *Pesquisa de campo*, n. 0 (1994); J.S. Leite Lopes, 'A vitória do futebol que incorporou a pelada', *Revista da USP*, 22 (1994).
2. R. Da Matta, 'Antropologia do óbvio: notas em torno do significado social do futebol brasileiro', *Revista USP*, 22 (1994), 17.
3. See R. Helal, *The Brazilian Soccer Crisis as a Sociological Problem*, Ph.D. thesis, New York University, 1994, p.12.
4. For example, see R. Helal, *The Brazilian Soccer Crisis as a Sociological Problem*; M. Murad, 'Futebol e Violência no Brasil' *Pesquisa de Campo*, n. 0 (1996); L.H. Toledo, *Torcidas organizadas de futebol* (São Paulo: Autores Associados/ANPOCS, 1996). According to Helal, the intensity with which Brazilians dramatized the decline in the number of spectators was evident in news coverage which spoke of the 'collapse of football', 'the bankruptcy of clubs' and the 'end of the greatest Brazilian passion'. All these phrases are titles of news articles published in the important Brazilian football magazine *Placar*; cited in R. Helal, *Passes e impasses: futebol e cultura de massa no Brasil* (Petrópolis: Vozes, 1997), p.16.
5. Helal, *Passes e impasses: futebol e cultura de massa no Brasil*, p.18.
6. The Parliamentary Commission of Inquiry is a judicial instrument guaranteed by the Brazilian Constitution (Section VII, Article 58) which permits the legislative power, through the House of Deputies and/or the Federal Senate, to investigate items of public interest.
7. In 1987, the main clubs rebelled against the CBF and tried to organize the Brazilian League. However, since sporting legislation at the time did not consider the measure legal, a compromise was agreed between the clubs and the CBF. In 2000, due to changes in the legislation, the clubs were able to organize the tournament. This fact was seen as a possible solution to the problems afflicting Brazil's football; as with greater autonomy, the clubs would organize a more coherent tournament. Unfortunately, this was not the result.
8. H. Lovisolo, *O Globo*, 1 Oct. 2000.
9. In relation to this, but concerning the technical aspects of the game rather than its place in the national imagery, Tostão, football commentator and former player, has recently featured in Brazilian newspapers emphasizing the decline of Brazilian football on the international stage. The same idea was admitted by Wanderley Luxemburgo, Brazil's former manager, before the qualifying round of the 2002 World Cup. Both suggest that Brazil is loosing its place as the major force in world football. These declarations may be taken as further evidence that Brazilians themselves are beginning to question the claim that Brazil is the land of football.
10. R. Da Matta, 'Esporte na sociedade: um ensaio sobre o futebol brasileiro' in R. Da Matta (ed.), *Universo do Futebol*, p.21.

11. Slavery was abolished by a law passed on 13 May 1888. The military proclaimed the Republic on 15 Nov. 1889. Football began to be played in 1894.

12. Those who favoured professionalism were benefited by widespread discussions advanced by the Vargas government concerning the new labour legislation. They made full use of the political moment to establish new regulations.

13. T.S. Di Tella, 'Populism' in W. Outhwait and T. Bottomore (eds.), *The Blackwell Dictionary of Twentieth Century Social Thought* (Oxford: Blackwell, 1993).

14. See Gilberto Freyre, *The Masters and the Slaves* (New York: A.A. Knopf, 1946 [1933]); D. Pierson, *Negros in Brazil* (Chicago: University of California Press, 1942); and, more recently, J.H. Rodrigues, *Brasil e África: outro horizonte* (Rio de Janeiro: Nova Fronteira, 1980).

15. The concept of 'ethnic group' was not widespread at the time. Brazil was divided into groups according to 'race'.

16. On Mário Filho, his career and his prominent role as a major promoter of football during the 1930's–1940's, see J.S. Leite Lopes, 'A vitória do futebol que incorporou a pelada', *Revista da USP*, 22 (1994).

17. Leite Lopes, 'A vitória do futebol que incorporou a pelada', 77.

18. The Maracanã Stadium was named after Mário Filho in 1966, the year of his death.

19. See Leite Lopes, 'A vitória do futebol que incorporou a pelada'.

20. Leite Lopes, 'A vitória do futebol que incorporou a pelada'.

21. It was not by accident that writers such as Gilberto Freyre drew parallels between the Brazilian style of playing football and other cultural manifestations, such as samba and capoeira. (Mário Filho, *O Negro no futebol brasileiro* [Rio de Janeiro: Editora Civilizagão Brasileira, 1964], Preface). In this same preface, Freyre describes the history of Brazilian football as the history of 'two forces in conflict: rationality and irrationality' – football being the element which 'sublimates the irrational impulses' of our society, 'hybrid, mestizo, with Amerindian and African roots, and not only European ones'. See also C. Gordon, 'História dos Negros no futebol brasileiro', *Pesquisa de Campo*, 2 (1995).

22. See Gordon, 'História dos Negros no futebol brasileiro'. The author illustrates how characteristics thought to be typical of Brazilian football are directly associated to the representation of blacks and mestizos in our society. In the past, they were thought of as aesthetic contributions deriving from specific racial characteristics; today they are seen to be part of the contribution of a 'black culture' as conceived in a generic, diffuse manner. See also, R. Helal and C. Gordon, 'Sociologia, história e romance na construção da identidade nacional através do futebol', *Estudos Históricos*, 13, 23 (1999).

23. Filho, *O negro no futebol brasileiro*.

24. See Gordon, 'História dos Negros no futebol brasileiro'; A. Vogel, 'O momento feliz: reflexões sobre o futebol e o ethos nacional', in Da Matta, *Universo do Futebol*.

25. The so-called Sports Lottery was, in fact, a football lottery. Each week, 13 games were selected, contestants had to predict the results of all thirteen games. See Lever, *Soccer Madness*.

26. According to government census, Brazil's population at the time stood at 90 million.

27. This song is now so much part of the football world that an updated version is currently the theme accompanying football transmissions in the country's largest television network, Rede Globo.

28. The clearest evidence reported by the press was the declining turnout in football matches during the Brazilian tournament: 1971 saw an average of 20,360 spectators; 1972 saw 17,590; 1973 saw 15,460; 1974 saw 11,601. See Helal, 'Estádios vazios, ausência de ídolos: notas sobre uma reflexão sobre a crise do futebol brasileiro'.

29. On the relationship between club presidents and Brazilian politics see Lever, *Soccer Madness*.

30. The principal clubs are divided among the main urban centres. In Rio de Janeiro: Flamengo, Fluminense, Vasco da Gama and Botafogo. In São Paulo: Corinthians, Santos, Palmeiras and São Paulo. In Minas Gerais: Atlético Mineiro and Cruzeiro. In the south: Internacional and Grêmio.

31. *O Globo*, 17 Sept. 1978–22 Sept. 1978.

32. *Jornal do Brasil*, 10 July 1974.

33. *Estado de São Paulo*, 28 July 1974.

34. *Estado de São Paulo*, 25 Aug. 1974.

35. *O Globo*, 16 Feb. 1975.

36. *Visão*, 4 Aug. 1975.
37. *Estado de São Paulo*, 24 June 1976.
38. *Estado de São Paulo*, 30 Aug. 1976.
39. *Jornal do Brasil*, 10 Nov. 1976.
40. *Veja*, 10 Sept. 1978.
41. See L.H. Toledo, 'Transgressão e violência entre torcedores de futebol', *Revista USP: dossiê futebol*, 22 (1994).
42. On the theme of violence in stadiums related to the growth of the 'torcidas organizadas', see Murad, 'Futebol e Violência no Brasil'.
43. The debate concerning the relationship between television and the public has re-surfaced recently due to the high number of television sets being sold in the country and the popularization of cable television among the Brazilian middle class. In 1997, clubs began to take notice of this and to negotiate more lucrative contracts with television stations. (It should be noted that North American sports are unable to survive without television: theirs is a 'symbiotic' relationship which benefits both parties.) See Wenner, *Media, Sports & Society* (California: Sage, 1989).
44. See C. Lessa, 'Globalização e crise: alguma esperança?', *Ciência Hoje*, 27, 162 (2000).
45. This phrase was coined in 1986 by the journalist João Saldanha during an interview with R. Helal. Even then the journalist claimed that 'the current legislation is obstructing the development and the modernization of Brazilian football'.
46. The Decree number 3,199 impeded the professionalization of administrators and, at the same time, created what was then the National Council for Sports with the aim of 'guiding, fiscalising, and incentivating the practice of sports throughout the country' (Art.1). Law 6251 (1975) ratified various points from this Decree and instituted the practice of unitary voting within federations.
47. This law regulated the contracts between athletes and clubs, prohibiting the athlete from choosing which club he intends to play in.
48. In 1996, Pelé, as Extraordinary Minister of Sports, outlined another project which ratified the more 'modernizing' aspects of the 'Zico Law' and resubmitted some of the amendments which had been previously rejected by the Congress.
49. The data and analysis which follows were first noticed by R. Helal, 'The Brazilian Soccer Crisis as a Sociological Problem', Ph.D. thesis, New York University, 1994.
50. In order to develop this point we have drawn our inspiration from a recent, compelling debate about globalization and crisis in Brazil. See Lessa, 'Globalização e crise'; Otávio Velho, 'Mistura ou difereriça: Qual esperança na globalização e na crise?', *Ciência Hoje*, 166 (2000).

7

Sport in Latin America from Past to Present: A European Perspective

ROBERT CHAPPELL

Latin America is defined as, 'everything in the Western Hemisphere south of the United States.'[1] Although referring to one regional entirety in terms of socioeconomic and cultural factors, the reality of the situation is far more complex. Due to social, economic, ethnographic, cultural and environmental factors, immigration currents and natural resources, C.V. Guardia maintains that Latin America can be divided into at least five differentiated sub-regions.[2] Consequently, it is important to remember that Latin America is not a homogeneous region. There may be distinctive similarities in the problems experienced by each nation but the collection of nations contained within the collective of Latin America varies considerably in wealth, tradition, historical circumstances, ethnicity, economic development, cultural awareness and political outlook. There are common problems but no universal solutions.[3]

STANDARDS OF LIVING AND CULTURAL DIVERSITY

Standards of living in Latin America range from Venezuela's oil-financed $4,000 annual per capita gross national product to Haiti's impoverished $300.[4] Indeed, J. Coghlan, in the United Nations Educational and Cultural Organisation (UNESCO) Report entitled 'The Reduction of Disparities between Developed and Developing Countries in the field of Sport and Physical Education', claims that 'there is no such homogenous group as developing countries; virtually every country that is formally defined thus for economic reasons is different. There are wealthy developing countries and there are poor developing countries. In between in terms of wealth there is every possible situation.'[5] Most countries in Latin America, with the exception of Brazil, are described by the World Bank as lower- to middle-income developing countries. Wealth is generated in a variety of ways. Some, such as Argentina and Peru have many people employed in agriculture. Large areas of Argentina are fertile and the main agricultural products are beef, maize and wheat. Peru employs 35 per cent of the population in agriculture where the crops include beans, maize, potatoes and rice. Agriculture is also the chief activity in Bolivia where it employs 47 per cent of the population. Latin America is relatively rich in natural resources. For example, copper is the most important export in Peru and Chile; Colombia exports coal and oil and produces emeralds and gold; Bolivia has several natural resources including tin, silver and natural gas, and in Mexico and Argentina, oil and oil products are important exports.[6]

Manufacturing industries are important throughout Latin America. Factories near the northern border of Mexico assemble car parts and electrical goods for US companies; Argentina manufactures cars, electrical equipment and textiles and Chile produces processed foods, metals, iron and steel, transport equipment and textiles. In Mexico, increasing co-operation with the US and Canada led to the establishment of the North American Free Trade Association (NAFTA) on 1 January 1994.[7]

In terms of economic development Brazil is unique in Latin America; it has been described by the United Nations as a 'rapidly industrialising country'. Its total volume of production (GNP) in 1995 was $579,787 million – the eighth largest in the world. Brazil is among the world's top producers of bauxite, chrome, diamonds, gold and tin. It is also a major manufacturing country. Aircraft and cars have been the major exported products from Brazil since 1992. Chemicals, iron and steel, paper and textiles are also produced. Brazil is also one of the world's richest farming countries – 28 per cent of the population are employed in agriculture. Soya beans are the major export commodity along with bananas, citrus fruits, coffee, maize, rice, beans and sugar cane. Paper is also a major manufacturing industry.

Wealth in Latin America often resides in the hands of the few. In most cities, such as Rio de Janeiro and Sao Paulo, there are extremely cosmopolitan areas but there are also shanty towns on the edge of most conurbations. Widespread poverty amongst farmers and residents of *favelas* (city slums), together with the high inflation rate and unemployment cause political problems. Partly as a result of the shanty housing, some areas of Latin America are particularly susceptible to natural disasters. For example, up to 30,000 people died in the floods that affected Venezuela in December 1999. Entire villages along the country's Caribbean coast were washed out to sea. Many of the victims were residents of the tin-roofed shanty towns that perch precariously on mountainsides.[9] In 1998, there was a similar tragedy in Honduras when it was struck by a hurricane. Poverty inhibits the widespread growth and availability of sport.

The cultural diversity of the peoples of Latin America has resulted from a wide variety of ethnicity. For example, 85 per cent of the people in Argentina are of European ancestry; Brazil is more diverse – it is composed of 53 per cent white, 22 per cent mulatto, 12 per cent mestizo (people of mixed white and Amerindian ancestry), 11 per cent African American and one per cent Japanese. Mestizo are the dominant group in Bolivia (31 per cent), Columbia (58 per cent), Chile (92 per cent) and Mexico (60 per cent).[10] This cultural diversity has influenced the development of modern sport. In Brazil, for example, modern sport was introduced by European immigrants in the second half of the nineteenth century. The first German sports clubs were established during this period in the southern part of Brazil. The clubs grew rapidly so that by the end of the nineteenth century nearly 300 German sports clubs had been founded in the southern state of Rio Grand do Sul alone. Italian immigrants to Brazil preserved their cultural traditions and traditional sports events, especially in rural areas. The maintenance of cultural identity through sport also occurred with other ethnic groups notably Portuguese, African and Spanish. For those living in poverty in *favelas*, active participation in soccer has provided a form of special identity and a means of 'adhesion to social, political and religious associations, and group identity'.[11]

POLITICAL INSTABILITY

The politics of Latin America reflect a history of turbulence and periodic instability. A brief review of recent Latin American history illustrates this state of affairs. Only recently, in 1982, Argentina invaded the Falkland Islands. Much of Latin America became involved in one way or another. Britain regained control of the islands within a year. Argentine elections were held in 1983 and constitutional government was restored and political stability largely assured. Brazil has faced many political difficulties since the 1930s, including a military dictatorship between 1964 and 1985. Until quite recently, Bolivia was ruled by a series of civilian and military governments, which regularly violated human rights. A constitutional government was restored in 1982, but Bolivia, like Argentina a year later, then faced problems of poverty and high inflation.[12] Colombia's recent history has also been unstable; rivalries between the main political parties led to civil wars between 1949–57. This period of strife was followed by a coalition government which was superseded by a single party government in 1989. Today Colombia faces many economic problems including a large illicit drug industry run by violent dealers, which has political consequences of instability and corruption. Chile became a unique political system in 1970 when Salvador Allende became the first Communist leader to be elected democratically. He was overthrown in 1973 by the dictator General Augusto Pinochet.[13] A new Constitution was introduced in 1981 and elections were held in 1989. Peru too has also been subjected to totalitarian rule during the twentieth century; civilian rule was restored in 1980 but a left-wing group known as the Sendero Luminoso began guerrilla warfare against the government. In 1990 Alberto Fujimori became president. He suspended the constitution in 1992 but it was restored in 1993 although the president retained much individual power. Peru now faces problems in rebuilding its economy.[14]

Political instability and authoritarianism in Latin America has had an adverse affect on the development of sport. Following the *coup d'état* that overthrew the Chilean government of Salvador Allende in 1973, the new Pinochet-led junta suppressed various forms of cultural activity, including sport. In Brazil in 1970 and Argentina in 1978, 'incumbent military regimes sought to exploit the emotional and nationalistic sentiments that followed their country's victories in soccer's World Cup in order to divert attention from their own failings or to prove the capability of their own leadership'.[15] Of course, sport has been used as a part of the foreign policy of other Latin American countries, as elsewhere in the world, in order to promote the country's nationalistic feelings. This practice is ironic since:

> Latin American countries were attempting to develop nationalistic feelings … by increasing the practice of European sports. Latin American countries still set their political and cultural goals in terms of those set in Western Europe and North America. Leaders

in Latin America began to embrace European sports as visible means of developing their own national societies and displacing the cultural policies of Latin America's 'folk communities'.[16]

The hosting of international sports events is among the most visible sports policies which governments use to develop nationalism. This is, in part, because it involves improving the infrastructure such as roads, railways and air-routes and partly because it generates a feeling of national pride in being directly involved with a major international event. It has been contended that the 1968 Olympic Games was one of Mexico's best investments. The nation hosted the Olympic games in order to develop national pride, to gain political acceptance abroad, to attract foreign investment and promote tourism. These ambitions, however, were certainly harmed when there was a violent crackdown, just two weeks before the games, against students and workers who had protested about the political and economic conditions in the country.[17]

In 1950, Guatemala hosted the Central American and Caribbean Games which, 'permitted a self-style revolutionary regime to present itself at home and abroad as a competent, democratic, peace-loving nation'.[18] But this was not sufficient to prevent internal political splits which resulted in the overthrowing of the regime in 1954. It also did little for the development of sport. Argentina hosted the soccer World Cup in 1978 which, despite national aspirations, did not result in economic prosperity nor establish 'domestic, social and political tranquility'.[19] It is probably not unconnected that no Latin American country has made a successful bid to host a world sports event since 1986. There is evidence in recent Latin American history to suggest that sports competitions have exacerbated international political tensions among nations. For example, Cuba participated in the 1980 Olympic games in Moscow in an attempt to align with the USSR. Along with Soviet countries, they boycotted the 1984 Games and supported the North Korean claim to share the hosting of the 1988 Olympic games in Seoul.[20]

EARLY DEVELOPMENTS OF SPORT

In his careful and comprehensive review of the early evolution of modern sport in Latin America, J.A. Mangan has stated that for much of the nineteenth and for the early part of the twentieth century, Britain was the dominant economic foreign power in Latin America. This power declined following the First World War. By 1945, Latin America was of little significance to the British government or British business interests.[21] According to Mangan, there was a 'British Informal Empire' in Argentina between 1806 and 1914.[22] Even before the mid-1800s, British technology and culture were evident in the urban areas around the Rio de la Plato estuary.[23] There were massive British investments in shipping, banking, public services and education. The British community in Argentina was the most numerous outside of the Empire.[24] In 1914, of a registered foreign population of 2.3 million, 28,000 were Britons. This was not a particularly large number but the influence was significant. Britain displaced Spain and Portugal in order to sell industrial products and to control the commercial networks. There were only a few missionaries, a few teachers, no soldiers and no administrators among the British immigrants. Profit, not politics was the concern. Britain gained control over the economy and indirectly became the ruling power in Argentina.[25] New technologies, monopolistic structures and power imbalances gave way to general processes of cultural domination.[26] According to M. Ferro, 'with financial capital and cultural creations, modern forms of imperialism can be influential even in situations of political independence. This constitutes imperialism without colonization and has been developed in its purer form in Latin America.'[27] From the eighteenth century, Britain's role in the development of modern sport in Latin America was more important than any other nation.[28] More specifically, the English middle class were pre-eminent early international innovators of the development of modern sport, especially in Argentina. The Scots, Welsh and Irish were less involved. Therefore, there is a case for separating the role and influence of the English middle-class sporting 'imperialism' from that of Britain's other ethnic groups.[29] It should be remembered that the majority of this group had attended English public school and were undoubtedly influenced by their experiences. Further, some schools in the Latin American countries catering for the ex-patriot middle classes, at least initially, adopted the practices of the English public schools. It was the English, as mentioned above, who were particularly responsible for the initiation of developments in modern sport in Argentina. The English middle class were inspired by public school practices in which sport was perceived to have important social and moral attributes.[30] From the second half of the nineteenth century, M. Huggins maintains that, 'English middle-class sport increasingly functioned as a powerful cultural bond, moral metaphor and political symbol. The contribution of the English middle classes to the development of sport is under-valued and under-appreciated'.[31] In Argentina, the British played sport mostly for their own enjoyment but they did teach the indigenous population how to play. Some sports, such as soccer, were enthusiastically assimilated whilst others, such as cricket, were only played within the British community. British naval officers introduced cricket in 1806 in the neighbourhood of San Antonio de Areco. The first cricket club was established by English residents in 1839, the Anglo-Potemo Club at Palermo de San Benito and the Buenos Aires Club were established in the 1850s and more clubs were formed throughout the 1870s. These clubs were exclusive and generally did not welcome non-British players.[32]

After its mainly British introduction, soccer became the national game in many Latin American countries. It seduced both the masses and the middle classes. Its evolution can be reasonably well traced in Argentina.[33] It was first played there in 1867. The first organized game was played by 16 British players on the cricket field of Palermo Cricket Club. Soccer developed in British schools, social clubs, sports clubs and British companies. Its popularity increased and, by 1891, there were enough clubs to establish a league. The Argentine Football League was formed in 1893 and the first President was a Scot, Alexander Watson Hutton.[34] As far as is known, its development was much the same elsewhere in Latin America. Its popularity has been described in the following words: 'Soccer offers the people an opportunity to have fun, to enjoy themselves, to get excited, worked up, to feel intense emotions that daily routine rarely offers them'. 'Soccer is a human drama in which people see themselves and their complex existence reflected in the struggles, triumphs, failures, and pains of their daily life'.[35] Rugby Union, too, also introduced by the English middle-class public school elite, became very popular in Argentina. It was first played in 1873 although initially teams consisted of English players. The game had its ups and downs; it was banned by the Argentine government in 1875 due to excessive casualties but was re-introduced in 1886.[36] Other British sports such as polo, tennis and golf became an important part of cultural life in Argentina. Polo prospered in the farming districts and in 1854 a match between teams from Bahia and Buenos Aires took place at the Buenos Aires Polo Club.[37] British middle-class families in Buenos Aires were usually prominent members of the swimming club, the golf club (created at Hurlingham Club in 1892) and the Buenos Aires Athletic Club (which had its first meeting in 1869). Rowing first became popular in the 1860s, an English Boat Club was established in 1870 and the first regatta was held on the River Leijan in 1871. Hockey was introduced to Argentina by the English in 1905 and the first competition was organized in 1908.[38]

Thus in the particular case of Argentina, there is ample evidence of sport being introduced by the English middle class. Early modern sport in Argentina *de facto* was essentially English. The middle-class cultural influence of the English has lasted to the present day. Of course, Argentine sport has undergone a profound process of diffusion, assimilation and adaptation but its origins lie indisputably with the nineteenth-century English middle class who had such great enthusiasm for, and involvement in, sport. Of course, with the single exception of soccer, there were variations in the enthusiasm shown for different sports between Latin American countries. English schools became agents of cultural transmission which spread the Games Cult throughout Argentina and other countries of Latin America.[39]

THE EUROPEAN INFLUENCE

Other European nations also played their part in the spread of European sport. As Spanish immigration to Latin America increased in the second half of the twentieth century, Basque-based sports such as *pelatto* became popular. A combination of indigenous and Spanish games and pastimes were played in Chile. As in Argentina and Brazil, animal-based sports were popular – these included rodeo, horse-racing, jousting, bullfighting and cockfighting. The indigenous activities included *Araucanian chueca* (which is similar to field hockey) and various other ball games. In Mexico and Peru, bullfighting remained popular throughout the nineteenth century although it was later perceived to be brutal and corrupt. Despite this change in attitude, 'the festival of the bulls retained a place in both popular and elite culture'.[40] Sports of European origin were common but geographical isolation and the lack of institutional control over the population resulted in indigenous activities continuing and surviving. In the late nineteenth century, cycling became popular in Mexico, Brazil, Colombia, Argentina, and Uruguay partly due to the desire to imitate European sport but partly due to the sport's connection with 'technology, fitness, precision in measuring time and distance and commercialisation'.[41]

In part due to the desire to imitate the British, the most powerful people in the world at the time, the Argentines and the Uruguayans organized clubs based on the British models. By 1900, cities such as Buenos Aires and Montevideo organized sports competitions among national populations, resident foreign communities and visiting European athletes.[42] As the Argentines adapted European economic and social values, the sports of the *pampean* society gradually decreased in popularity.[43] Similar processes of diffusion are seen in the case of baseball in Yucatan, Mexico which was introduced via Cuba in the 1890s[44] (but that is part of the Americanization of Latin American sport and is dealt with elsewhere in this volume); in the case of soccer in Paraguay which was introduced by a Dutch physical education teacher in 1900, initially played in the capital Asuncian and later in other parts of the country; and in the case of boxing in Chile which was introduced in the late nineteenth century by British sailors through the cities of Valpariso and Santiago.

During the first part of the nineteenth century, popular European sports spread throughout Latin America mainly from ports and capital cities. Imported sports began as amateur activities within the elite sections of the population but gradually became popular among the masses. Some amateur sports became professionalized and, in time, all sports became institutionalized, commercialized and technologically-based. Northern European urban team games did not win total control of Latin American sport. Bullfighting has continued to be popular in Mexico, Peru, and Venezuela. In some areas there has been resistance to the modernization of some sports. However, modern bullfighting takes place in large stadiums with large crowds. The intense media coverage reflects its popularity with the general population. Argentina's reputation for superior horsemanship is reflected in the games of polo and *pato*. These games are 'stylised versions of long established games which perpetuate rural equine traditions'.[45]

So now that we have dealt with the past and the European heritage, what of the present European influences? European models serve as exemplars for Latin America but are adapted to local conditions. There is an ongoing debate in many developing countries as to whether priority should be given to developing sport for the masses or sport for elite performers. These objectives are not mutually exclusive but where resources are scarce, choices have to be made. Cuba is one of the few countries in Latin America that has made progress in both areas. Sport in Cuba is controlled by the Instituto Nacional Deportes Education Fisica Recreation (INDER) which was established in 1961 and is still affiliated to central government. This model owes much to the former Soviet Union. It allows central government to fund athletes and to operate talent discovery programmes. To stimulate participation and discover talent, INDER organized physical tests called *Listos Para Vencer* (LPV, Ready to Win). A scheme entitled 'The Plan of the Mountains' was established in 1963 to encourage sports participation in rural areas. The scheme developed simple facilities to encourage the playing of football, baseball, basketball and volleyball – sports which do not require expensive facilities or equipment. INDER-MINED was launched in 1964 by President Fidel Castro in order to provide more qualified coaches. The scheme ensured that every elementary school had a qualified physical education teacher. Another plan to encourage participation in sport was the 'Plan of the Streets' launched in 1966, in which children were encouraged to play organized sport in the streets every Sunday morning. The 'Plan of the Mountains', INDER-MINED and the 'Plan of the Streets' were, and are, all aimed at providing 'sport for all'.

Young elite performers are sent to the Escuales d'Iniciacion Deportia Escolar (EIDE, Schools for the Initiation into Scholastic Sport), and those students with the most potential graduate to one of Cuba's Escuales Superior Perfeccion Athletisme (ESPA, Superior Schools of Athletic Perfection) where they remain until the age of 19. Top athletes can then transfer to the National Training Centre in Havana known as the Cuidad Deportivo which also serves as the headquarters of INDER. It is at the Cuidad Deportivo that the best athletes are given the necessary attention and highly specialist coaching so that they may represent Cuba internationally. The organization of sport in Cuba is based on the political ideology. Griffiths quite rightly comments that 'Cuba's success in the development of sport has to be located in the social context in which they occur'.[46] Sport in Cuba is bound up with politics, reflecting and maintaining the prevailing ideology under the one political party, the Partido Comunista Cuba (PCC).[47]

The ideology of sports participation in Nicaragua is similar to that of Cuba. Resources are limited and therefore success in international sport is rare. The government recognize that sport can be reformed and promoted in order to achieve revolutionary political ends. Some suggest that the new sports programmes in Cuba and Nicaragua are elitist and sexist[48] but recent research[49] would indicate that this is certainly not the case in Cuba. Whatever the revolutionary political impulse, it is clear that the Cubans and, at times, the Argentine, Brazilian and Chilean military have manipulated sport for political purposes that help to maintain the government in power and exclude alternate systems. Evidence certainly suggests that sport in Latin America has existed as a cultural form of power struggle. Cuba has witnessed the decline of indigenous activities and the introduction of sports institutions by Europeans and Americans.

MODERN SPORT IN LATIN AMERICA

The legacies of European and North American influences co-exist in modern Latin America. Today, soccer is the most popular sport for both participants and spectators. Latin America has hosted the soccer World Cup on several occasions (in Argentina, Brazil, Chile and Mexico) and Mexico hosted the Olympic Games in 1968. In Argentina, rugby is played at club and international level. The Argentine 'Pumas' regularly compete in the final stages of the rugby World Cup and occasionally beat supposedly superior teams in 'friendly' internationals. Among the Argentine wealthy elite, polo, sailing, golf and hockey are popular. Polo reflects Argentina's reputation for superior horsemanship and highlights the grassy pampa as a unique feature in the country. In Mexico, baseball competes with soccer as the most popular sport; is also a very popular activity in the Dominican Republic, Mexico and, to a lesser extent, in Venezuela. Argentina has produced some fine professional boxers who use the sport 'as a means of escape from poverty'.[50] Basketball and volleyball are now played throughout Latin America; Brazil is an international basketball force and the Brazilian women are considered to be amongst the best volleyball players in the world (although the Peruvian women's team won the silver medal at the 1988 Olympic Games). The Brazilian wealthy elite have also produced champions in motor racing, sailing, tennis and show jumping.

Both Argentina and Brazil have produced some outstanding tennis players. In Anglo-Caribbean areas, cricket is the most popular sport, although the 1990s have witnessed the gradual erosion of the former pre-eminence of the West Indian cricket team as the best team in the

TABLE 1
MEDALS WON BY LATIN AMERICAN COUNTRIES
IN THE 2000 OLYMPIC GAMES

Position	Country	Gold	Silver	Bronze	Total
9th	Cuba	11	11	7	29
39th	Mexico	1	2	3	6
50th	Colombia	1	0	0	1
52nd	Brazil	0	6	6	12
57th	Argentina	0	2	2	4
65th	Uruguay	0	1	0	1
72nd	Chile	0	0	1	1
(1st	USA	39	25	33	97)

world. This may be in part due to the popularization of basketball. Poor black people, especially in Trinidad and Tobago,[51] are enthused by watching games on local television from the United States (National Basketball Association).[52]

Countries in Latin America have tried to expand their domestic sports facilities and institutions to promote sport. For example, the National Sports Games in Quito, Ecuador in November 1974 were held in an attempt to stimulate friendship and build national unity among all Ecuadorians. A sports festival held in Mexico in 1941 entitled 'Juegos Deportivos Nacionales de la Revolucion' included several traditional games and national dances and was, for the same reasons, an attempt to promote an appreciation of Mexico's cultural heritage in the search of a distinct identity.[53] Such events are established to engender prestige and develop pride among the population, however, some commentators have argued that 'Latin Americans often lack an adequate and necessary "sporting mentality" to produce high level athletes'.[54] Further, K. Heinemann maintains that 'financial factors lead to a lack of opportunity, and therefore success at international sport is most improbable in Latin America'.[55] At a non-professional level, the lack of administrative and financial support in Latin America has limited the development of some sports. Some countries have good sports facilities and are able to host major international sports events such as the Olympic Games, the soccer World Cup, the VI Central American and Caribbean Games (Guatemala, 1950), and the Junior IAAF Athletics Championships (Santiago, Chile, 2000). In Latin America, there are an excessive number of stadia for soccer but some countries do not have good, or even fair, facilities across the full range of international sports.

Marked economic and social disparities have limited access to both sports events and facilities. Bolivia, Peru, Ecuador and Paraguay have extremely poor facilities for any sport other than football. The greater proportion of the nations' wealth is concentrated on a relatively small number of people and regions. Recent studies in the city of Porte Alegre, Brazil, for example, highlight critical issues regarding sports participation in metropolitan areas. The findings suggest that sports participation does not rank high on the social agenda when it is in competition with other problems such as education, transport and housing.[56] In consequence, in an increasingly urbanized environment there is a growing lack of space and facilities for organized sport which deprives many people of the opportunity to participate.

Furthermore, in some huge cities such as São Paulo, Brazil, there is a growing problem of crime and violence. In Mexico City, over a third of the population live in dwellings without running water and nearly a quarter of buildings lack the facility to dispose of sewerage. The shanty towns are occupied by recent migrants and families from rural areas, or by families displaced by urban renewal and highway construction. In the poorest sections of Latin American society, the basic needs of food, housing, clothing and education are lacking.[57] It is therefore hardly surprising that this significant percentage of the Latin American population (in all countries except Argentina, Uruguay and Costa Rica) do not have access to, or indeed time for, sports facilities. They are more concerned with survival. Paradoxically, a reverse trend of urban to rural migration is beginning among young Latin American professionals and early retirees. This is creating a demand for luxury facilities such as gymnasiums, health clubs, golf courses and tennis clubs in semi-rural and small resort areas.

A number of international organizations, such as the International Labour Sports Confederation (CSIT) at its seminar in June 1999 in Jyväskylä, Finland, stressed the need for participation in sport as a basic human right. This sentiment re-iterated the International Charter of Physical Education and Sport as was issued by the United Nations Educational and Scientific Organisation (UNESCO) in 1978. Article 1 of the Charter stated, 'Every human being has a fundamental right to access to physical education and sport which are essential for the development of his [*sic*] personality. The freedom to develop physical, intellectual and moral powers through physical education and sport must be guaranteed within the educational system and in other aspects of social life'.[58] According to the Charter, there should be an equal opportunity to participate in sport regardless of sex, age, race or financial status. Participation in sport in Latin America needs to be integrated into the social policies of all the constituent countries. Participation in sport must be seen as part of the total education process in Latin America. The associated benefits of participation such as the development of teamwork, loyalty and the maintenance of health and hygiene are of great importance.[59] Another important consideration is the potential foreign investment that a successful sports programme or positive sports image can attract.

PRESENT EUROPEAN AND NORTH AMERICAN INFLUENCES

J. Coghlan[60] quite rightly said that 'children are children the world over, so they will play and demand activity, they will run, chase, kick anything and throw anything'. The task of the providers in Latin America is to harness and develop their energy by providing facilities, safe environments and qualified coaches. Unfortunately in some cases there is a deficiency in the provision of facilities which is exacerbated by problems of maintenance. The demise of physical education, for example, was addressed at the World Summit on Physical Education in Berlin in November 1999 and has been the subject of much research.[61] The final document of the Summit served as an official working document for the 3rd International Conference of Ministers and Senior Officials responsible for Sport and Physical Activity (MINEPS III) organized by the United Nations Educational Scientific and Cultural Organisation (UNESCO) in Uruguay, in December 1999. The low status of physical education in relation to academic subjects and the difference between official government policy and school practice appears to be a problem in Latin America. Statements of objectives are not always implemented. According to Guardia,[62] for example, as a result of socioeconomic and cultural reasons, only a limited number of the school age population are actually in school during the required years. A lack of involvement in physical activity is aggravated by the fact that a large number of children have to leave school during the first years of education to support the family financially. Consequently, physical activity is informal rather than formal. Several countries in Latin America have changed their school schedule so that students attend school for only half a day. This has affected opportunities for physical education and sport at school because as the school day is so short, academic subjects take priority over sport. Physical education, if it exists at all, is very much a subsidiary subject in state schools. It is rare to find institutions with good sports programmes except in expensive private schools and private universities. It is therefore unsurprising that Guardia maintains that the population of Latin America does not realize the importance of physical activity to the life of individuals.

All Latin American countries have some provision for teacher training. In rural areas, however, the training is of the informal variety and consists of the would-be-teacher observing lessons and practising directly with the children. There is no training in educational theory. In wealthy urban areas, teacher training institutes are advanced, sophisticated and highly technologized. Most formally trained physical education teachers instruct at secondary level as they are better paid; there are therefore insufficient teachers at elementary level. Most of their efforts are directed at coaching teams in sports such as soccer, volleyball, basketball, swimming and tennis. More recently there have been indications of an understanding of the importance of physical activity in the well-being of the people. However, increased involvement will only be achieved by training more teachers and improving facilities. Under the Constitution (Article 217), all Brazilians have the right to take part in sport and the government is responsible for educational and leisure sports. Physical education comes under the jurisdiction of the Ministry of Education. There are a number of governmental programmes for sport run by the Instituto Nacional de Desenvolvimento de Desorto (INDESP). These are 'Sport for All' programmes and include approximately 160,000 children from poor communities.[63] Brazilian provision for sport is slowly developing in the states of the east and south but remains very poor in the states of the north, north-east and mid-west.[64] Facilities in other parts of Latin America are variable in both quantity and quality.

There are many examples of positively implemented programmes and good practices in Latin America. Unfortunately, in many countries, such as Brazil considered above, the statutory requirements are in place but the actual implementation does not meet obligations and expectations. Financial constraints, inadequate resources and the limited number of teachers result in the gap between statutory policy and the implementation of programmes. As J. Arbena maintains, 'those who control the allocation of necessary funds just have not desired to make a long term commitment in that area'.[65] The matter of implementing sports programmes was discussed during the 'Regional Forum on Physical Activity and Sport' in Mexico in 1994 as preparation for the World Forum held in Quebec, Canada in 1995.[66] Recommendations made at the Forum included promoting 'the cause of physical education world-wide in a sense of shared and mutually beneficial interests'.[67]

A model sports programme is commendable but all of the governments in Latin America must demonstrate the political will to improve programmes as a basic need. A preliminary undertaking would be for governments to guarantee physical education lessons in schools. If traditions of physical activity were further developed in schools, children would then be better disposed to take part in sports activities in the post-school situation. The importance of sport and organized post-school activities in relation to the resultant health and well-being of the community cannot be over emphasized. Sport would have important implications on health, would improve the quality of life and would develop a broad range of participation from which elite athletes might develop.

Research in sport sciences in now undertaken at a number of universities in Latin America and at the Centre of Research Laboratory of Vocation Physical Ability of São Castano do Sul (CELAFISCS) in Brazil. CELAFISCS has also initiated a programme entitled 'Agita São Paulo', considered to be one of the best programmes initiating physical activity in the world as it involves one million participants in the state of São Paulo, Brazil. Such initiatives at regional, national and international level should provide powerful lobbying groups for the cause of sport. Unfortunately, a substantial portion of the research conducted in Europe and North America does not reach Latin America. This is mainly due to the lack of financial resources that make it difficult to maintain proper libraries or to participate at international sports conferences. Despite some institutional and individual attempts to establish international dialogues, substantial links are lacking. Financial constraints have also resulted in a lack of postgraduate study programmes. For example, the first Brazilian doctoral programmes in scientific research began in 1989. Presently, there are 13 master's courses and four doctoral programmes offered in departments of physical education and sport in Brazil. Until recently, most Latin American academic personnel received their formal training abroad, usually in North America or Europe.[68]

Several international organizations are involved in the development of sport in Latin America. For example, the Fédération Internationale d'Education Physique (FIEP) organizes many courses and conferences throughout the region. The International Council for Sports Science and Physical Education (ICSSPE) has a strong presence in Latin America due to the work of Dr Victor Matsudo, the co-ordinator of its Working Group on Developing Countries. Thus, North America and Europe continue to extend their influence on certain aspects of modern sport as they did in the past.

PRESENT INTERNATIONAL INVOLVEMENT

The countries of Latin America vary widely and, they are all special cases. It would be convenient to be able to devise a master plan to develop sport and seek its implementation through such organizations as the International Olympic Committee (IOC), International Federations or through bi-lateral agreements. Such an enormous task would need to be co-ordinated as a rolling programme and amended as it unfolded. In order that the quality of sport be improved, both governmental and non-governmental aid needs to be expanded.[69] Importance should be attached to organizations such as CELAFISCS since they understand the local conditions and what steps need to be taken in order to improve the situation. In order to make greater strides to promote physical activity, a number of collaborative initiatives should be considered. According to K. Hardman,[70] these should be initiated by an international body and composed of representatives from world agencies such as ICSSPE, FIEP and others. This lobby should include medical and related associations in order that the health benefits of a lifelong involvement in sport may be encouraged.

The UNESCO 'International Commission on Education for the 21st Century' provides a potential vehicle for promoting sport in the future. In 1997, the General Assembly of the United Nations proclaimed the year 2000 the 'International Year for the Culture of Peace'. It is anticipated that under its guidance, organizations will be able to develop grass roots activity programmes throughout the world, thus stressing the importance of sport in the lifecycle of all individuals. It is essential that developed countries do not overwhelm the Latin American nations; support for sport should only be granted if it is requested by the host country. There is a need for partnership if there is to be co-operation. Developing counties that wish to co-operate must exhibit the will to promote sport and physical education. Individual statements are not enough; there needs to be a clear continuation of government policy; there must be a 'shopping list' of needs and priorities; the policy development must embrace 'Sport for All' as well as sport for the elite and indicate commitment to the long term. In the past, Europe and North America have greatly influenced the early development of modern sport in Latin America. In the future there will be a pressing need for the international community to shoulder responsibility to ensure that the masses of Latin America are able to enjoy the sports of modern world. The twenty-first century has a role for the powerful and privileged continents of Europe and North America which is arguably just as significant as that of the nineteenth century.

CONCLUSION

An historical analysis of the evolution of sport in Latin America reveals the role of Europeans in the early establishment of modern sports. More specifically, evidence suggests that Britain's role in the development of modern sport in Latin America has been, since the eighteenth century, more significant than that of any other nation. The English rather than the Scots, Irish or Welsh were pre-eminent innovators of sport, especially in Argentina. The English became the agents of cultural transmission that spread the English Games Cult, developed by the public schools, throughout Latin America. Sport has undergone a process of diffusion, assimilation and adaptation but recent historical evidence suggests that its origins lie with the nineteenth century, English middle-class enthusiasm for sport. The later evolution of sport saw the increasing influence of North America which, as already mentioned, is the subject of another chapter in this volume.

The further development of sport in Latin America is hindered by a number of significant problems. The World Bank defines all of the countries of Latin America as developing countries. This means that the standard of living is not high and a significant proportion of the population live in poor housing. Sport is not a high priority and, in any case, the rapidly growing cities limit suitable facilities. Some Latin American countries boast good facilities but others do not even have fair facilities across a full range of sports. If sport is to be popularized, it needs to be seen as a basic need which has a beneficial effect on the lives of individuals. Assistance from international sports federations should be sought as appropriate in order to produce more qualified sports personnel.

It is clear that many governments in Latin America are eager to promote sport for the masses but that the problems they face are immense and, in some cases, overwhelming. Governments and international organizations in the developed world should offer assistance but they must be aware that real problems will result if the West sets the agenda. The reality of the situation in Latin America is complex and may not be appreciated by 'outsiders'. It is extremely difficult to offer advice from afar but any civilized developed society has a moral obligation to make suggestions and offer financial help where appropriate so that the provision of sport in Latin America is improved. The influence of Europe and North America, directly or indirectly, is far from over.

ACKNOWLEDGEMENT

While the ideas and arguments are wholly mine, I would like to thank Professor J.A. Mangan of Strathclyde University for his continued assistance in preparing this chapter for publication.

NOTES

1. J.L. Arbena, 'Sport and Social Change in Latin America' in Alan Ingham and John Loy (eds.), *Sport in Social Development: Traditions, Transitions and Transformations* (Champaign, IL: Human Kinetics, 1993), p.97.
2. C.V. Guardia, 'Physical Education in Latin America and the Caribbean', *ICSSPE Bulletin*, 19 (1995), 18–19.
3. J. Lillis, 'Assessment of Needs in Physical Education and Sport in Africa and Proposals for Implementation of the First International Conference of Ministers and Senior Officials Responsible for Physical Education and Sport in the Education of Youth', UNESCO.
4. Arbena, 'Sport and Social Change', 97. Venezuela's GNP is distorted by income from petroleum. Venezuela is a poor country. Agriculture is the primary activity. The average standard of living is far lower than is Argentina, Uruguay and Chile.
5. J. Coghlan, *The Reduction in Current Disparities between Developed and Developing Countries in the Field of Sport and Physical Education* (London: UNESCO, 1986).
6. The Royal Geographical Society, *World Atlas and Gazetteer* (London: George Philips Ltd, 1998).
7. Ibid., pp.2–48.
8. Ibid., p.6.
9. *Times*, 20 Dec. 1999, 13.
10. The Royal Geographical Society, *World Atlas and Gazetteer*, pp.2–48.
11. L.P. DaCosta, 'The State versus Free Enterprise in Sports Policy: The Case of Brazil' in L. Chalip, A. Johnson and L. Strachura (eds.), *National Sports Policies: An International Handbook* (London: Greenwood Press, 1996), p.25.

12. The Royal Geographical Society, *World Atlas and Gazetteer*, p.5.
13. In September 1998, General Augusto Pinochet arrived in Britain intending to receive surgery. On 16 October, the Spanish authorities requested his extradition to Spain on charges of murder and torture alleged to have taken place during his 17-year rule over Chile. On 11 January 2000, the British Home Secretary Jack Straw decided to allow Pinochet to return to Chile. The Home Office concluded that he was physically unfit to stand trial. This decision was welcomed by the Pinochet's supporters but condemned by human rights campaigners – see *Times*, 12 Jan. 2000. On 1 December 2000, General Pinochet was placed under house arrest in Chile. He was charged with ordering the kidnapping and execution of 75 political prisoners – see *Times*, 1 Dec. 2000.
14. The Royal Geographical Association, *World Atlas and Gazetteer*, p.10.
15. Arbena, 'Sport and Social Change', 110.
16. J.L. Arbena, 'Nationalism and Sport in Latin America, 1850–1990: The Paradox of Promoting and Performing 'European' Sports', *International Journal of the History of Sport*, 12 (1995), 220–38.
17. Ibid., 227.
18. Ibid.
19. Ibid.
20. Ibid., 230.
21. J.A. Mangan, 'The Early Evolution of Modern Sport in Latin America: A Mainly English Middle-Class Inspiration', Paper presented at the Seventh Brazilian Conference of the History of Sport, Physical Education, Leisure and Dance, Porto Alegre: 29 May–1 June 2000, 1–70.
22. Ibid., 23. See J.A. Mangan (ed.), *The Cultural Bond: Sport, Empire, Society* (London and Portland, OR: Frank Cass, 1992).
23. Ibid., p.18.
24. A. Graham-Yooll, *The Forgotten Colony* (London: Hutchinson, 1981).
25. M. Ferro, *Colonisation: A Global History* (London: Routledge, 1997), p.345. See A. Hennessy and J. King (eds.), *The Land that England Lost* (London: British Academic Press, 1992).
26. Mangan, 'The Early Evolution', 4.
27. M. Ferro, *Colonisation, A Global History* (London: Routledge, 1997), p.9.
28. A. Guttman, *Games and Empires: Modern Sports and Cultural Imperialism* (New York: Columbia University Press, 1994), p.2.
29. Mangan, 'The Early Evolution', 28. See J.A. Mangan, *Athleticism in the Victorian and Edwardian Public School: The Emergence and Consolidation of an Educational Ideology* (London and Portland, OR: Frank Cass, 2000).
30. Ibid.
31. M. Huggins, 'Second Class Citizens? English Middle Class Culture and Sport 1850–1910: A Reconsideration', *International Journal of the History of Sport*, 17, 2 (2000), 1.
32. Mangan, 'The Early Evolution', p.30.
33. See the essay by Vic Duke and Liz Crolley in this volume, pp.93–116.
34. Ibid.
35. J. Arbena, 'Meaning and Joy in Latin American Sports', *International Review for the Sociology of Sport*, 35, 1 (2000), 88–9. The first national association, the Argentine Football Association retained English as its official language until 1906. In 1934 a new and definitive association was created and Spanish became the official language. Between 1900 and 1930, English clubs such as Southampton, Nottingham Forest, Everton and Chelsea visited Argentina to play football.
36. Mangan, 'The Early Evolution', 30.
37. Ibid., 35.
38. Ibid., 47.
39. Ibid., 50. See Mangan, 'The Early Evolution' on the role of St. Georges College, Buenos

Aires, in the encouragement of playing sport.
40. Arbena, 'Sport and Social Change', 102.
41. Ibid., p.103. See William Beezley, 'Bicycles, Modernisation, and Mexico' in J. Arbena (ed.), *Sport and Society in Latin America* (Westport: Greenwood Press, 1988), pp.15–28. Colombia has had excellent results in the Tour de France and other major cycling events in recent years.
42. Arbena, 'Sport and Social Change', 104.
43. Ibid.
44. Ibid. See G.M. Joseph, 'Forging the Regional Pastime: Baseball and Class in Yucatan' in J. Arbena (ed.), *Sport and Society in Latin America* (Westport: Greenwood Press, 1988), pp.29–61.
45. Arbena, 'Sport and Social Change', 108.
46. J. Griffiths and P. Griffiths, *Cuba: The Second Decade* (London: Writers and Redeemers Books, 1979).
47. R. Chappell, 'The Soviet Protégé: Cuba, Modern Sport and Communist Comrades', *European Sports History Review*, 3 (2001), 181–204.
48. Arbena, 'Sport and Social Change', 110
49. Chappell, 'The Soviet Protégé', 181–204.
50. Arbena, 'Sport and Social Change', 107.
51. J.R. Mandle and J.D. Mandle, *Caribbean Hoops: The Development of West Indian Basketball* (New York: Gordon and Breach, 1995).
52. M. Malec, *The Social Roles of Sport in Caribbean Societies* (New York: Gordon and Breach, 1995).
53. Arbena, 'Nationalism and Sport in Latin America', 229.
54. Ibid., 224.
55. E. Dunning, J. Maguire and R. Pearton (eds.), *The Sports Process, A Comparative and Developmental Approach* (Champaign, IL: Human Kinetics, 1996), p.149.
56. A. Reppold, 'A Comparative Analysis of the Future of Sport and the Olympic Movement: South America', Paper presented at the British Olympic Association Conference, Loughborough: 19 March 1997.
57. H. Digel, *Sport in a Changing Society: Sociological Essays* (Schorndorf: Meyer and Meyer, 1995).
58. UNESCO, *International Charter for Physical Education and Sport* (New York: UNESCO, 1978).
59. V. Matsudo, 'Physical Activity Patterns among Young Adults in a Developing Country', Paper presented at the International Congress on Sport Science, Sports Medicine and Physical Education, Brisbane: 7–12 Sept. 2000.
60. J. Coghlan, 'Physical Education needs in Africa', *FIEP Bulletin*, 51 (1981), 28–31.
61. K. Hardman, 'The Fall and Rise of Physical Education in International Context', Paper presented at the Pre-Olympic and International Scientific Conference, Malaga: 1–14 July 1996; K. Hardman, 'School Physical Education: Current Plight and Future Directions in International Context', Paper presented at the 11th Commonwealth and International Scientific Conference, Kuala Lumpur: 3–8 Sept. 1998; K. Hardman, 'Threats to Physical Education! Threats to Sport for All', Paper presented at the VII Congress 'Sport for All', Barcelona: 19–22 Nov. 1998.
62. C.V Guardia, 'Physical Education in Latin America and the Caribbean', *ICSSPE Bulletin*, 19 (Fall 1995), 18–19.
63. M. Tubino, 'Sport and Physical Education in Brazil', *ICSSPE Bulletin*, 27 (Sept. 1999), 50. See J.A. Mangan and V. De Melo, 'A Web of the Wealthy: Modern Sport in the Nineteenth Century Culture of Rio de Janeiro', *International Journal of the History of Sport*, 14, 3 (1997), 168–73.
64. DaCosta, 'The State Versus Free Enterprise in Sport Policy: The Case of Brazil', 23–37.
65. Arbena, 'Sport and Social Change', p.154.

66. C.V. Guardia, 'Physical Education in Latin America and the Caribbean', *ICSSPE Bulletin*, 19 (Sept. 1995), 18–19.
67. Hardman, 'The Rise and Fall of Physical Education'.
68. Reppold, 'A Comparative Analysis'.
69. J. Coghlan, *The Reduction in Current Disparities between Developed and Developing Countries in the Field of Sport and Physical Education* (London: UNESCO, 1986).
70. Hardman, 'The Fall and Rise of Physical Education'.

Hegemony, Emancipation and Mythology

LAMARTINE P. DaCOSTA

'Where are the blacks?' That was the pointed question asked by Allen Guttmann after watching a video of a 'Sport for All' activity organized in Sorocaba, Brazil. The question came during a presentation I gave at the Congress of 1995 to commemorate the seventy-fifth anniversary of the German Sport University in Cologne. On that occasion Guttmann and myself were among the speakers charged with reporting on the image of sport on different continents.[1]

The simple and direct question summarized, at least for me, the prejudice characteristic of some scholars in the more developed world regarding the alleged elitism of sport in many lesser developed countries outside Europe, USA, Canada, Australia and Japan. Guttmann sought to highlight the absence of the unprivileged – either because of racial prejudice or because of disadvantage – in recreational and competitive sport. In the view of such commentators, sport in South America, in Africa and in most of Asia, is a middle-class pastime or, occasionally, the activity of talented individuals from the working class.

My reply drew Guttmann's attention to the social context of the region in which the recreational event took place. The economic prosperity of the region was close to average for the developed world. 'Sport for All' activities had begun here in the 1960s, before the subsequent European movement. Since these pioneering Brazilian initiatives, the promotion of sport in Sorocaba had concentrated on those economically-disadvantaged groups with most acute need for recreational opportunities.

In reality, the limited participation of the Afro-Brazilian was due more to the nature of the local population than to any demonstration of racial discrimination. Although Brazil is a patchwork of ethnic groups, most of the population is of European descent. Portuguese, Spanish and

Italians add up to 27 million and Germans to 9 million. There are also 9 million Lebanese, 2 million Japanese and a number of descendants of other nationalities. Brazil has more poor whites than any other multiracial nation. Blacks constitute a minority. Over the years, the intermingling of blacks with other ethnic groups has produced numbers that equal half of Brazil's 170 million population.

So in the case of Sorocaba, Guttmann's question was irrelevant. Sorocaba was a very particular situation but it could have relevance for the whole of Brazil. Brazilian society has certainly evolved in stages similar to those typical of the recent South African apartheid or of the Black and Latin ghettos of the United States. The result has been general upheavals, protests and public demonstrations. Latin American countries, Brazil included, have been noted for their violence and racial prejudice as results of historical social inequality. However, racial injustice has produced a number of social changes that have contributed to a new social re-configuration of an entire continent. Clearly some international scholars are insufficiently aware of the current situation that illustrates steady improvement in the lot of the disadvantaged.

Nevertheless, it is true to say that ethnicity is one of the keys to understanding the development of sport in Brazil and indeed in most of Latin America. Racial prejudice in Brazil is still practised through covert exclusion. This process is more difficult to deal with than the overt exclusion that took place in South Africa and still takes place in the United States. It is for this reason that Guttmann's question would never be asked by a Brazilian scholar. In Brazil, the myth of racial democracy has been promulgated and subtly promoted as a national reality but it has also had to co-exist with an elitism that is reinforced by the slogan 'black people know their place'. Myth is one thing; reality is another.

DEVELOPMENT BIAS

Helmut Digel gave a presentation on the 'Modernization of Co-operation in Sport' at the same Congress of 1995. According to Digel, a comparative analysis of the most advanced countries reveals 'modernization as a set of desirable values' and a model for the development of sport in economically-disadvantaged countries and cultures. As a result, Digel proposes that this group of nations should adopt a policy of 'specific rationality' to develop sport through the natural sciences.[2] This proposition reflects a high degree of prejudice in relation to the development of sport in developing countries. It fails to take into account cultural traditions, practices and beliefs, amenities, facilities and incomes. In other words, Digel postulated the existence of a direct relation between industrialization and the development of sport. This assumption earned my personal criticism expressed below, as I phrased it to the Congress:

> The 'six theses on sport development' presented by Digel refer more to problem-solving mechanisms than to values which relate to aspirations and needs. What is missing in Digel's proposal is a vision of the relevance of his mechanistic view for economically disadvantaged cultures and their communities. I suggest giving as much credit to social sciences as to hard sciences. Instead of struggling to adapt managerial tools to this technological world in flux I propose to bring so-called 'sports development' into a sharp and different focus, namely, the context defined by cultural relativism.[3]

Pluralism of perspective is required. Cultural relativism has often stood as a healthy counterpoint to absolutist approaches in sport, which claim to account for the expansion and development of sport as a result of the growing rationalization of industrialized societies. Guttmann has become one of the most quoted authors whenever theoretical consistency is brought to any discussion about the modernization of sport. Digel's thesis overlaps with Guttmann's, thus it is not surprising that both Guttmann and Digel interpret sport which takes place in less developed countries according to data which do not fit the actual reality. Both dismiss too readily cultural background especially in terms of Latin America. Guttmann's public rejection of an activity supposedly practised only by the happy few as he saw it in Brazil and Digel's determinist attitude toward the requisites to be complied with in order to ensure sport's success leave much to be desired. Both claim that the modernization of elite sport is a universal manifestation.

EMANCIPATION

The approaches of Guttmann and Digel have been mentioned here as examples of current tendencies. However, misleading interpretations of sport in alien cultural settings are commonplace, even among commentators in *Sport in Latin American Society*. It is possible to consider the Latin American development of modern sport from another viewpoint. The approach I propose considers the development of sport as a result of the reaction against poverty and other social constraints. I use emancipation, as opposed to rationality, as an analytical concept although both approaches are not mutually exclusive. My proposed model includes the following premises: that the growth and development of sport were a means of social emancipation throughout Latin America and that rationality has only appeared, and appears, in specific areas. In addition, I argue that the suggested universality of Guttmann's model has not yet been put to the test in the context of Latin America only because the history of sport in Latin America is not widely investigated. The sparse literature that does exist focuses mostly on Brazil which, in terms of population and income, represents half of South America. Brazil shares ethnical and cultural features with Uruguay, Argentina and Chile in the south and with Venezuela, Colombia and Peru in the north. Moreover, cultural patterns of north-eastern Brazil are similar to those of Mexico and Central America while the strip of land between Bahia and Rio de Janeiro shares features in common with the Caribbean. In short, Brazil is a fascinating analytical mix with an attraction all its own.

EMANCIPATION V. HEGEMONY

J. Arbena's approach to 'The Later Evolution of Modern Sport in Latin America' has several characteristics in common with Guttmann's theory of modernization. It is possible to understand Arbena's approach through the attention he gives to the importance of the development of sport in England and to the later Anglo–American re-inventions but also through the priority he attributes to power relations and political manoeuvrings.

In his most recent writing, Arbena has examined the paradox that exists in the reinforcement of Latin American nationalism through the utilization of English sport.[4] He has also studied the predominance of modern sport over indigenous cultural manifestations of the societies that share the Latin American continent.[5] In the case of Latin America, while Arbena does not consider sport as 'a major battleground on which the hegemonic culture has struggled against residual or emergent deviations', he does consider it to be one of the most obvious repercussions of such disputes.[6] Arbena agrees with the classical view that identifies sport as a product of both emancipation and hegemony and favours the idea of social confrontation once sport is 'a mechanism by which the hegemonic sectors, consciously or not, manipulate the factors of production and consumption'.[7] However, Arbena makes a curious exception of traditional sports and games in his generalizations about hegemonic power. Using examples of Hispanic America – mainly Mexico and Chile – he emphasizes, for example, the efforts of the Sandinista revolutionary movement of Central America during the 1970s, when it promoted folk sports in an attempt to 'revive traditional values and popular expressions by linking sports/games to activities associated with traditional festivals'.[8]

My criticism of Arbena's approach[9] has to do with the overemphasis he places on the English and North American influence on Latin American sport. In this regard, the development of sport is understood as a fundamental step forward in understanding the influential process of diffusion. Arbena runs the risk of generating interpretations of submission, imitation or cultural dependence that do not sufficiently differentiate sport from other cultural phenomena and do not fit the facts. His writing reveals that his problems are related more to the historical research methodology he employs than to the sociological analyses that he uses.

Arbena's use of primary sources is insufficient. Furthermore, past sport is interpreted using data from the present. In such circumstances, issues relating to hegemony are a valid concern but results are shadows of the past not the substance of the past and lead to generalizations such as 'the history of "modern" organized sport in Latin America is the history of the diffusion, adoption and manipulation of sports invented and/or codified and institutionalized by Europeans, mainly by the British'.[10] It is far safer and more accurate, of course, to do as J.A. Mangan has done and limit such generalizations tentatively to the 'early' history of modern sport on the continent.

It is possible to justify Arbena's argument in the case of the assimilation of sport imported from England by the elite clubs of the Rio de la Plata region. There, sports such as rugby and polo have reached levels comparable to those of their country of origin. In the case of football, however, the English influence was undoubtedly replaced when the game was reinvented as the national sport of Argentina and Uruguay. Mangan also has an interest in the diffusion and adoption of English sport in various parts of the world. As a cultural historian, among other things, Mangan is interested in the introduction, assimilation, adaptation, rejection and various repercussions of English sport but his tone is far more qualificatory and he roots his evidence more deeply in the empirical soil. Arguably, any concern with examples across the globe of cultural transfer is more productive for the history of English sport than it is for its Latin American counterpart. Of course the early significance of this extraordinary cultural importation can hardly be denied but Latin American sport is recognized for its eclecticism and cultural hybridism – any exaggerated focus on one particular theme runs the danger of losing sight of others.[12] However, it is important to appreciate that one focus can be more useful than another at certain moments in history and that to focus too closely on emancipation at the wrong moment runs the same risk.

Happily, Arbena's simplifications are not shared by Mangan in his cautious consideration of the English influence on the continent. Mangan identifies a clear absence of moral hegemony in the British economic domination of nineteenth-century Latin America. In marked contrast to Africa, Asia and the Antipodes, there was no imperial moral mandate in Latin America. Sport was not caught up in political priorities. The British simply conducted business in South America.[13] Thus, the 'manipulation' depicted by Arbena in the process of cultural transfer of sport is singularly and sensibly absent in Mangan's depiction of the early evolution of modern sport in Latin America and the associated English influence.

In sum, Arbena assigns data to a hegemonic explanation too readily and offers fragmentary evidence without the substance or continuity that would grant it historical value. In his reductionism, Arbena cannot be included among the scholars from other continents sufficiently sensitive to Latin American cultures. He is part of a long tradition established first in the late eighteenth century of outsider comment when German, French, Spanish and Portuguese social scientists and artists were living and researching on the continent. Those scientific studies and works of art postulated a multifaceted and original Latin America as a re-creation of social relations brought to the continent by European immigrants and colonizers. Over time, however, those influences were adjusted either by assimilation or by confrontation.[14]

This is the reason why, until its recent inclusion in the generic group of less developed regions, Latin America was considered a European social-cultural experiment, sometimes perverse, sometimes productive, sometimes beneficial. The consideration of the role of sport in this sometimes controversial interaction is long overdue. Pierre de Coubertin set the proper tone in the early twentieth century. He was greatly concerned to typify Latin American sport in a way that reflected an acknowledgement of its cultural specificity. During his campaign to consolidate the modern Olympic Games in the 1910s and the 1920s he gave priority to Latin America often using the French expression *'intelligent eclecticism'* to describe sport in that part of the world.[15]

Today, the tradition of seeking nuances in Latin American social and cultural contexts in which eclecticism is dominant still survives in the case of a few North American and European scholars. The so-called 'Brazilianists' represent a significant element of a group of scholars trying to treat diversity as the central element of Latin American history, sociology, economics and political science.[16] In this context, the recent investigations of Richard McGehee on the modernization of sport in Central America[17] and of Eduardo Archetti on meanings, values and symbols of football in Argentina are stimulating in their respective approaches.[18] Both have dealt with primary sources in a way that avoids oversimplification and provide cultural interpretations that fit the facts of sport in Latin America.

Because of the many contrasts present in Latin America historiography, it is impertinent to attribute the core meaning of sport as a social phenomenon to hegemonic conflict. The question remains, therefore, as to whether Arbena's approach is yet another instance of interpreting Latin American facts without adequate reference to the past due in turn to the fact that it has not as yet been thoroughly investigated. Does this 'ahistorical' interpretation expose a too narrow empiricist and instrumental tradition to which Arbena appears to subscribe?

EMANCIPATION V. INSTRUMENTALISM

The same question may be asked in the context of the problems in Latin America associated with the development of physical education in the work of R. Chappell.[19] He too has adopted a reductionist view in his analyses of Latin America – for his part he is concerned exclusively with social inequality. Chappell lists the unquestionable constraints on Latin America and then concentrates on the provision of basic needs. He states that the development of sport and leisure is to be understood as a process of supplying needs in terms of health, education and nutrition. This is yet another 'ahistorical' interpretation that is certainly compassionate and also constructive since Chappell makes suggestions for a way forward which would alleviate present shortcomings but which lacks an accurate sense of the complexity of 'eclectism'.

According to Chappell's view, there is an instrumentalist pre-condition in society that allows sport to find its own way. The essential element of this structural and functionalist position is to be found in subscription to the health benefits of sport; otherwise how would it be possible to legitimate its successful growth around the world? However, the lack of a historical perspective – as equally evident in Chappell's case as in Arbena's – concerning Latin America, overlooks libertarian and communal impulses as important in the pursuit of emancipation as education, health and nutrition.

It remains to be reiterated that sociological analyses of sport in Latin America have neglected history. Chappell overlooks improvised communality in his examples of deprivation in Latin American sport, he fails to provide the variety of approaches by which sport becomes intelligible. At this point it is worth mentioning the work of Richard Holt. Holt has criticized shortcomings in our understanding of the appeal of sport. He has suggested that there should be a 'balance between the inner development of the activity and sporting body – its playful and institutional dynamics – and the social and ideological context in which it took place'.[20] In my view, this balance should be set within a general methodological order in which an investigation of cross-cultural comparisons should seek to ensure that the various meanings of sport within a historical perspective are adequately explored.

HISTORY V. VALUES

It is a matter of regret that historical inquiries into the evolution of sport in Latin America are in short supply. In view of this, historians from other parts of the world with an interest in Latin America could usefully occupy this 'vacant space' to the advantage of historians of culture, society, politics and sport globally. To an extent, of course, this is precisely what *Sport and Society in Latin America* has set out to bring about. However, it has also set out to give space to Latin American historians and social scientists. Thus the volume views the evolution of sport on the continent – from both inside and outside and in the past and in the present. Of course there is much to be done by way of historical investigation but this bilateral approach offers a greater wealth of topics to be further investigated.

The presentation I gave in Cologne in 1995 highlighted the shortage of studies in the history of sport in Latin America. Latin American scholars have singularly failed to investigate the evolution of sport in their countries. In one survey, about half of the national sports leaders, and 100 per cent of local scholars with international experience, ignored the existence of historical studies carried out in their own countries or in neighbouring nations. Approximately 80 per cent of the total number of respondents were unable to relate sport in their own countries to the development of their local culture yet items concerning social, professional and legal changes, in addition to scientific and pedagogical practices were tackled specifically and knowledgeably.[21]

This lack of interest in history produced another investigation that identified the construction of social values as the central focus of sport analysts in Brazil, and very probably, in Latin America as well. In short, academics in Latin America consider themselves social reformers – they give priority to present problems in order to create appropriate and pragmatic interventions. In this context it is not surprising perhaps that prominent scholars have neglected history.[22]

In all honesty, in view of the criticism made of certain 'external' interpreters throughout this epilogue, the concentration on values due to past hegemonic struggles must also be acknowledged. Despite its 'ahistorical' approach, this kind of inquiry might well reflect the injustices and social inequalities that have characterized Latin America in the past.

THE RISE OF EMANCIPATION

There are grounds for optimism regarding an interest in historical research. In the last few years things have been changing – at least among Brazilian sport historians who have extended their research into primary sources producing and stimulating fresh reinterpretations. The transfer of their historical findings to other nations in Latin America is speculative but evidence from Brazilian investigations does indicate validity for other regions on the continent. Various sports recreated by European immigrants in the south of Brazil may share features with neighbouring countries of the Southern Cone because of geographical and sociocultural circumstances. The construction of a local and communal identity through sport, in conjunction with religion, education, festivities and the like, has been demonstrated by G. A. Oliveira for German groups[23] and by Regina De Rose for Italian immigrants.[24] Lothar Wieser, a German historian who has studied the creation and survival of 57 clubs in the south of Brazil, came to similar conclusions about social identity through sport.[25] In 1998, after reviewing documents related to the Fascist movement in Brazil dating back to the 1930s, P. Labriola and I confirmed the ethnicity, culture, religion and sport as phenomena that segregated, distinguished and unified the German and Italian populations in vast areas of the states between Rio Grande do Sul and São Paulo.[26] The accuracy of this view is attested in a doctorate thesis by Leomar Tesche, in which the *Turnen* movement was re-examined in the light of new evidence. His study demonstrated that the *Turnen* meshed with other interests and determined with them typical local identities.[27]

ELITE CLUBS AND POPULAR SPORTS

There is an effective convergence of data that illustrates how ethnic groups used sport as a means of corporate self-protection and as a means of construction of their own communal identity. In 1995, this evidence led me to re-interpret the creation of sporting clubs in South America using two perspectives. The first views the club as the place of social memory in which sport was remembered as one of its foundations. The second views the club as the meeting place where imported sports were adopted in order to promote social cohesion.[28] The first model embraces the communal club, available to all, and the second includes the elite club, where entrance is selective and frequently associated with social status symbols.

The often-mentioned English influence in Latin American sport was strong in the elite club found throughout Latin America. That English influence was subject to greater adaptation in the working-class clubs. In the Southern Cone the working-class clubs were primarily Italian and German and later Spanish and Portuguese. In Brazil, specifically, the blacks and poor whites became part of the assimilation process at a later period. Furthermore, adaptation was consolidated by the introduction and expansion of football into the Spanish- and Portuguese-speaking countries during and after the late nineteenth century. One result was that football became the most popular game in Latin America.[29]

It is then possible to observe that the majority of English sports in Latin America were voluntarily appropriated by local populations in contrast to the process of imposition that took place in Africa and Asia. As already suggested by Mangan, the 'moralistic ideology of athleticism' was not imposed on the local populations by – mostly – the English during the period of their successful entrepreneurial endeavours in Latin America before the First World War.[30] This fact puts in perspective Arbena's triumphalist claim that to spend 'only one weekend in Buenos Aires (or perhaps Montevideo or Santiago)' is sufficient to appreciate the popular preference of the sports 'institutionalized' by the British and Anglo-Americans and the lesser role played by Iberian and indigenous sports as 'recreational curiosities'.[31]

As a working hypothesis, the de-traditionalization of English sport in Latin America involved a shift of authority from 'without' to 'within'. In other words, the subscription to a 'tradition-maintenance' view should be set aside in favour of subscription to an assimilation–adaptation view.[32] The appropriation of football and baseball occurred in the early twentieth century in the countries located north of the Equator (Venezuela, Colombia, Peru, Central America, Caribbean and Mexico). Baseball clearly reveals the direct impact of American culture. However, it is important to mention here that the popularization of modern sport in Venezuela, Colombia, Peru, Central America, the Caribbean and Mexico was not initiated by clubs since Spanish colonization did not use sports clubs as a means of socialization. Furthermore, the immigration of other ethnic groups was much less important in the north than it was in the south. In contrast to the southern countries, the northern countries of Latin America constructed their sport traditions from directly imported foreign influence rather than from indirect immigratory influence.

The situation of sport clubs in Latin America revealed by my investigation of 1995 may be represented by two basic models. The first model depicts a club stronger than the sports that represent its traditions (southern Latin America). The second suggests that sport regulates the internal relations of the club that justify its existence (northern Latin America). Clubs in Latin America understandably still operate according to trends that date back to the second half of the nineteenth and early twentieth centuries but most of them have experienced the all-conquering process of adaptation. In Latin America, clubs and sports clearly reflect the historical elements of autonomy, self-assertion and self-realization despite the occasional example of confrontational relations with their social and cultural class environment.

In my view there is an emancipatory continuity suggested by the historical evidence in addition to confrontational change suggested by Arbena and dictated by the satisfaction of basic needs that Chapell suggests. Of course, it might be useful to recognize the place of all three, and of other perspectives in the evolution of Latin American sport, in keeping with subscription to 'eclecticism'. Nevertheless, to the surprise of Brazilian scholars, since the beginning of the 1990s the importance of the quest for emancipation has been increasingly revealed by the empirical investigations of sport historians. It is wise to recognize this as an important dimension of the evolution of modern sport – at least in Brazil.

Victor Melo has made a particularly interesting and valuable contribution to the Brazilian history of sport by making use of primary sources on horse-racing and rowing in Rio de Janeiro between 1849 and 1903. His conclusions illustrate these sports as essentially a re-creation of the European world in Brazil for the social elite of that city rather than a hegemonic strategy. This view accords with the situation that Mangan suggests took place in Buenos Aires.[33] Moreover, Melo closely examined the practice of traditional sports – capoeira, for instance – among the poorest segments of the population. He concluded that such games meaningfully promoted communal, collective and group identity. In this regard, this was much more than a simple reaction against hegemonic insistence.[34]

THE MYTHOLOGICAL APPROACH

My criticism of the simplifications associated with the development of Latin American sport has referred to studies demonstrating too little concern for a historically appropriate treatment and resulting in unsatisfactory conclusions. These studies display fractured, or even mythological, features. It is regrettable that Latin American scholars often imitate the wrong colleagues from other parts of the world and adopt approaches similar to those of Arbena and Chappell.

Football is an emblematic example, which, in Latin America's case, has involved on occasion mere reproduction of mythological narratives without adequate historical assessment. By way of example, the Englishman Charles Miller was considered to be the 'founder' of 'British' football in Brazil at the end of the nineteenth century. As such, Miller promoted football among the elite in the style in which it was played in its original country. However, recent historical inquiries have discredited this mythological view. In reality football was introduced to Brazil by the Jesuits, who arrived two decades before Miller.[35] In 1999, Heglison Toledo and I made enquiries in an attempt to verify the religious source of football. Our efforts ended up confirming the hypothesis that English football had been brought to Brazil at least as early as 1893, via Episcopalian educational institutions located in Juiz de Fora.[36]

Such inquiries reveal that the origins of activities can fade into 'oblivion', can be assimilated into the local culture and then be forgotten completely. Adaptation by recipients result in a 'taken for granted' activity, the beginnings of which are no longer important but the present satisfactions of which are unquestionable. Evidence not only from Latin America but from Europe offers support for this assertion.[37] In Brazil, 'religious' football was smoothly and swiftly assimilated throughout certain country regions only to be 'discovered' by middle-class elitist clubs of the urban centres some time later. All this points to the need for in-depth local studies to ensure that a comprehensive and accurate depiction of the evolutionary process is available.

Another perspective recently receiving criticism and re-evaluation involves the role played by Afro-Brazilians in the development of football. Antonio Soares, a scholar from Rio de Janeiro, examined documentary sources from the first half of the twentieth century and concluded that Brazilian social scientists shared with the press a subscription to the creation of myths when discussing the roots of football in the country. According to Soares, the scientists have adhered uncritically to the so-called 'democratisation, ascension and affirmation of Negroes in football'.[38] Soares argues that historical sources were simply neglected for the sake of a mythical construction of the supremacy of Negroes and their singular style in football – a form of inverse racism.

CONCLUSION

In summary, some 'outside' interpreters of Latin American sport have demonstrated academic positions revealing prejudice and exaggeration while 'inside' interpretations produced by locally scholars frequently neglect or even manipulate historical sources. Both those 'external' and 'internal' shortcomings should be dealt with in appropriate concern for the accumulation of careful and accurate research. Guttmann, Arbena and Chappell are not without their value; they raise issues for future inquiry but the onus is now on Latin American scholars to correct, improve and advance the inadequate efforts of past and present scholars – both non-indigenous and indigenous (as emphasized by Mangan in his earlier chapter).

This conclusion is intended to provoke a response from both 'outsiders' and 'insiders' concerned with Latin American sport. There will be more on this subject in due course. The development of modern sport in Latin America cannot be adequately dealt with in a short overview. The purpose of this short comment is to highlight both adequacies and inadequacies in current inquiries and to point the way forward to better scholarship.

Happily, it may be stated that in the light of recent developments associated with the study of the history of sport on this continent, historians of sport no longer occupy 'marginal' but increasingly 'mainstream' status in academia.

Behind this comment lies the considerable growth in investigations presented at Brazilian national conferences on the history of sport during the 1990s. More recently, these annual events have reached the level of nearly one hundred selected presentations per conference, preparing the ground for the growth of a prestigious group of intellectuals in Latin American sport and physical education.[39]

This innovative set of historians has shown a clear-sighted advance with regard to the influence of sport in society. Many of the inquiries now available record the autonomy and self-realization of participants in sport at every level of Brazilian society.[40] These inquiries cannot be interpreted as odd or exceptional or peculiar. After all, sport of various kinds has been available to communities, rich and poor, large and small in varying degrees across the world. That sport includes elements of hegemony, mythology and also emancipation should not come as a surprise. What is required of Latin American studies in the future is an appreciation of appropriate complexity. This is the way forward. Hopefully *Sport in Latin American Society* has revealed something of this complexity and itself will point the way forward to more advanced and sophisticated publications in the future. This is certainly its ambition.

NOTES

1. L..P. Dacosta, 'The Image of Sport in South America' in J. Mester (ed.), *Images of Sport in The World* (Cologne, 1995), pp.75–97.
2. H. Digel, 'Guidelines for a Reflexive Modernization of the Development Co-operation in Sport' in DaCosta, *Images of Sport*, pp.315–24.
3. L..P. DaCosta, 'Cultural Identity and Globalisation – A Counter-Statement to Helmut Digel's Guidelines for Development Co-operation in Sport' in DaCosta, *Images of Sport*, pp.325–6.
4. J.L. Arbena, 'Nationalism and Sport in Latin America, 1850–1990: The Paradox of Promoting and Performing European Sports' in J.A. Mangan (ed.), *Tribal Identities: Nationalism, Europe, Sport* (London and Portland, OR: Frank Cass, 1996), pp.220–38.
5. J.L. Arbena, 'Sport and Social Change in Latin America' in G. Ingham and J.W. Loy (eds.), *Sport in Social Development Traditions, Transitions and Transformations* (Champaign, IL, 1993), pp.97–100.
6. Ibid., p.113.
7. Ibid., p.100.
8. Arbena, 'Nationalism and Sport', p.229.
9. L.P. Dacosta, *Emergencia e Difusao do Desporto Moderno na America Latina – Influencias Britanica e Norte Americana: uma Revisao Critica*, VII Congresso Brasileiro de Historia do Esporte, Educacao Fisica e Lazer, Gramado,RS, Brasil, junho de 2000.
10. Arbena, 'Nationalism and Sport', p.221.
11. J.A. Mangan, *The Early Evolution of Modern Sport in Latin America: a Mainly English, Middle-Class Inspiration?* VII Congresso Brasileiro de Historia do Esporte e Educacao Fisica, Gramado-RS, Brasil, junho de 2000. An expanded version of this paper features in this volume as Ch.1.
12. For further elaboration on this topic concerning Latin America, see N.G. Canclini, *Hybrid Cultures* (Minneapolis, MN, 1995), pp.3–6.
13. Mangan, *The Early Evolution*, pp.1–6.
14. Canclini, *Hybrid Cultures*, pp.273–81.
15. For a fuller description of Coubertin's involvement with Latin America, see L.P. DaCosta, '*Exposicao Internacional do Rio de Janeiro em 1022: um Marco Historico do Movimento Olimpico ma America do Sul*', Coletanea do IV Encontro Nacional de Historia do Esporte, Lazer e Educacao Fisica, Belo Horizonte-Brasil, 1996, pp.411–16.
16. For a succinct review of Brazilianists' standpoints, see J.L. Love, *Crafting the Third World* (Stanford, CA, 1996), pp.10–21.
17. R.V. McGehee, 'The Rise of Modern Sport in Guatemala and the First Central American Games', *International Journal of the History of Sport*, 9, 1 (1992), 132–40.
18. E. Archetti, 'In Search of National Identity: Argentinean Football and Europe', in Mangan, *Tribal Identities*, pp.201–18.
19. R. Chappell, 'An Overview of the Problems and Issues Involved in Developing Physical Education in Latin America', *ICSSPE Bulletin* (28 Jan. 2000), 26–8.
20. R. Holt, 'Towards a General History of Modern European Sport: Some Problems and Possibilities' in A. Krueger and A. Teja (eds.), *La Comune Eredità dello Sport in Europa*, Proceeding of the Second CESH Conference (Roma, 1997), p.31.
21. DaCosta, *Images*, pp.82–3.
22. For the role of sport intellectuals, see L.P. DaCosta, 'The State versus Free Enterprise in Sports Policy: the Case of Brazil' in L. Chalip, A. Johnson and L. Stachura (eds.), *National Sports Policies – an International Handbook* (Westport, CT, 1996), pp.23–38.
23. G.A. Oliveira, 'A Imigração Alema e a Introdução de Punhobol no Rio Grande do Sul', unpublished Masters dissertation, University of Santa Maria, Brazil, 1987.
24. R.A De Rose, 'A Influencia da Imigracao Italiana no Desenvolvimento do Esporte no Rio Grande do Sul', unpublished Masters dissertation, Federal University of Rio Grande do Sul, 1996.
25. L. Wieser, *Deutsches Turnen in Brasilien* (London, 1990), pp.282–6.
26. L.P. DaCosta and P. Labriola, 'The Bodies from Brazil – The Making of Fascist Aesthetics' in J.A Mangan (ed.), *Shaping the Superman: Fascist Body as Political Icon – Aryan Fascism* (London and Portland, OR: Frank Cass, 2000), pp.163–80.

27. L. Tesche, 'O Turnen, a Educação e a Educação Física nas Escolas Teuto – brasileiras no Rio Grande do Sul, 1852–1940', unpublished doctoral thesis, Unimep – Piracicaba, Sao Paulo, Brazil, 1999, pp.98–151. See also his chapter on the topic in J.A. Mangan (ed.), *Europe, Sport, World: Shaping Global Societies* (London and Portland, OR: Frank Cass, 2001).
28. DaCosta, *Images*, pp.91–2.
29. Ibid., p.92.
30. For a discussion of this point, see J.A. Mangan, *The Games Ethics and Imperialism* (London and Portland, OR: Frank Cass, 1998), pp.168–92.
31. Arbena, 'Nationalism in Sport', p.221.
32. For further examples of traditions' replacement, see P. Heelas, S. Lash and P. Morris, *Detraditionalization* (Oxford: 1996), *passim.*
33. V. Melo, 'Cidade Sportiva – O Turfe e o Remo no Rio de Janeiro –1849 / 1903', unpublished doctoral thesis, University Gama Filho, Rio de Janeiro, Brazil, 1999, p.272.
34. Ibid., pp.14–19.
35. V. Melo, 'Futebol: que Historia e essa?', unpublished paper, 1998.
36. H.C. Toledo and L.P. DaCosta, 'O Futebol no Brasil antes de Charles Miller – O Caso do Instituto Granbery de Juiz de Fora-MG no Marco de 1893', *Dinamis*, 7, 26 (1999), 83–90.
37. A. Grafton and A. Blair, *The Transmission of Culture in EarlyModern Europe* (Pennsylvania: 1999), *passim.*
38. J.A. Soares, 'Historia e Invencao de Tradicoes no Campo do Futebol', *Estudos Historicos*, 13, 23, (1999), 119.
39. For further clarification of this point, see V. Melo and L.P. DaCosta, 'Brief Notes on the History of Sport and Physical Education in Brazil', *ISHPES Bulletin*, 15 (1998), 1–2.
40. Besides the examples of emancipation revealed in the more developed southern areas of the country, there have been others found in poor regions such as Belem, capital of the state of Para, located in Amazon region, as described by J.L. Vallinoto, 'Origens da Institucionalizacao Esportiva: a Vida Recreativa em Belem do Para de 1840 a 1905', unpublished Masters dissertation, University Gama Filho, Rio de Janeiro, 2000.

Select Bibliography

**The Early Evolution of Modern Sport in Latin America:
A Mainly English Middle-Class Inspiration?
J.A. MANGAN**

N.B. Dirks, *Colonialism and Culture* (Michigan: University of Michigan Press, 1992).

A. Pagden, *Lords of all the World: Ideologies of Empire in Spain, Britain and France c.1500-1800* (New Haven: Yale University Press, 1995).

A. Guttmann, *Games and Empires: Modern Sports and Cultural Imperialism* (New York: University of Columbia Press, 1994).

J.A. Mangan, *The Games Ethic and Imperialism: Aspects of the Diffusion of an Ideal* (London: Viking Penguin, 1986; and Frank Cass, 1998).

J.A. Mangan, *Athleticism in the Victorian and Edwardian Public School: The Emergence and Consolidation of an Educational Ideology* (Cambridge: Cambridge University Press, 1981; Brighton: Falmer, 1986; and London and Portland, OR: Frank Cass, 2000).

J. King, 'The Influence of British Culture in Argentina' in A. Hennessy and J. King (eds.), *The Land That England Lost* (London: British Academic Press, 1992).

A. Graham-Yooll, *The Forgotten Colony* (London: Hutchinson, 1981).

J.T. Stevenson, *The History of St. George's College, Quilmes, Argentina 1898-1935* (London: Church Missionary Society, 1936).

Richard Graham, *Britain and the Onset of Modernization in Brazil: 1850–1914* (Cambridge: Cambridge University Press, 1968).

**The Later Evolution of Modern Sport in Latin America:
The North American Influence
JOSEPH L. ARBENA**

J.L. Arbena (ed.), *Latin American Sport: An Annotated Bibliography, 1988–1998* (Westport, CT: Greenwood Press, 1999).

J.L. Arbena, 'Nationalism and Sport in Latin America, 1850–1990: The Paradox of Promoting and Performing "European" Sports',

International Journal of the History of Sport, 12, 2 (Aug. 1995), 220–38.

J.L. Arbena (ed.), *Sport and Society in Latin America: Diffusion, Dependency, and the Rise of Mass Culture* (Westport, CT: Greenwood Press, 1988).

W.H. Beezley, *Judas at the Jockey Club and Other Episodes of Porfirian Mexico* (Lincoln: University of Nebraska Press, 1987).

P.C. Bjarkman, *Baseball with a Latin Beat: A History of the Latin American Game* (Jefferson, NC: McFarland & Co., 1994).

R. Gonzàlez Echevarría, *The Pride of Havana: A History of Cuban Baseball* (New York: Oxford University Press, 1999).

G.M. Joseph, 'Documenting a Regional Pastime: Baseball in Yucatan' in R.M. Levine (ed.), *Windows on Latin America: Understanding Society Through Photographs* (Coral Gables, FL: University of Miami Press, 1987), pp.76–89.

A.M. Klein, *Sugarball: The American Game, the Dominican Dream* (New Haven: Yale University Press, 1991).

M. Longorio, *Athletes Remembered: Mexicano/Latino Professional Football Players, 1929–1970* (Tempe, AZ: Bilingual Press, 1997).

R. Ruck, *The Tropic of Baseball: Baseball in the Dominican Republic* (Westport, CT: Meckler, 1991).

Tribulations and Achievements:
The Early History of Olympism in Argentina
CESAR R. TORRES

C. Diaz Alejandro, *Essays on the Economic History of the Argentine Republic* (New Haven, CT: Yale University Press, 1970).

A. Guttmann, *Games and Empires* (New York: Columbia University Press, 1994).

F. Luna, *Alvear* (Buenos Aires: Hyspamerica, 1986).

J. MacAloon, *This Great Symbol* (Chicago: The University of Chicago Press, 1981).

J. Saraví Riviere, *Aportes para una Historia de la Educación Física, 1900 a 1945* (Buenos Aires: IEF No.1 'Dr. Enrique R. Brest', 1998).

D. Rock, *Politics in Argentina, 1890–1930* (London: Cambridge University Press, 1975).

C.R. Torres, 'Mass Sport Through Education or Elite Olympic Sport? José Benjamín Zubiaur's Dilemma and Argentina's Olympic Sports Legacy', *Olympika: The International Journal of Olympic Studies*, 7 (1998), 61–88.

C. Viale, *El Deporte Argentino* (Buenos Aires: García Santos, 1922).

D. Young, *The Modern Olympics* (Baltimore: The Johns Hopkins University Press, 1996).

Fútbol, Politicians and the People:
Populism and Politics in Argentina
VIC DUKE and LIZ CROLLEY

P. Alabarces and M. Rodriguez, *Cuestión de Pelotas* (Buenos Aires: Atuel, 1996).

E. Archetti, *Masculinities: Football, Polo and the Tango in Argentina* (Oxford: Berg, 1999).

E. Archetti and P. Romero, 'Death and Violence in Argentinian Football' in R. Giulianotti, N. Bonney and M. Hepworth (eds.), *Football, Violence and Social Identity* (London: Routledge, 1994).

O. Bayer, *Fútbol Argentino* (Buenos Aires: Editorial Sudamericana, 1990).

V. Duke and L. Crolley, 'Football Spectator Behaviour in Argentina: a Case of Separate Evolution', *Sociological Review*, 44 (1996), 272–93.

V. Duke and L. Crolley, *Football, Nationality and the State* (Harlow: Longman, 1996).

J. Frydenberg, 'Redefiniciün del fútbol aficionado y del fútbol oficial: Buenos Aires, 1912' in P. Alabarces, R. Di Giano and J. Frydenberg (eds.), *Deporte y Sociedad* (Buenos Aires: Eudeba, 1998).

T. Mason, *Passion of the People?* (London: Verso, 1995).

A. Romero, *Las Barras Bravas y la Contrasociedad Deportivo* (Buenos Aires: Nueva América, 1994).

A. Scher and H. Palomino, *Fútbol: Pasión de Multitudes y de Elites* (Buenos Aires: CISEA, 1988).

J. Sebreli, *La Era del Fútbol* (Buenos Aires: Editorial Sudamericana, 1998).

Baseball Arguments:
Aficionismo and Masculinity at the Core of *Cubanidad*
THOMAS CARTER

V. Burstyn, *The Rites of Men: Manhood, Politics, and the Culture of Sport* (Toronto: University of Toronto Press, 1999).

R. González Echevarría, *The Pride of Havana: A History of Cuban Baseball* (New York: Oxford University Press, 1999).

M.C. Gutmann, *The Meanings of Macho: Being a Man in Mexico City* (Berkeley: University of California Press, 1996).

M.H. Jamail, *Full Count: Inside Cuban Baseball* (Carbondale: Southern Illinois University Press, 2000).

S.M. Low, 'Spatializing Culture: The Social Production and Social Construction of Public Space in Costa Rica', *American Ethnologist*, 23, 4 (1996), 861–79.

L.A. Pérez, *On Becoming Cuban: Identity, Nationality, & Culture* (Chapel Hill: University of North Carolina Press, 1999).

E. Torres-Cuevas, 'En Busca de la Cubanidad', *Debates Americanos*, 1 (1995), 2–17.

E. Torres-Cuevas, 'En Busca de la Cubanidad (II)' *Debates Americanos*, 2 (1996), 3–11.

Unión de Escritores y Artistas de Cuba (UNEAC), *Cuba: Cultura e Identidad Nacional* (La Habana: Ediciones UNION, 1995).

The Crisis of Brazilian Football and Post-modernity: Perspectives for the Twenty-first Century
CESAR GORDON and RONALDO HELAL

R. DaMatta (ed.), *Universo do Futebol: esporte e sociedade brasileira* (Rio de Janeiro: Pinakotheke, 1982).

G. Freyre, *The Masters and the Slaves: a Study in the Development of Brazilian Civilization*, translated by Samuel Putnam (New York: A.A. Knopf, 1946).

R. Helal, *The Brazilian Soccer Crisis as a Sociological Problem* (Ph.D. Dissertation, Department of Sociology, New York University, 1994).

R. Helal, *Passes e Impasses: futebol e Cultura de Massa no Brasil* (Petrópolis: Vozes, 1997).

J. Lever, *Soccer Madness* (Chicago: The University of Chicago Press, 1983).

M. Filho, *O Negro no Futebol Brasileiro* (Rio de Janeiro: Editora Civilização Brasileira, 1964).

L. Toledo, *Torcidas Organizadas de Futebol* (São Paulo: Autores Associados, ANPOCS, 1996).

E. Galeano, *Football: in Sun and Shadow* (London, 1997).

C. Gordon and R. Helal, 'Sociologia, historia e romance na construção da identidade nacional através do futebol', *Estudos Históricos*, 23, 13 (1999).

C. Gordon, 'Eu já fui preto e sei o que é isso', *Pesquisa de Campo*, 3–4 (Revista do Núcleo de Sociologia do Futebol, IFCH, UERJ, 1996).

C. Gordon, 'História social dos negros no futebol brasileiro', *Pesquisa de Campo*, 2 (Revista do Núcleo de Sociologia do Futebol. IFCH, UERJ, 1995).

Sport in Latin America from Past to Present:
A European Perspective
ROBERT CHAPPELL

J.L. Arbena, 'Sport and Change in Latin America' in A. Ingham and J. Loy (eds.), *Sport in Social Development: Traditions, Transitions and Transformations* (Champaign, IL: Human Kinetics, 1993), pp.97–119.

J.L. Arbena, 'Nationalism and Sport in Latin America, 1850–1990: The Paradox of Promoting and Performing "European" Sports', *International Journal of the History of Sport*, 12 (1995), 220–38.

J.L. Arbena, 'International Aspects of Sport in Latin America: Perceptions, Prospects and Proposals' in E. Dunning, J. Maguire and R. Pearton (eds.), *The Sports Process: A Comparative and Developmental Approach* (Champaign, IL: Human Kinetics, 1996), pp.151–69.

A. Graham-Yooll, *The Forgotten Colony* (London: Hutchinson, 1981).

C.V. Guardia, 'Physical Education in Latin America and the Caribbean, *ICSSPE Bulletin*, 19 (1995), 18–19.

L.P. DaCosta, 'The State versus Free Enterprise in Sports Policy: The Case of Brazil' in L. Chalip, A. Johnson and L. Strachura (eds.), *National Sports Policies: An International Handbook* (London: Greenwood Press, 1996), pp.23–39.

J.A. Mangan, 'The Early Evolution of Modern Sport in Latin America: A Mainly English Middle-Class Inspiration', Paper presented at the Seventh Brazilian Conference of the History of Sport, Physical Education and Dance, Porto Alegre, 29 May–1 June 2000.

J.A. Mangan and V. DeMelo, 'A Web of the Wealthy: Modern Sport in the Nineteenth-Century Culture of Rio de Janeiro', *International Journal of the History of Sport*, 14 (1997), 168–73.

A. Reppold, 'A Comparative on the Future of Sport in the Olympic Movement: South America', Paper presented at the British Olympic Association Conference, Loughborough University, 19 March 1997.

Epilogue: Hegemony, Emancipation and Mythology
LAMARTINE P. DaCOSTA

L.P. DaCosta, 'The Image of Sport in South America' in J. Mester (ed.), *Images of Sport in the World* (Cologne: German Sport University, 1995).

L.P. DaCosta, 'Cultural Identity and Globalization – A Counter-Statement to Helmut Digel's Guidelines for Development Cooperation in Sport' in J. Mester (ed.), *Images of Sport in the World* (Cologne: German Sport University, 1995).

L.P. DaCosta, 'Emergencia e Difusao do Desporto Moderno na America Latina – Influencias Britanica e Norte Americana: uma Revisao Critica', VII Congresso Brasileiro de Historia do Esporte, Educacao Fisica e Lazer, Gramado-RS, Brazil, June 2000.

J.A. Mangan, 'The Early Evolution of Modern Sport in Latin America: a Manly English, Middle-Class Inspiration', VII Congresso Brasileiro de Historia do Esporte e Educacao Fisica, Gramado-RS, Brazil, June 2000.

L.P. DaCosta, 'Exposicao Internacional do Rio de Janeiro em 1022: um Marco Historico do Movimento Olimpico na America do Sul', Coletanea do IV Encontro Nacional de Historia do Esporte, Lazer e Educacao Fisica, Belo Horizonte-Brasil, 1996.

L.P. DaCosta, 'The State versus Free Enterprise in Sports Policy: the Case of Brazil' in L. Chalip, A. Johnson and L. Stachura (eds.), *National Sports Policies – an International Handbook* (Westport: Greenwood, 1996).

L. Wieser, *Deutsches Turnen in Brasilien* (London, 1990).

L. P. DaCosta and P. Labriola, Bodies from Brazil: Fascist Aesthetics in a South American Setting' in J.A Mangan (ed.), *Superman Supreme: Fascist Body as Political Icon – Global Fascism* (London and Portland, OR: Frank Cass, 2000).

L. Tesche and A.B. Rambo, 'Reconstructing the Fatherland: German Turnen in Southern Brazil' in J.A. Mangan (ed.), *Europe, Sport World: Shaping Global Societies* (London and Portland, OR: Frank Cass, 2001).

V.A. Melo, *Cidade Sportiva – Primordios do Esporte no Rio de Janeiro* (Rio de Janeiro: Relume Dumara, 2001).

H.C. Toledo and L.P. DaCosta, 'O Futebol no Brasil antes de Charles Miller – O Caso do Instituto Granbery de Juiz de Fora-MG no Marco de 1893', *Dinamis*, 7, 26 (1999).

J.A. Soares 'Historia e Invencao de Tradicoes no Campo do Futebol', *Estudos Historicos*, 13, 23 (1999).

Notes on Contributors

Lamartine P. DaCosta is Senior Professor in the Masters and Doctorate Programme on Physical Education at the University Gama Filho, Rio de Janeiro. During the 1990s he was a guest professor at the University of Porto in Portugal and a supervising professor at the International Olympic Academy in Greece. He is also a former consultant on sports, education and health projects located in Kuwait, Tanzania, the United States and Peru. As author or co-author he has written more than 100 articles and 36 books, most of them in Portuguese and on sports issues.

J.A. Mangan is Director of the International Research Centre for Sport, Socialisation and Society at the University of Strathclyde, Glasgow. He is founder and General Editor of the Cass series *Sport in the Global Society* and founding and executive academic editor of the Cass journals *The International Journal of the History of Sport*; *Culture, Sport Society*; *Soccer and Society* and *The European Sports History Review*. His *Athleticism in the Victorian and Edwardian Public School* and *The Games Ethic and Imperialism* have recently been reprinted by Frank Cass.

Joseph L. Arbena is Professor of History at Clemson University where he has taught since 1965. He holds degrees in Latin American History and Culture from the George Washington University (1961) and the University of Virginia (1970). He has compiled two annotated bibliographies of sports in Latin America (1989 and 1999), edited a collection of essays on Latin American sports and published some 30 articles on sports topics. He also served as editor of the *Journal of Sport History* (1993–96). His current research focuses on sport, politics and national identity in Latin America.

Cesar R. Torres received his BA and Senior Diploma in Argentina. He is in the Department of Physical Education and Sport at the State University of New York College at Brockport. His research interests and publications revolve around the connections between the sporting and

Olympic practices and the broader cultural, political, intellectual and economic forces at play across the Western hemisphere during the end of the nineteenth and early twentieth centuries.

Vic Duke is Senior Research Fellow in the Football Research Unit at the University of Liverpool. He is co-author of *Football, Nationality and the State* (1996) and *A Measure of Thatcherism* (1991), as well as the author of many articles on political and sociological aspects of football.

Liz Crolley is Senior Lecturer in Languages at Manchester Metropolitan University. She is co-author of *Football, Nationality and the State* (1996) and *Football, Europe and the Press: Imagined Identities?* (2001), as well as the author of several articles on Spanish football and football and gender.

Thomas Carter is currently an adjunct professor in the Department of Sociology and Anthropology at St. Cloud State University in Minnesota. He is one of the few cultural (social) anthropologists to have conducted fieldwork in Cuba since the Cuban Revolution. He is presently working on an ethnography on baseball in Cuba.

Cesar Gordon is a doctoral student at the Graduate Program of Social Anthropology, National Museum, Federal University of Rio de Janeiro. He holds a Master of Arts in Social Anthropology from the National Museum, Federal University of Rio de Janeiro. He is a member of the Editorial Board of *Soccer and Society* and the author of several articles on the history of Brazilian football.

Ronaldo Helal is Professor of the Department of Social Communication at the State University of Rio de Janeiro. He holds a Ph.D. in Sociology from New York University. He is a researcher of the National Research Council (CNPg) and the author of *Passes e Impasses: futebol e Cultura de Massa no Brasil*, (1997); 'The Brazilian Soccer Crisis as a Sociological Problem' (Ph.D. thesis) and *O Que É Sociologia do Esporte* (1990).

Robert Chappell is a lecturer in the Department of Sport Sciences at Brunel University, London. He has a keen interest in the evolution of modern sport in Latin America.

Index

Other Titles in the Series

Sport in Australasian Society
Past and Present

J A Mangan, *University of Strathclyde* and
John Nauright, *University of Queensland* (Eds)

This volume examines the emergence of sporting cultures in two of the
world's most prolific nations based on per capita international
performance. This is the first book to discuss the historical development
of sport in both Australia and New Zealand. These two countries both
have a long history of involvement in international sport through their
history as members of the British Empire and Commonwealth and the
Olympic movement. Australia and New Zealand inherited the games-
playing traditions of the English public schools but quickly developed
their own distinct sporting cultures. In this collection leading and
emerging scholars explore the establishment of the games ethic in
Australasian private schools and the emergence of Australasian physical
cultures based in schools, on sports fields, in the stands and at the
beach.

Contributors: *Stuart Macintyre, Martin Crotty, J A Mangan, Colm
Hickey, David Kirk, Peter A Horton, Frazer Andrewes, Rob Hess, Ian
Jobling, Douglas Booth, Angela Burroughs, John Nauright, Murray
Phillips, Frank Hicks, Ian Andrews, Malcolm MacLean, Bob Stewart,
Aaron Smith, Tara Magdalinski and Jock Phillips.*

376 pages 2000
0 7146 5060 9 cloth
0 7146 8112 1 paper
A special issue of The International Journal of the History of Sport
Sport in the Global Society No. 18

FRANK CASS PUBLISHERS
Crown House, 47 Chase Side, Southgate, London N14 5BP
Tel: +44 (0)20 8920 2100 Fax: +44 (0)20 8447 8548 E-mail: info@frankcass.com
NORTH AMERICA
5824 NE Hassalo Street, Portland, OR 97213 3644, USA
Tel: 800 944 6190 Fax: 503 280 8832 E-mail: cass@isbs.com
Website: www.frankcass.com

Shaping the Superman: Fascist Body as Political Icon – Aryan Fascism

J A Mangan, *University of Strathclyde* (Ed)

' ... an authoritative, thought-provoking and readable discussion of an aspect of Fascist ideology which has received comparatively little attention.'

Culture, Sport, Society

'Some superb insights into different aspects of this question.'

Contemporary Review

One of the central images of masculinity in the Western cultural tradition is the murderous hero, the supreme specialist in violence. A string of warrior-heroes – Achilles, Siegfried, Lancelot, Rambo – populate European and American film and literature. Governments can use this connection between admired masculinity and violent response to threat to mobilize support for war. The most systematic case in modern history was the Nazis' cult of Nordic manhood, reaching its peak in the propaganda image of the SS-man. This book is a study of masculinity as a metaphor and especially of the muscular male body as a moral symbol. It explores the Nazis' preoccupation with the male body as an icon of political power, and the ideology and theories which propelled it.

Contributors: *J A Mangan, Heinz-Georg Marten, Arnd Krüger, John Hoberman, Graham McFee, Alan Tomlinson, Peter Reichel and Allen Guttmann.*

232 pages 15 illus 1999
0 7146 4954 6 cloth
0 7146 8013 3 paper
A special issue of The International Journal of the History of Sport
Sport in the Global Society No. 14

FRANK CASS PUBLISHERS
Crown House, 47 Chase Side, Southgate, London N14 5BP
Tel: +44 (0)20 8920 2100 Fax: +44 (0)20 8447 8548 E-mail: info@frankcass.com
NORTH AMERICA
5824 NE Hassalo Street, Portland, OR 97213 3644, USA
Tel: 800 944 6190 Fax: 503 280 8832 E-mail: cass@isbs.com
Website: www.frankcass.com

Superman Supreme: Fascist Body as Political Icon – Global Fascism

J A Mangan, *University of Strathclyde* (Eds)

The Fascism of the 1930s was a major political force both within and outside Europe. It appealed to emotion and sentiment, to the love of adventure and heroism, the belief in action rather than words, self-sacrifice, the exultation of violence, even death. A neglected element of this international phenomenon is Fascism's projection of the martial male body as a symbol of state power. This sequel to the acclaimed *Shaping the Superman* shows that the idealised image of the Aryan Superman had a wide currency beyond Germany and reveals how Fascist movements in Europe, America and Asia made metaphorical and literal use of the male body for political purposes.

Contributors: *J A Mangan, Gigliola Gori, Wolfgang Weber, Paula Black, Vassil Girginov, Peter Bankov, Hans Bonde, Teresa Gonzalez Aja, Tony Collins, Lamartine P Da Costa, Plinio Labriola, Takeshi Komagome and Fan Hong.*

224 pages 38 illus 2000
0 7146 4955 4 cloth
0 7146 8014 1 paper
A special issue of The International Journal of the History of Sport
Sport in the Global Society No. 15

FRANK CASS PUBLISHERS
Crown House, 47 Chase Side, Southgate, London N14 5BP
Tel: +44 (0)20 8920 2100 Fax: +44 (0)20 8447 8548 E-mail: info@frankcass.com
NORTH AMERICA
5824 NE Hassalo Street, Portland, OR 97213 3644, USA
Tel: 800 944 6190 Fax: 503 280 8832 E-mail: cass@isbs.com
Website: www.frankcass.com

Freeing the Female Body
Inspirational Icons

J A Mangan, *University of Strathclyde* and **Fan Hong**, *University of De Montfort* (Eds)

This book tells the stories of remarkable women who devoted their lives to the cause of women's physical liberation. They each shared the same ambition: to free women's bodies through sport. Scholars have studied the paradoxical importance of sport in both reinforcing the male-dominated status quo and emancipating women from traditional repression in both Western and Eastern worlds, but the role that individuals played in achieving the political and economic freedom of women through sport has been neglected. This collection records the bravery of these forgotten inspirational figures whose determination helped to free women from the ranks of the sexualised, controlled and oppressed.

Contents: 'All the Freedom of the Boy': Elizabeth Cady Stanton, Nineteenth-Century Architect of Women's Rights *Roberta J Park*. A Martyr for Modernity: Qiu Jin, Feminist, Warrior and Revolutionary *Fan Hong* and *J A Mangan*. A Militant Madonna: Charlotte Perkins Gilman, Feminism and Physical Culture *Patricia Vertinsky*. A Lifetime of Campaigning: Ettie Rout, Emancipationist beyond the Pale *Jane Tolerton*. Breaking Bounds: Alice Profé, Radical and Emancipationist *Gertrud Pfister*. At the Heart of a New Profession: Margaret Stansfeld, a Radical English Educationalist *Richard Smart*. Alexandrine Gibb: 'In No Man's Land of Sport' *M Ann Hall*. A Glittering Icon of Fascist Femininity: Trebisconda 'Ondina' Valla *Gigliola Gori*. Ignoring Taboos: Maria Lenk, Latin American Inspirationalist *Sebastião Votre* and *Ludmilla Mourão*. In Pursuit of Empowerment: *Sensei* Nellie Kleinsmidt and Gender Challenges in South Africa *Denise E M Jones*. Epilogue: Prospects for the New Millennium: Women, Emancipation and the Body *J A Mangan*.

288 pages illus 2001
0 7146 5088 9 cloth
0 7146 8129 6 paper
A special issue of The International Journal of the History of Sport
Sport in the Global Society No. 20

FRANK CASS PUBLISHERS
Crown House, 47 Chase Side, Southgate, London N14 5BP
Tel: +44 (0)20 8920 2100 Fax: +44 (0)20 8447 8548 E-mail: info@frankcass.com
NORTH AMERICA
5824 NE Hassalo Street, Portland, OR 97213 3644, USA
Tel: 800 944 6190 Fax: 503 280 8832 E-mail: cass@isbs.com
Website: www.frankcass.com